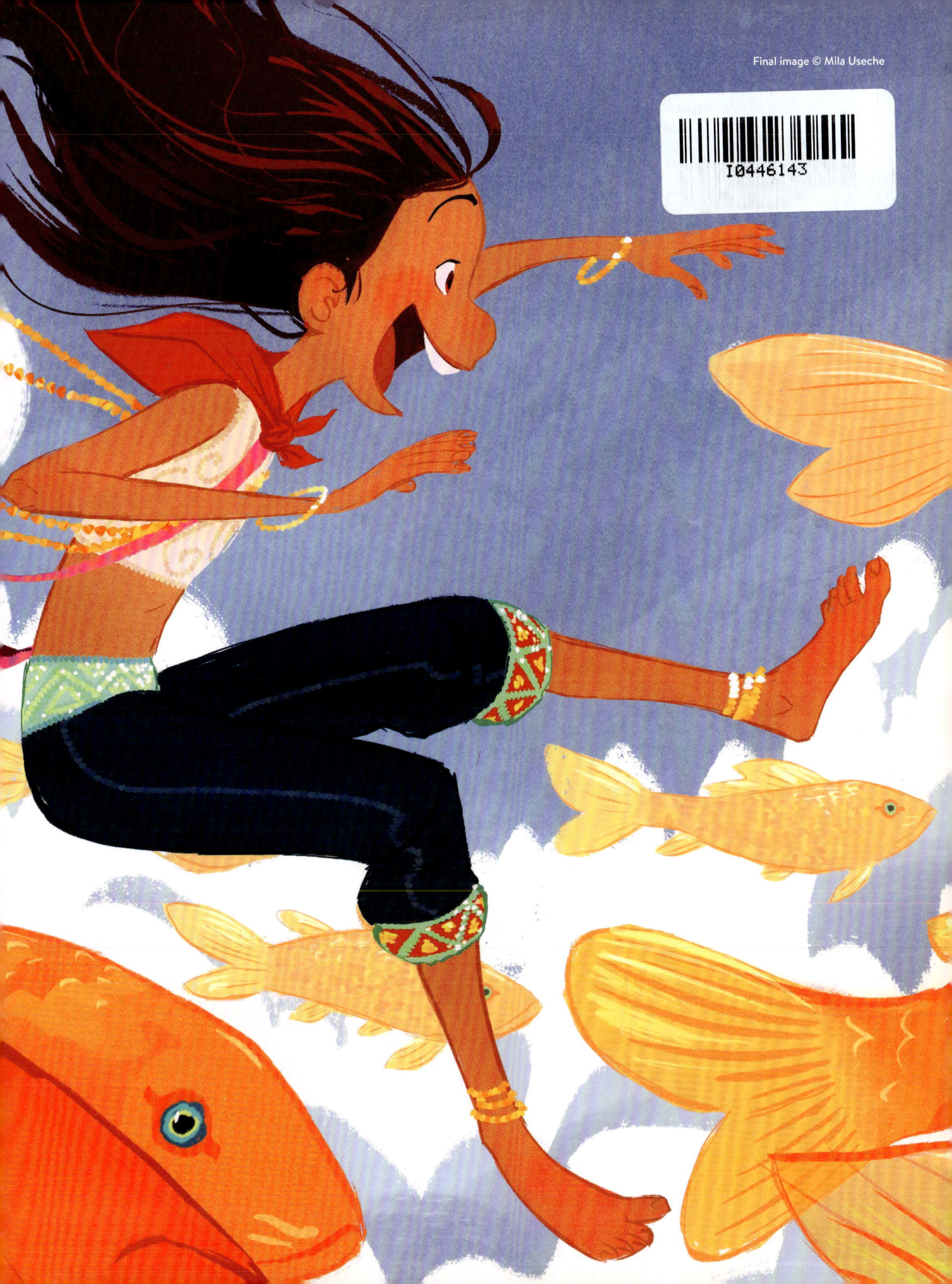

'I ALWAYS TRY TO CHALLENGE MYSELF TO TRY DIFFERENT STYLES AND RENDERING TECHNIQUES'

Hi Mila, thanks for creating this issue's cover! Can you tell us a little about your career to date?

Hi, thank you for the invitation! It's a huge honour for me. So, for the last couple years I've been mostly freelancing. I often get hired for short visual development in animation and sometimes in editorial illustration, designing book covers. In animation, most projects I get hired for are in very early development, which means I often get to design characters from scratch. In editorial, I often work on books aimed at children and teens. Before I started freelancing, I worked for a small video-game studio in Berlin. I quit that job right after releasing a game that I was art director on.

Do you have a favourite style of character to draw?

It really depends on my mood or what I want to communicate or express at that particular moment. In general, I like to simplify a lot, which often leads to a more traditional character for animation style. However, I also like drawing chunky, cute characters that aren't so dynamic, and instead are mostly just adorable. I get bored of things very easily, so it's hard for me to have a consistent style! I used to think that was a disadvantage, but it's become one of my strengths. I always try to challenge myself to try different styles and rendering techniques.

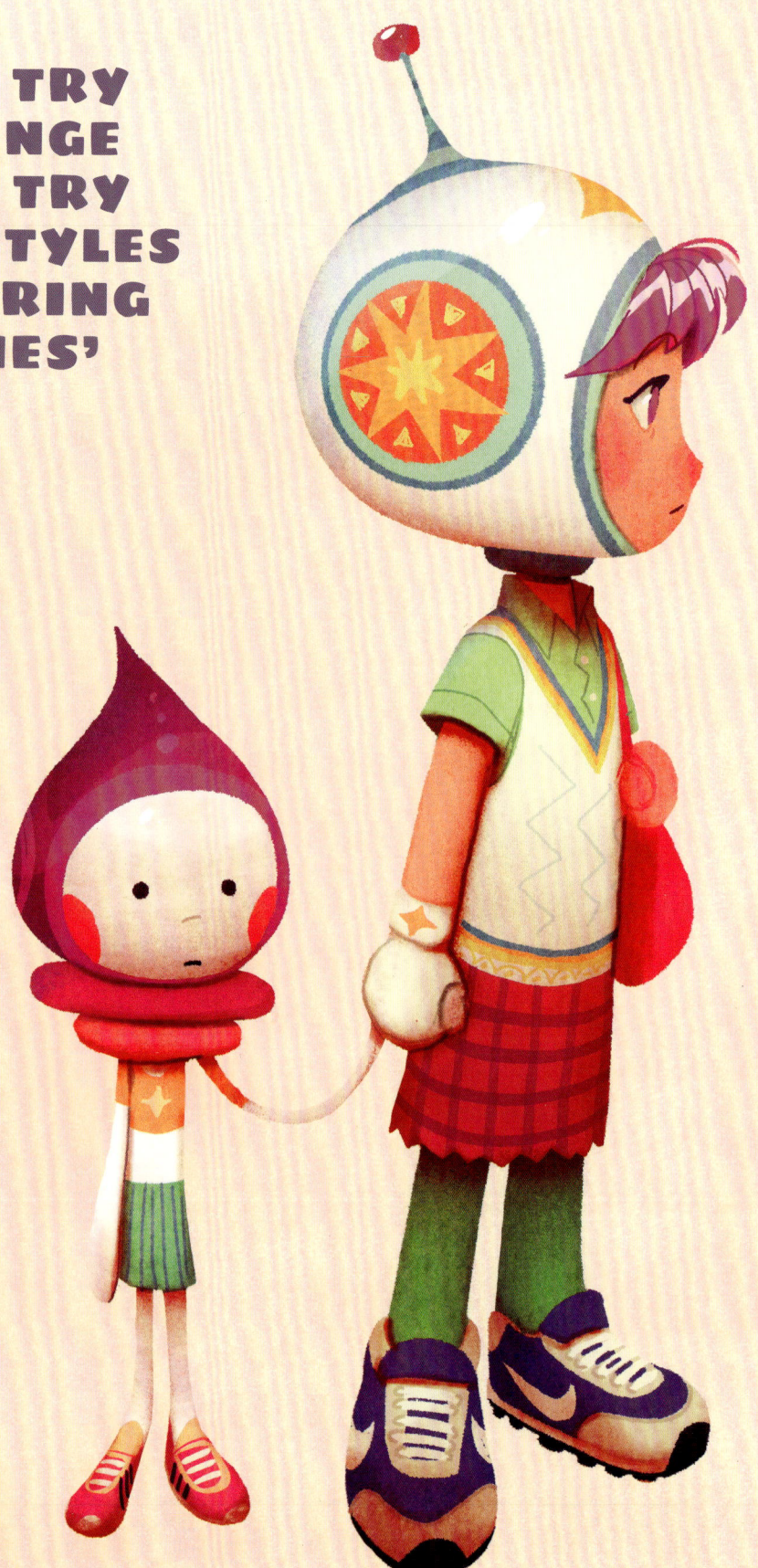

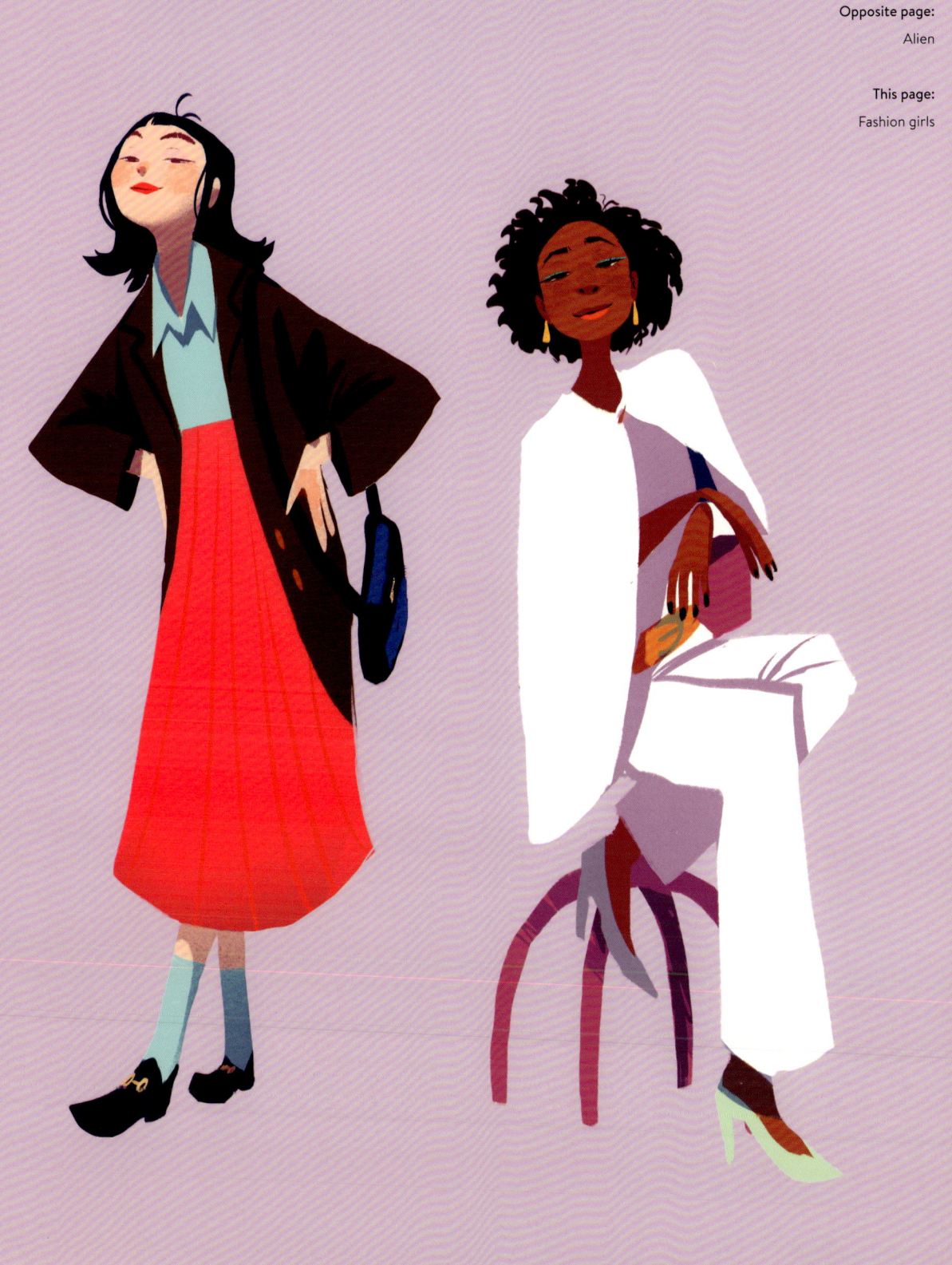

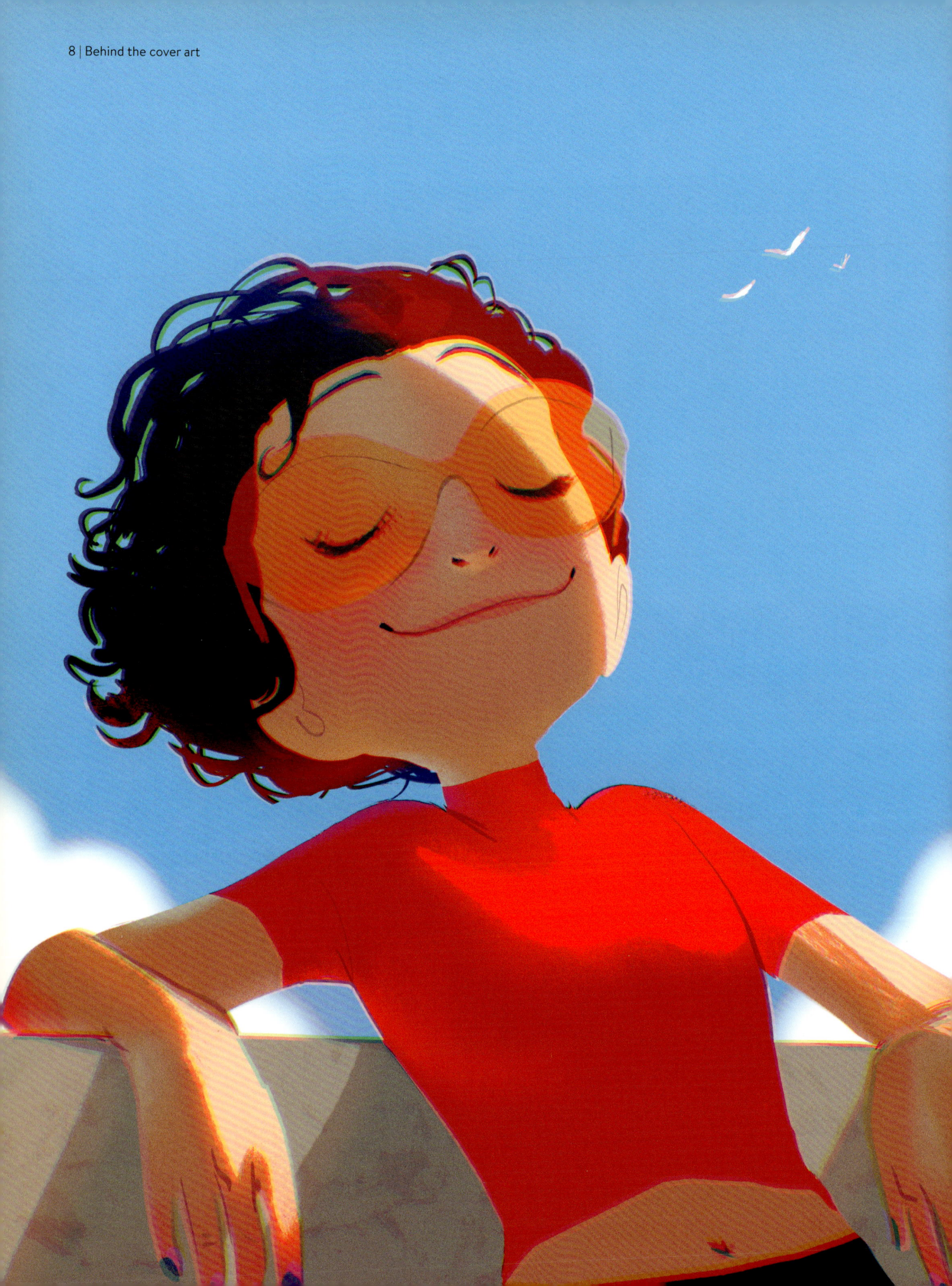

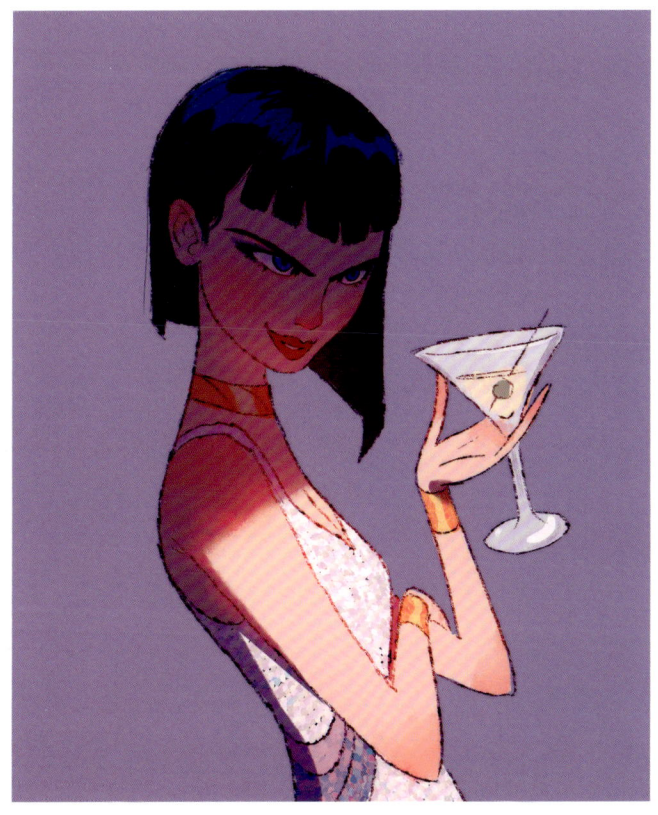

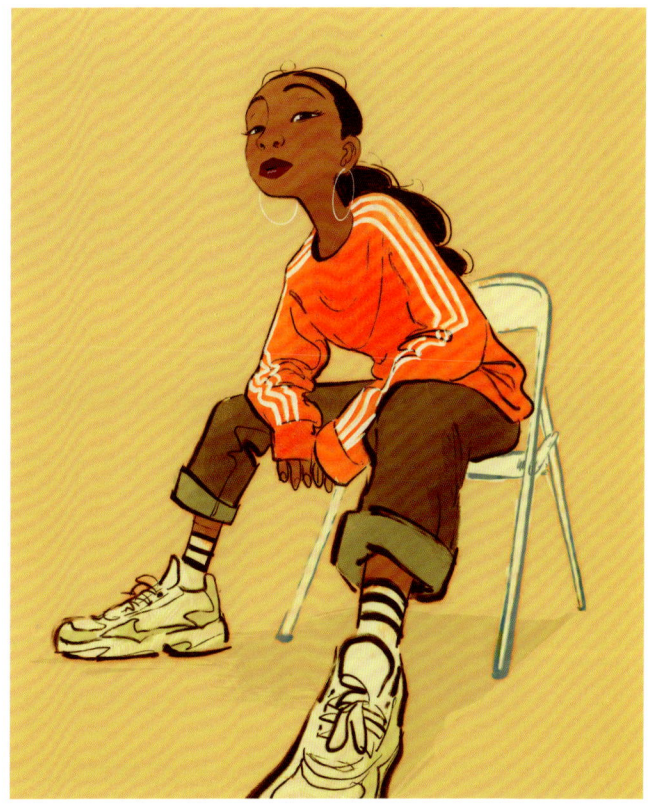

'WHEN IT COMES TO PERSONAL PROJECTS, I MOSTLY FIND INSPIRATION IN MY LIFE EXPERIENCES'

Opposite page: Self

This page (left): Day 3 of the Huevember challenge

This page (right): Day 26 of the Huevember challenge

Where do you find inspiration for your character designs?

It varies depending on whether I'm working on commissioned or personal art. When it comes to commissioned work, I spend a lot of time researching and studying references. I usually get inspired just from that – I'm a very curious person, so learning new things really gets my creative engine going. When it comes to personal projects, I mostly find inspiration in my life experiences – either from my day-to-day experiences or memories from my past.

My childhood in Colombia is an endless source of inspiration, as are the experiences of living far from home.

Do you have any tips for our readers to stand out and be noticed by the major studios?

I think it's all about creating honest art that you care about. In my case, I really got noticed the moment I started being true to myself with the kinds of projects I wanted to work on, and most importantly, the kind of stories I wanted to tell. I began working on very personal projects based on my life experiences and so felt a special connection with the characters and the worlds I was developing. This kept me motivated to continue my work, even when I was tired after spending all day at the game studio. This allowed me to have more artwork to share online and, after consistently posting artwork I cared about, I started getting a lot of attention on social media.

You mentioned your childhood in Colombia – how much do you find your cultural heritage influences your artstyle?

Oh yes, very much so – sometimes, without even realising! After I moved away from Colombia, almost ten years ago, I struggled with my identity and that was reflected in my art – it was generic and lacked intention. I've learned a lot about myself in these last few years and much of it has come from remembering my childhood in Colombia. I feel I've started romanticising my culture and it's showing more and more in my art over the years, especially when it comes to the way I use colour and the subjects of my personal projects.

What have been your favourite projects to work on so far, and what should we look out for from you in the future?

So far my favourite thing to work on has been my own short-film, *Epifania*. It's currently in development with Telescope Animation and it will be my first time writing and directing. I'm also doing all the art direction. It's been really fun to work on because it's a huge challenge and I'm learning a lot. It's also my first step into directing bigger productions, which is really my goal. Hopefully it will be finished by the end of 2023 and released in 2024. There's also a couple other projects of my own that I'm very excited to share, although it might be a few years before I'm able to mention anything.

This page (top):

Cocouy characters

This page (bottom):

Diablito

Opposite page:

Soledad

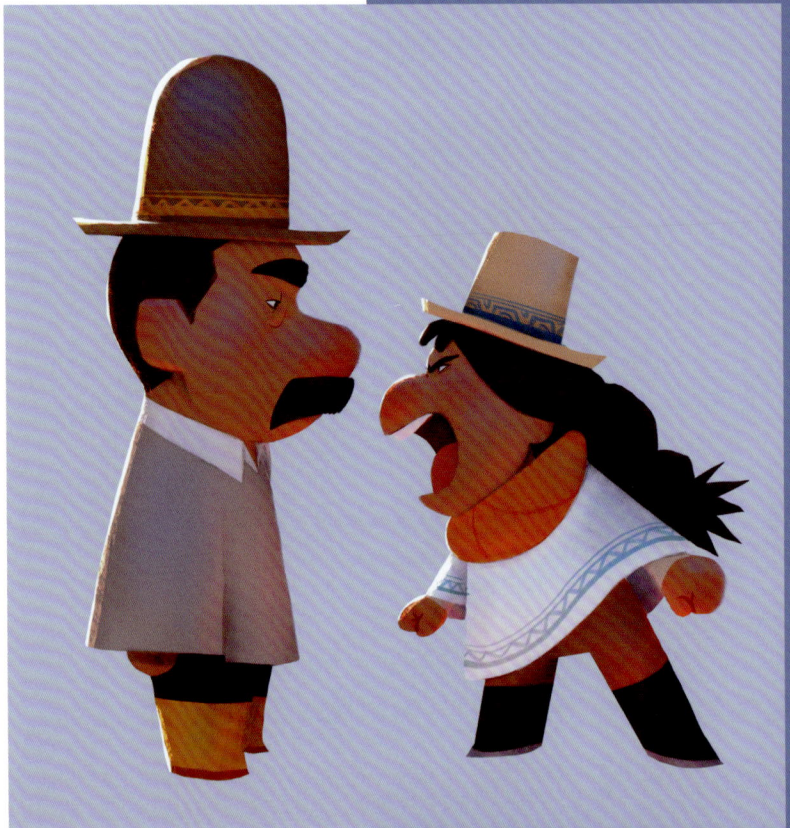

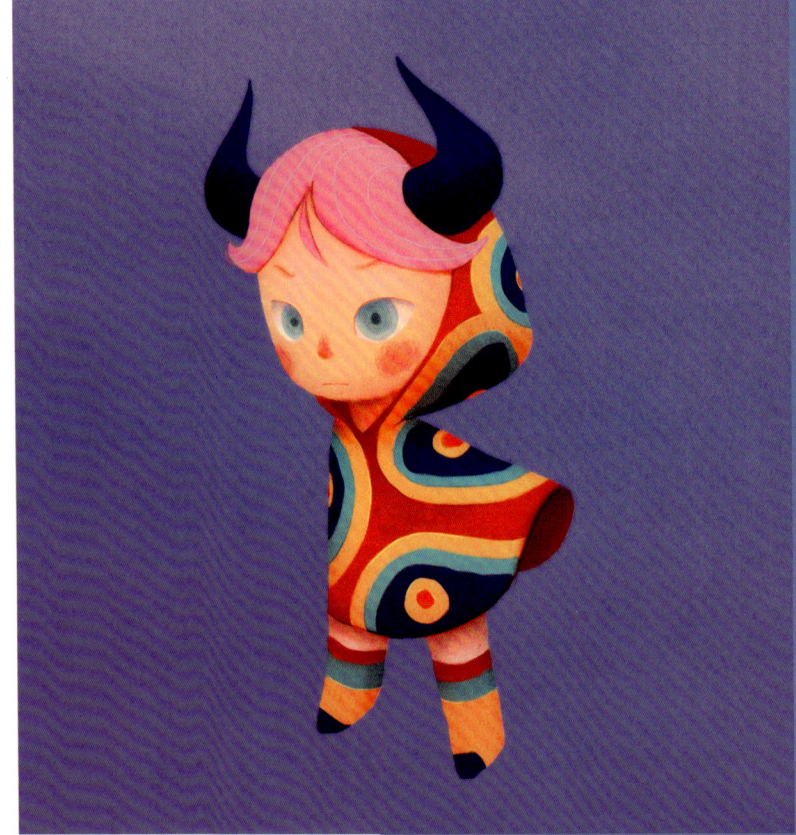

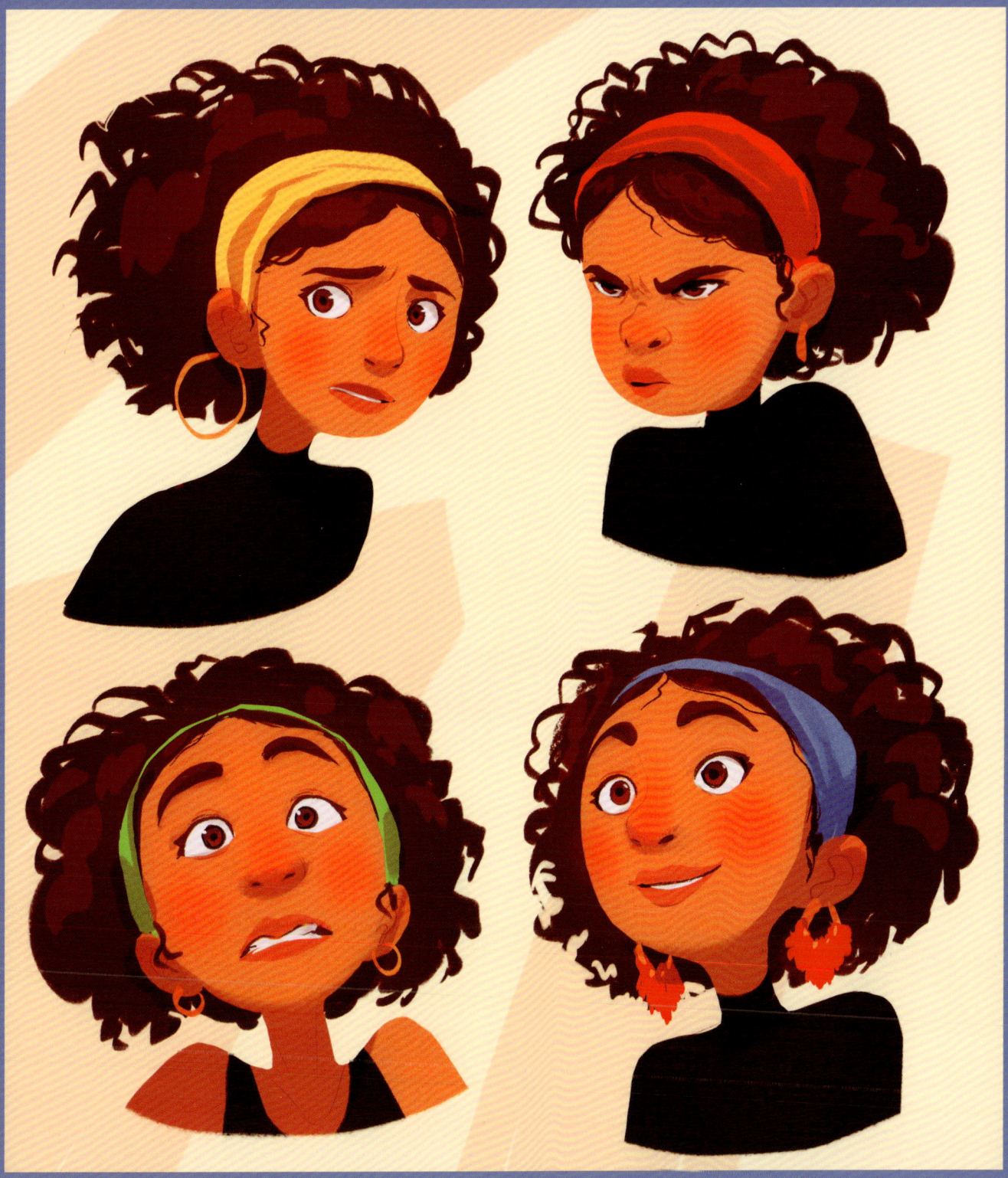

CRAFTING THE COVER

This tutorial will take you through how I created the magazine's cover art. I like to travel a lot and all the work I do as a freelancer is remote, so it's easiest for me to use a few powerful tools that I can carry with me. That's why I create all my art using an iPad Pro and carry a sketchbook for brainstorming and casual sketching. The cover art was made using Procreate.

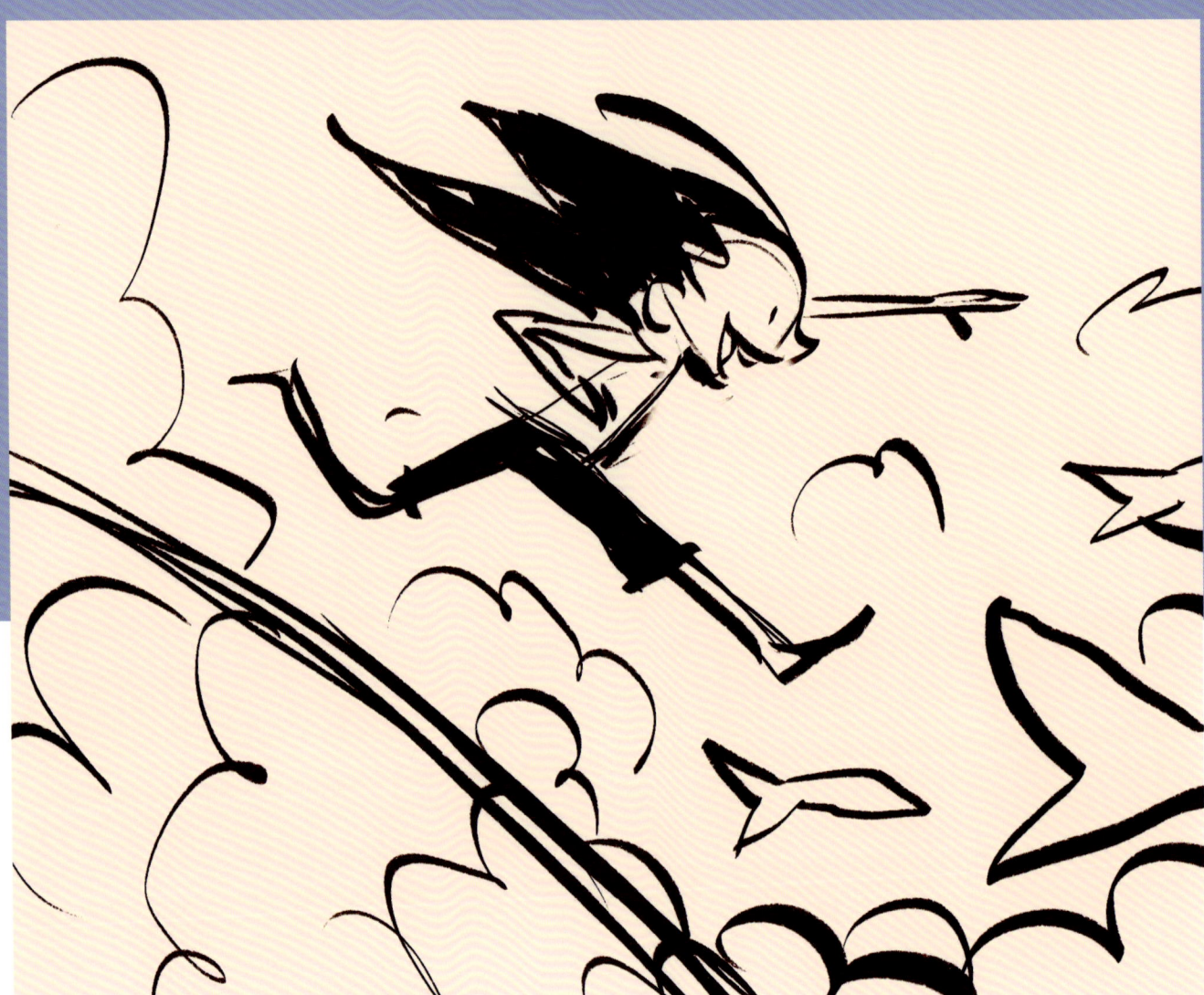

AN IDEA TAKES SHAPE

Coming up with an idea is usually one of the most demanding parts of the design process for me, but luckily I have a pretty good idea of a direction for the cover art: I want to create something fun and magical. At the beginning of a project, it's important to keep your thumbnails loose and very simple. These early drawings are worth more for the idea they convey rather than the technical skill they show. Keeping sketches simple will also let you quickly try different ideas and compositions.

This page: A very quick and rough thumbnail of my idea

Opposite page: A more polished layout of the cover based on my thumbnail

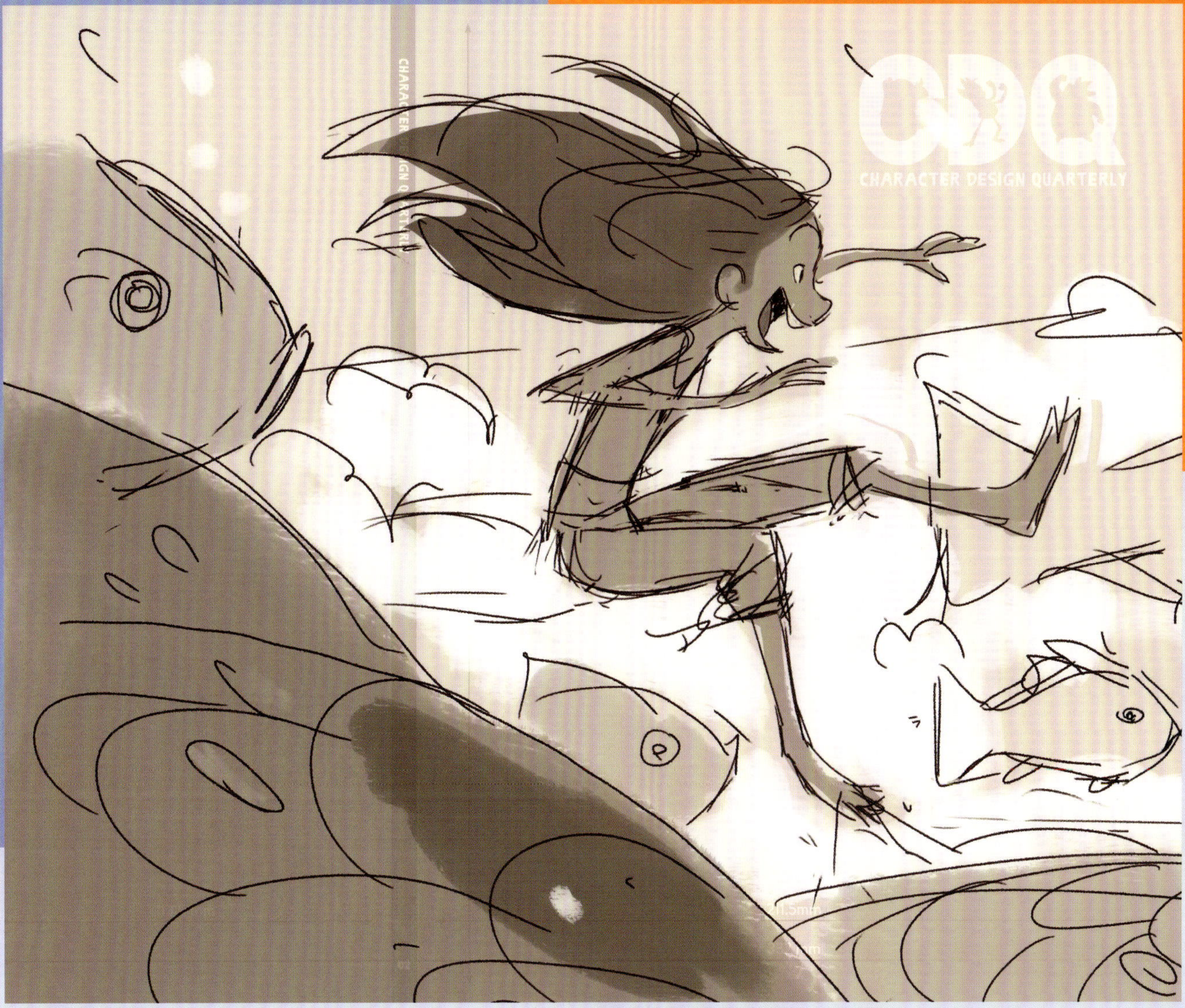

LAYING FOUNDATIONS

After deciding on a rough thumbnail idea and composition, the next step is to polish the bigger shapes and resolve poses and expressions. Because this is a character-based illustration, I have to be careful not to saturate the background with too many elements that could distract the viewer from focusing on my character. Also, because this is a cover, I have to be mindful from the start of where the title will go and where the image will fold. Considering these elements now will prevent me running in to trouble later on. Imagine this step as setting up the foundations of a house.

IT'S RAINING IDEAS

Early on in the process, I had the idea that the girl would be holding an umbrella. I thought it would add a more whimsical feeling to the image. However, the umbrella took a lot of space away from my character. I couldn't really find a good reason to keep it so I decided to go with a more dynamic pose for the final design.

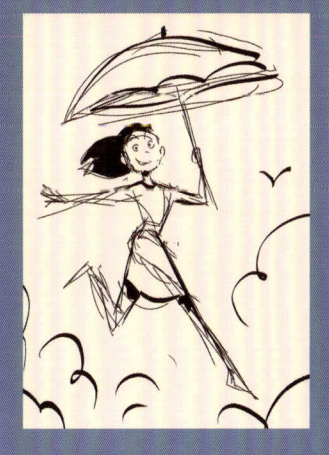

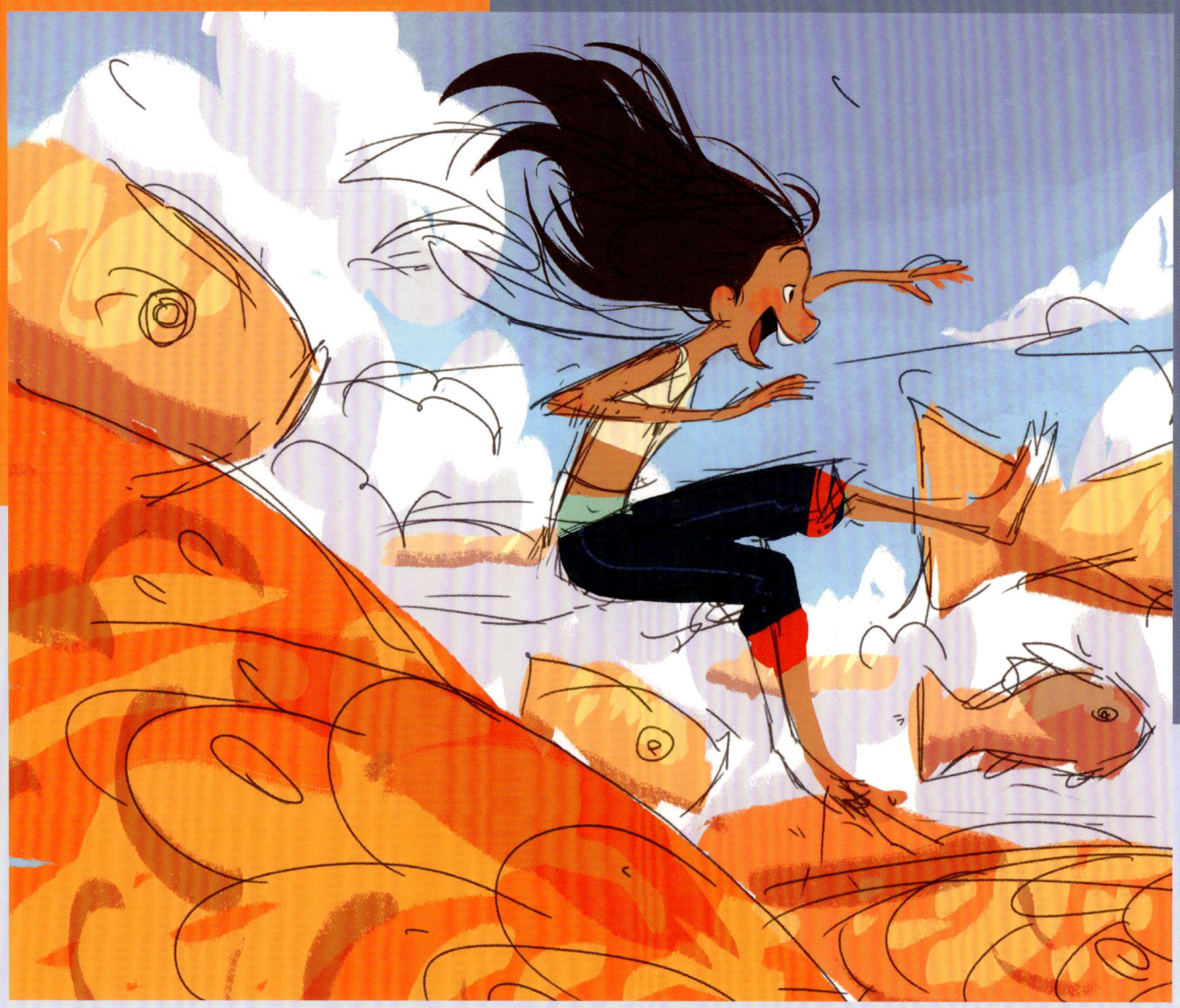

COLOUR BLOCKING

I haven't really changed my cleaned-up sketch but I add some rough colour to have a better idea of how to move forward with my colour choices. At this stage, it's very important to remember that my character is the focus of my illustration. This way, I can better manage the hues and values of the entire image to make my character stand out from the background. I superimpose the warm tones of the face over the cool tones of the sky and add small amounts of bright colour details on the character's clothing.

RIDING THE WAVE

After figuring out my colours, I start polishing the shapes and details of my character and the fish. I want to keep some of the rough, loose nature of my sketch, so I have to be careful not to be too clean. Therefore, I don't trace my sketch precisely, but rather paint under it with loose and expressive strokes. At this stage, I also make some small changes on the arrangement of some elements to further enhance the flow of the illustration. This is also a good moment to add details to my character, such as patterns and jewellery. These extra embellishments will make my character look unique and authentic.

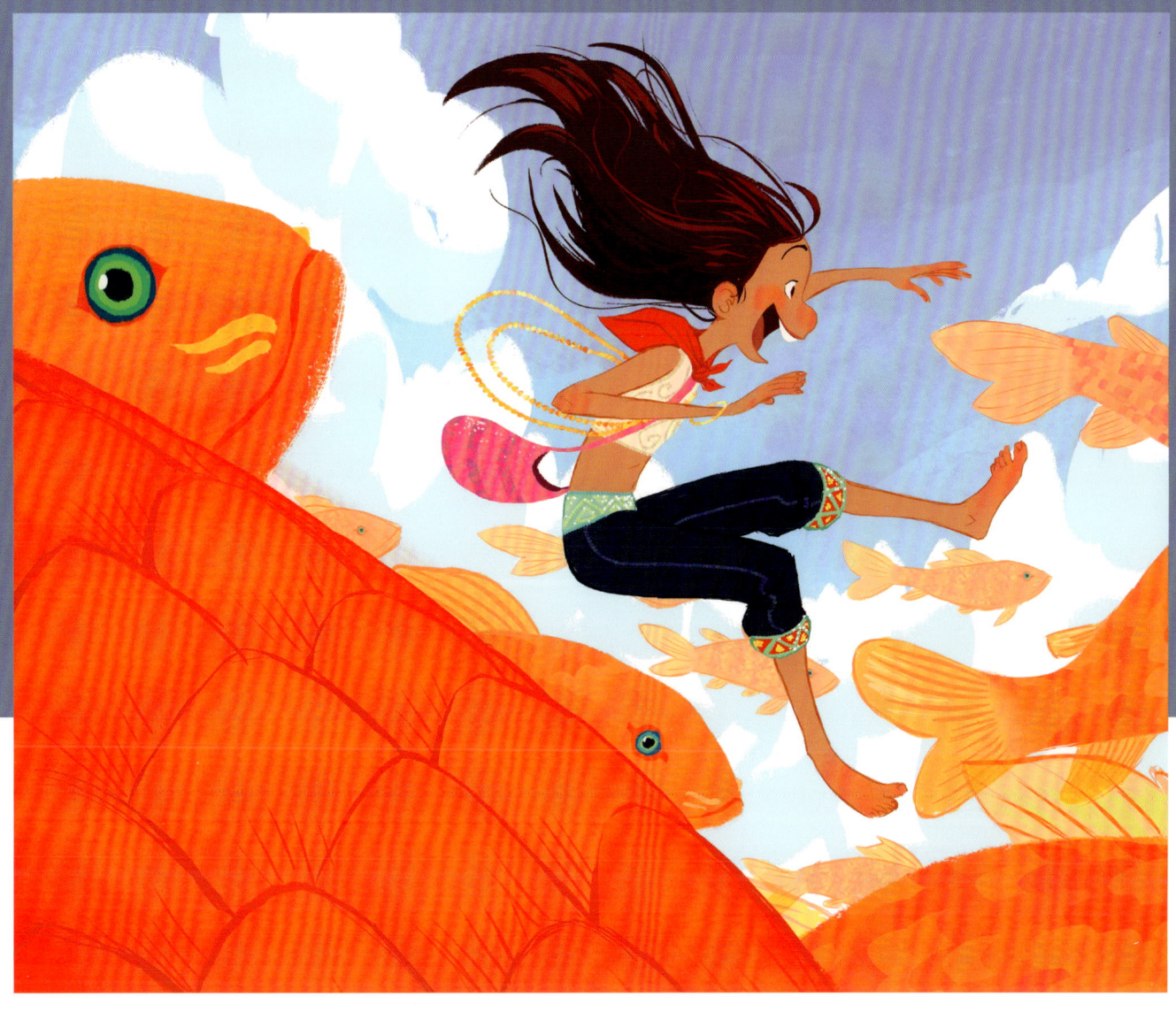

'I WANT TO KEEP SOME OF THE ROUGH, LOOSE NATURE OF MY SKETCH, SO I HAVE TO BE CAREFUL NOT TO BE TOO CLEAN'

Opposite page: A coloured version of my cleaned-up sketch

This page: A cleaned-up version of the illustration, using coloured lines and flat colours

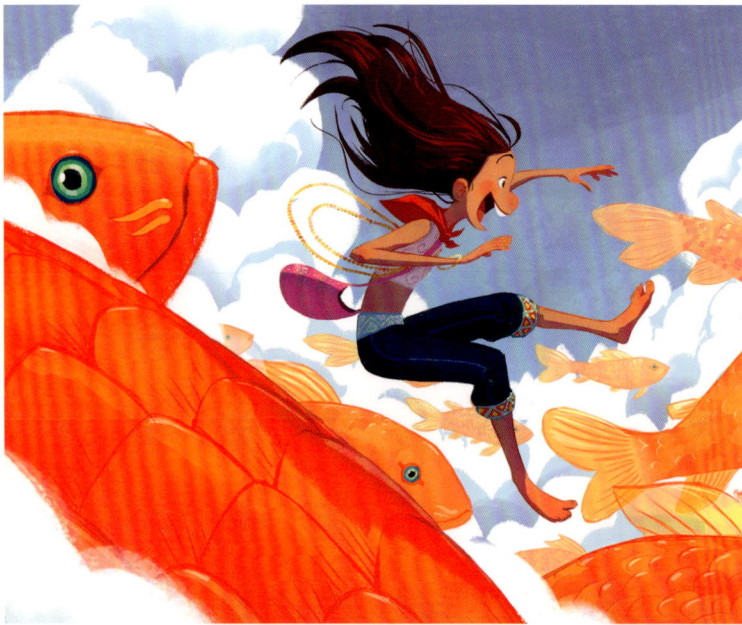

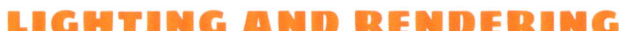

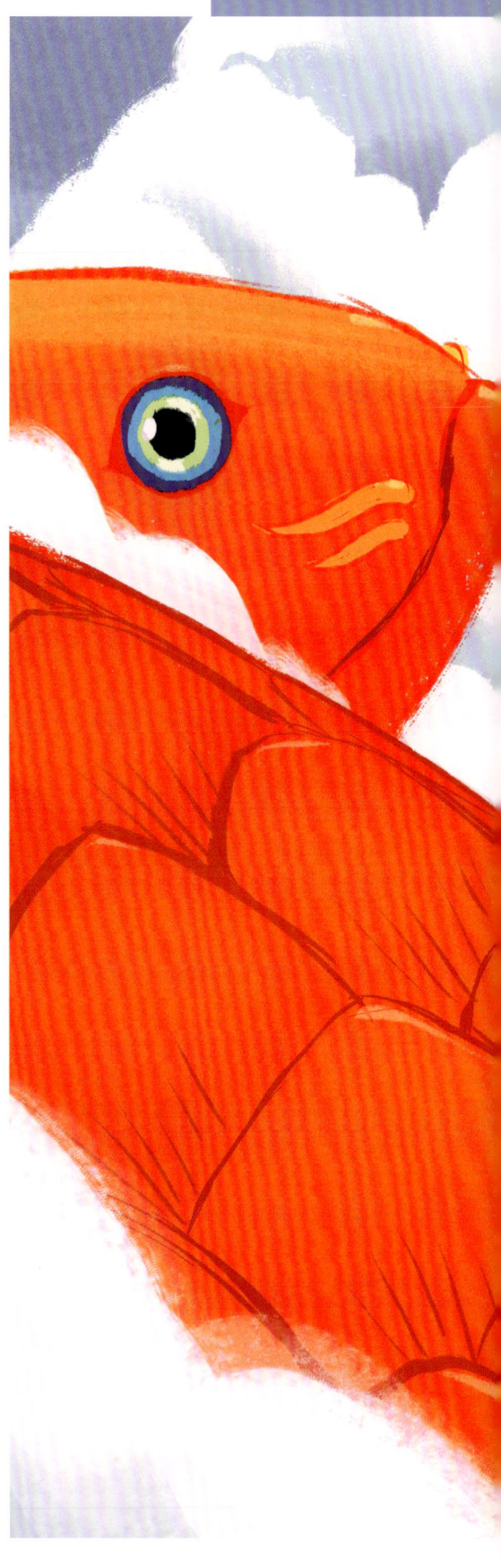

LIGHTING AND RENDERING

I want to keep the image as simple as possible, but I also want it to look magical. I add rough shadows and light effects that push the contrast of the image and add more of a cinematic feeling. To keep it simple, I use a single layer set to Multiply, filled with a light purple colour. This way, I can make sure that all the shadows stay balanced, both in hue and darkness. For some light details, I use a layer set to Colour Dodge and paint a few subtle gradients using a soft brush.

THE FINAL PUSH

I'm not happy with how the render light and shadows look, so I decide to go back to a flatter and more graphic style. Sometimes, going one step back is the way to move forward. I continue by further balancing the colours and values so the image is easy to read, even without the higher contrast of the shadows. At this final stage, I also add a few layers of texture and grain to give my illustration a nice hand-made textured look. For this, I use a watercolour paper texture that I created myself, plus a simple grey grain layer, both set to Overlay mode at around 50% opacity.

This page: A more rendered version of the image, with shadows, gradients, and light effects

Opposite page: The finished version of my illustration

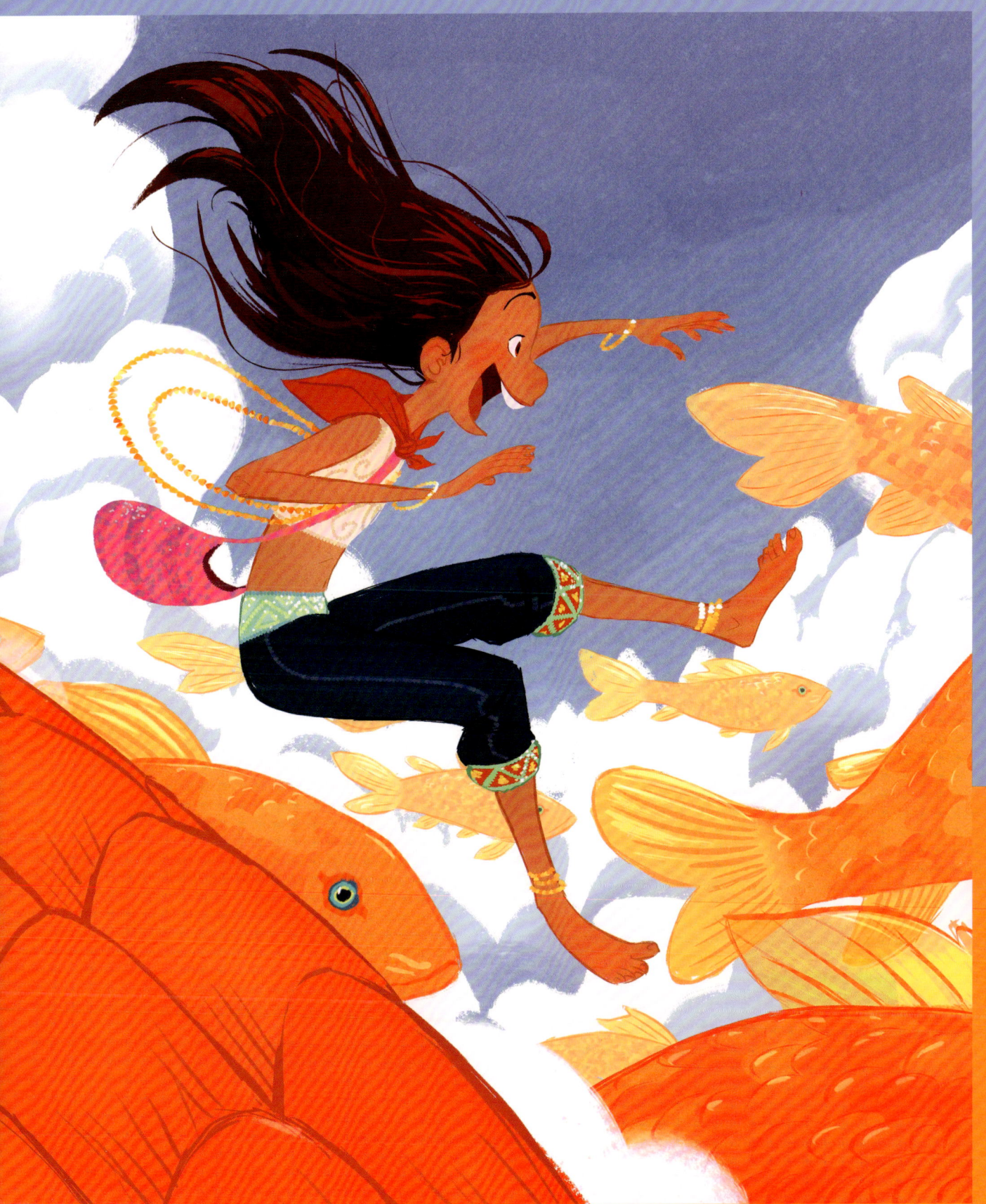

BAT TO BASICS

RAAHAT KADUJI

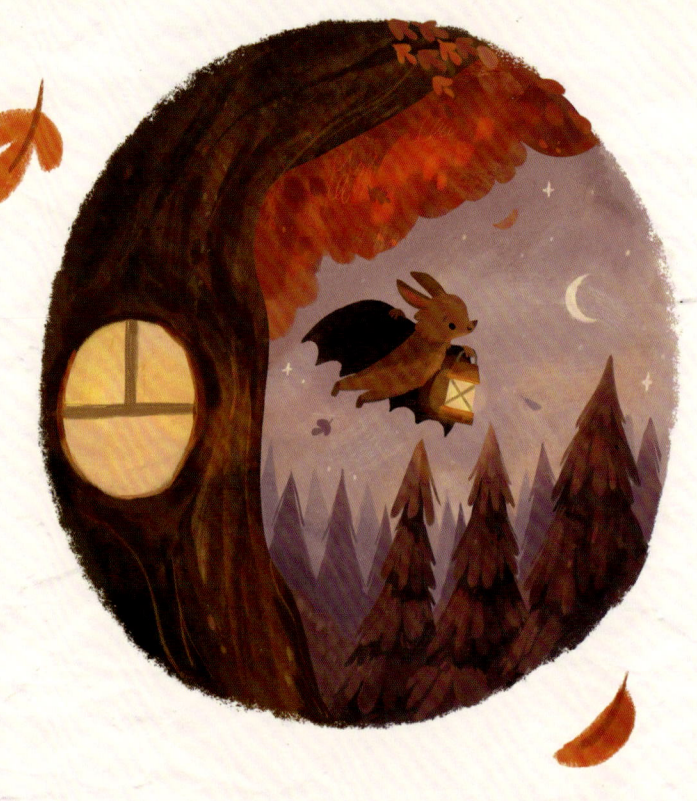

There's so much fun to be had in imagining and designing a character for children to enjoy. Let's take a closer look at how I designed the character Bat from my debut children's book, *I'm Not Scary*. I'll walk you through the process, starting simply, introducing emotion and personality, and experimenting with colour to help convey the character's narrative. I usually begin with pencil sketches in my sketchbook before moving to Photoshop for further design development and the final digital illustration.

SIMPLE SHAPES

For a solid foundation, start with basic shapes. These can be transformed into anything, but at their core they are easy for children to recognise. Think which shape best represents your character. Are they smooth and gentle like a circle, or are they pointy and sharp like a triangle? My character Bat is gentle and kind, so he's rounded in shape.

'FOR A SOLID FOUNDATION, START WITH BASIC SHAPES'

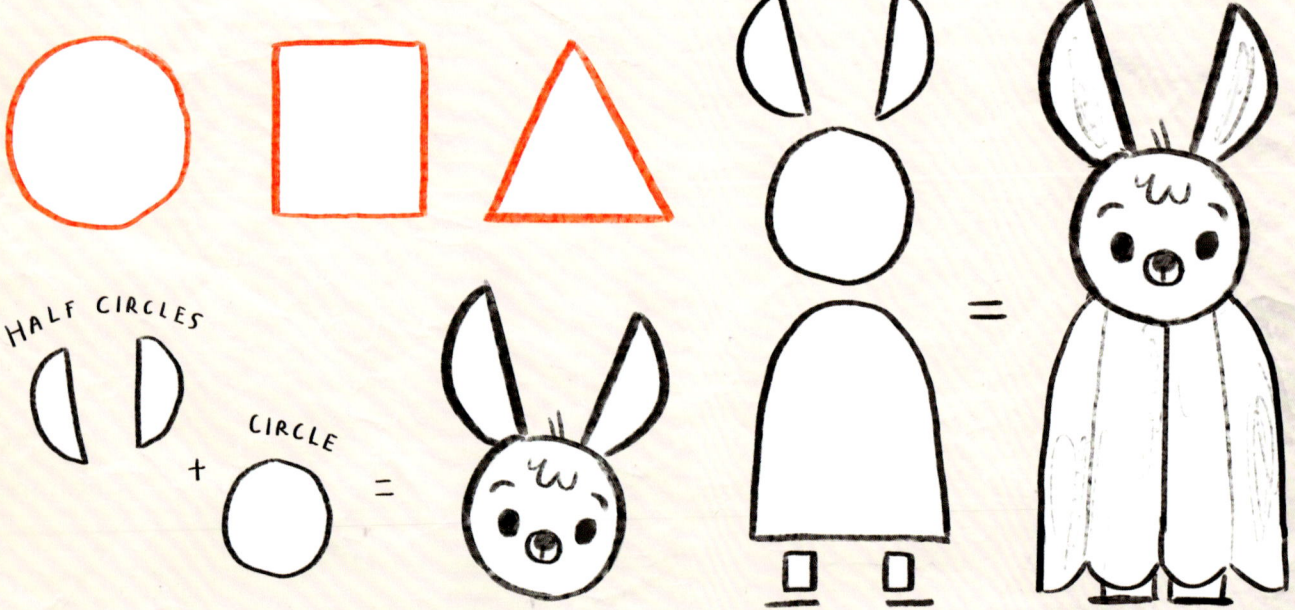

CHILD-LIKE PROPORTIONS

Characters don't need to be realistic. Exaggerate or simplify their proportions to make them more playful. A big head and shorter limbs will make your character appear younger and more familiar to an audience of children. You can apply this technique to both human and animal characters.

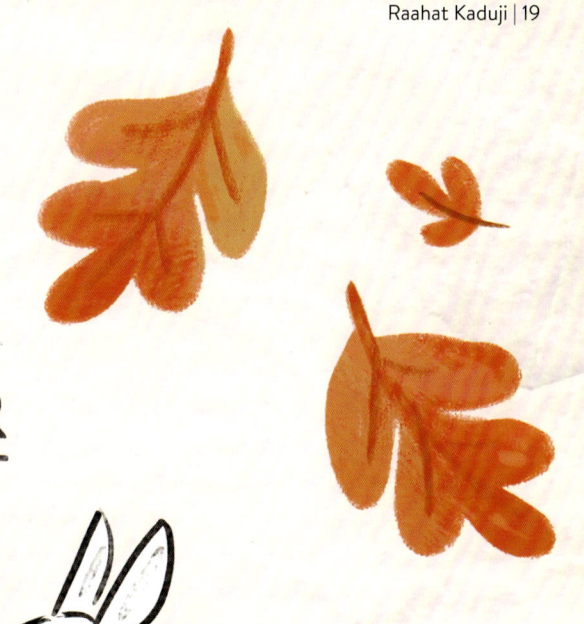

OLDER

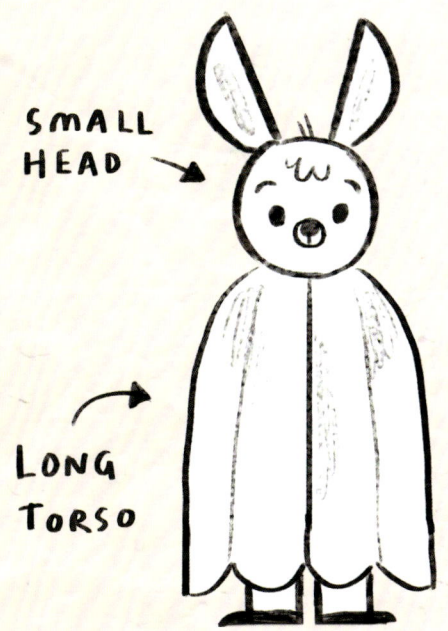

SMALL HEAD

LONG TORSO

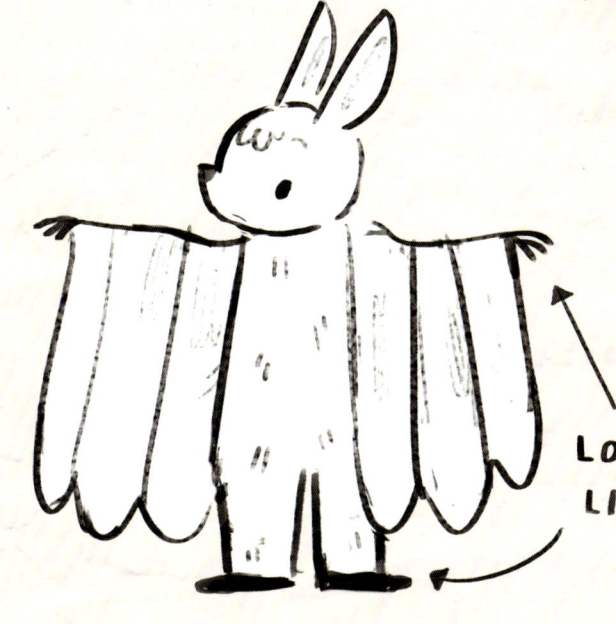

LONG LIMBS

YOUNGER

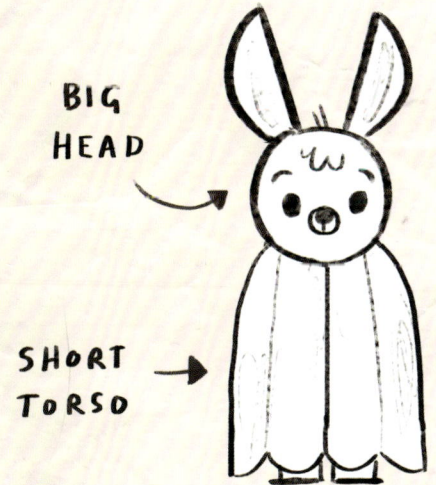

BIG HEAD

SHORT TORSO

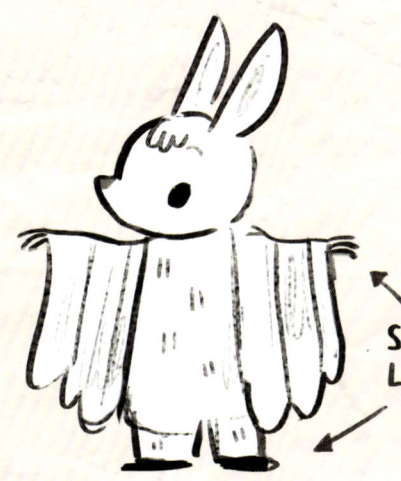

SHORT LIMBS

'CHARACTERS DON'T NEED TO BE REALISTIC'

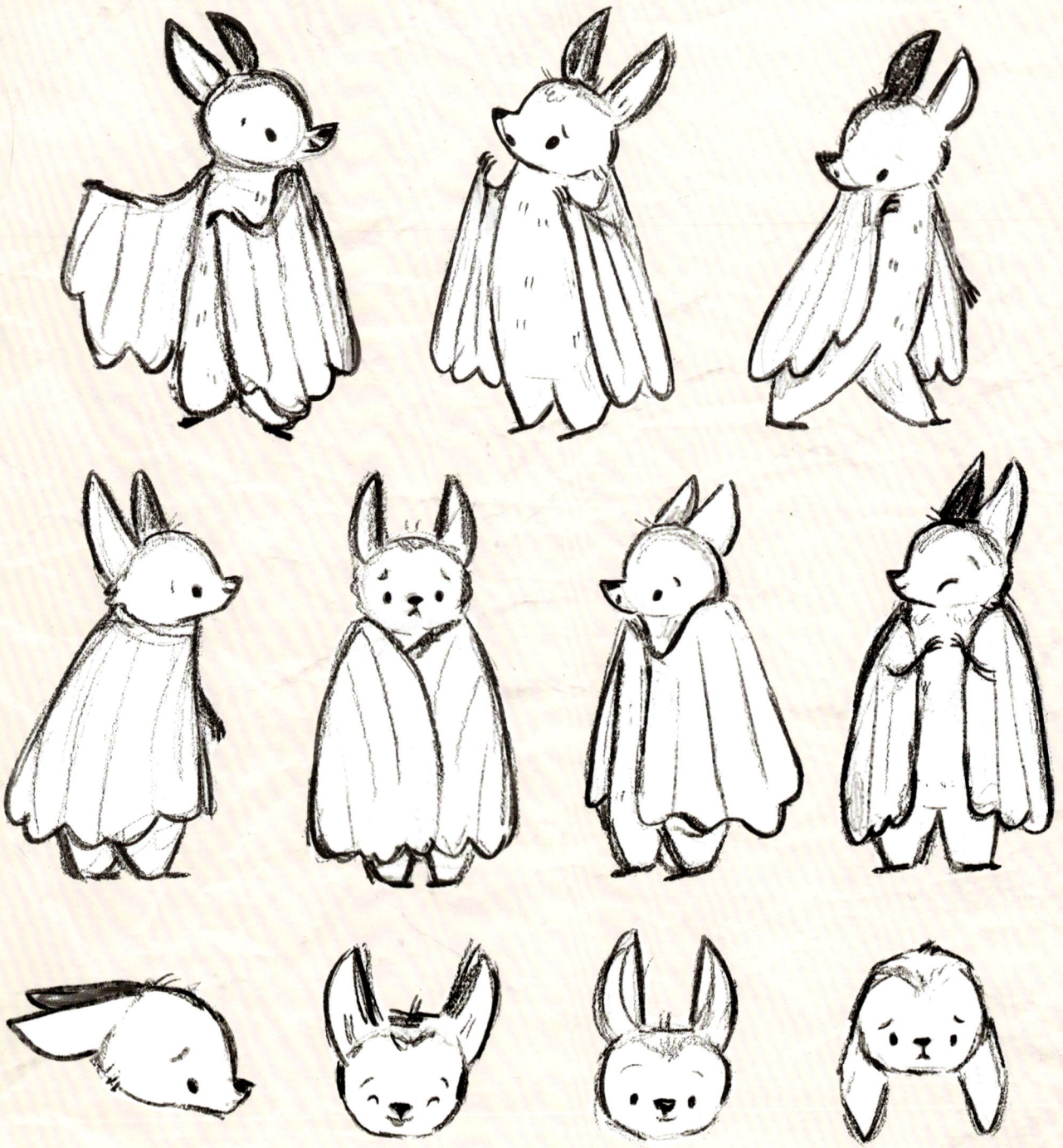

EXPRESSIVENESS

Begin to explore different facial expressions and poses to introduce feeling. It's important to explore a whole range of emotions to establish your character's nature. These are sketches of Bat from my sketchbook. Notice how expressions make him appear more animated and alive as his shape continues to evolve.

PROPS AND PERSONALITY

Become familiar with your character's narrative and really dig into who they are. Consider their likes and dislikes, their hobbies and interests, and where they live. Think about items, clothing, or possessions that you might see them with. Bat lives in a forest and enjoys baking, so I've sketched some baked goods, berries, and a lantern that he carries to see at night.

'BECOME FAMILIAR WITH YOUR CHARACTER'S NARRATIVE AND REALLY DIG INTO WHO THEY ARE'

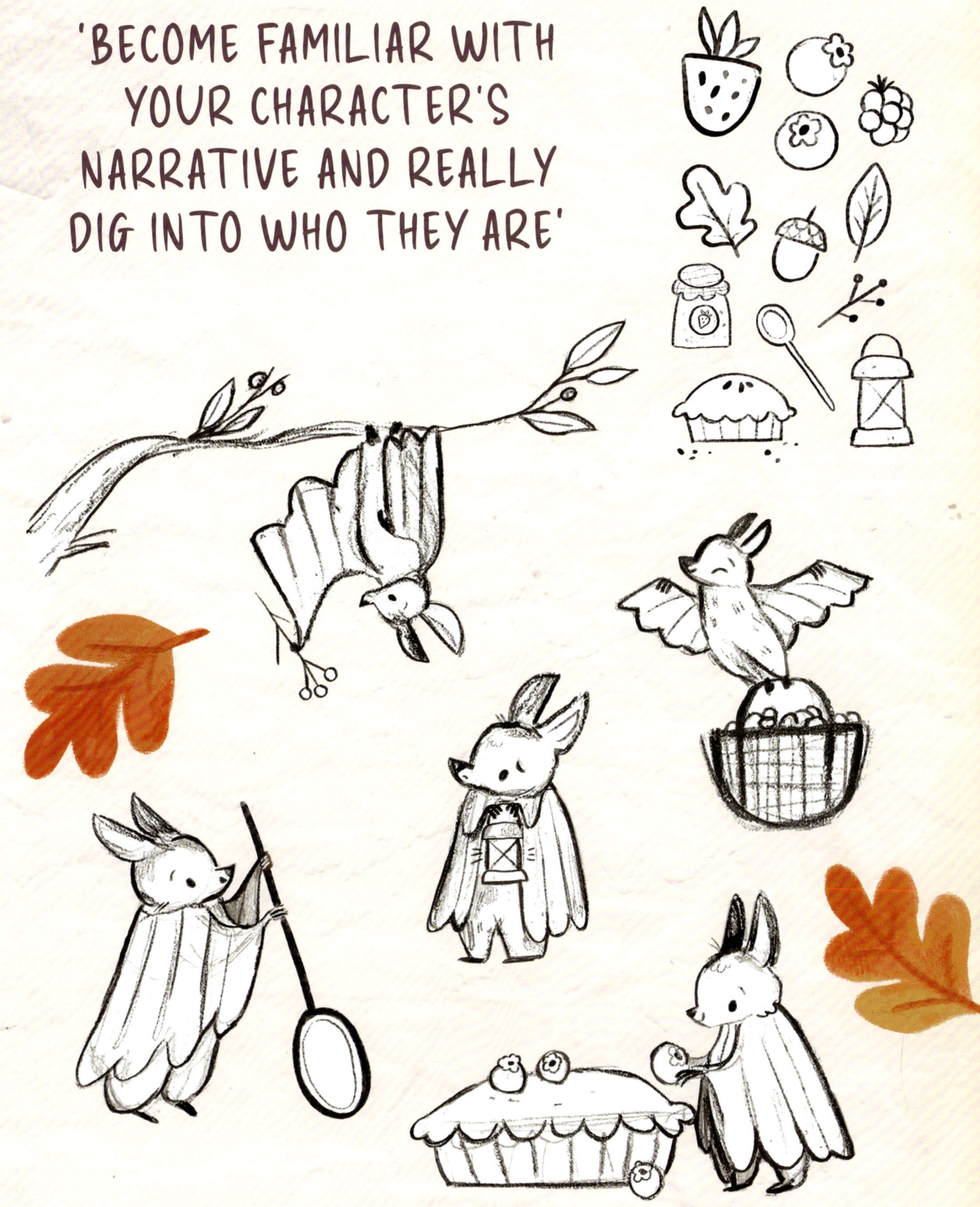

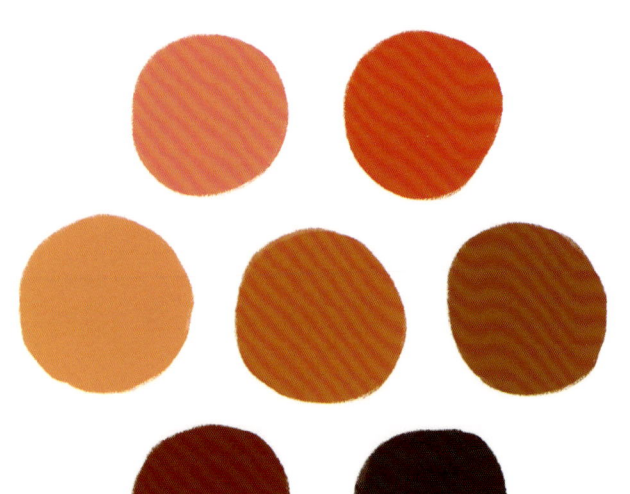

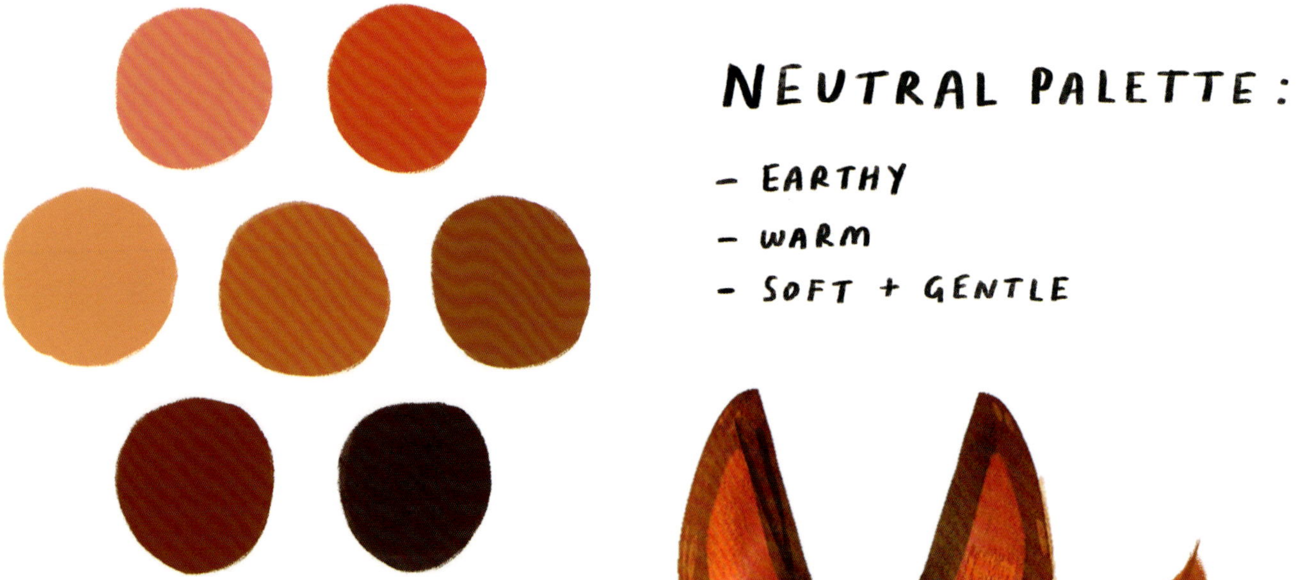

NEUTRAL PALETTE:

- EARTHY
- WARM
- SOFT + GENTLE

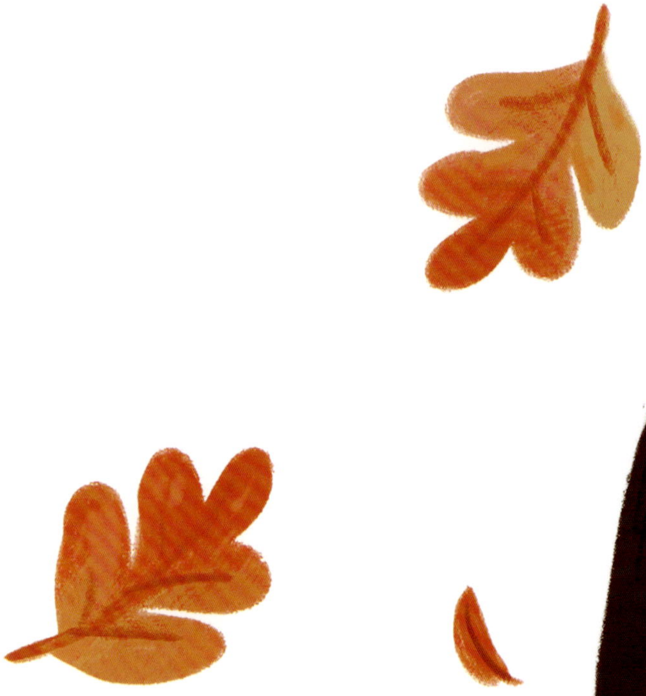

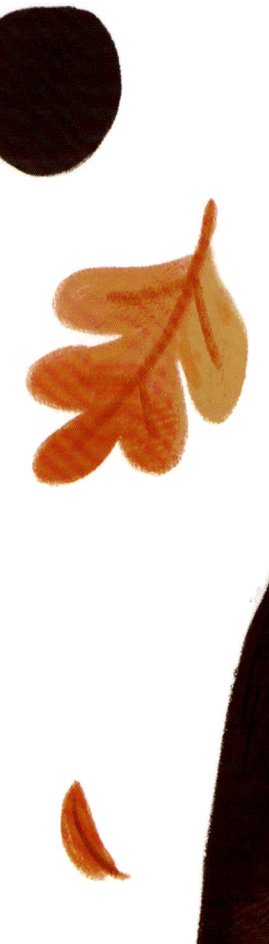

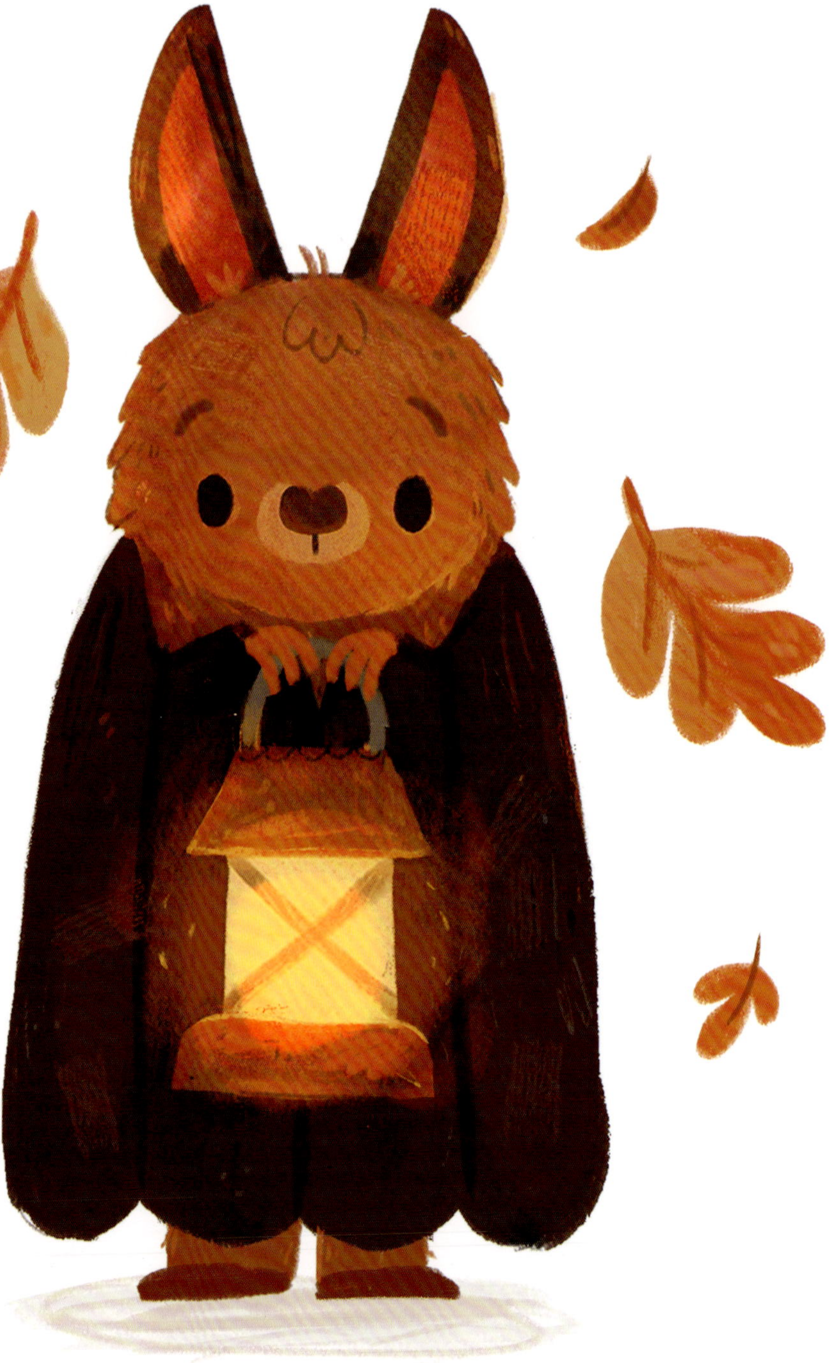

COLOUR EXPLORATION

Now it's time to use colour to bring your character to life. Colour is an important part of children's character design as it's what makes your character stand out on the page. Use a colour palette that best contributes to their mood and story. For example, a bright palette is fun and exciting, while a neutral palette is more gentle and mellow. I've opted for the latter with Bat's design.

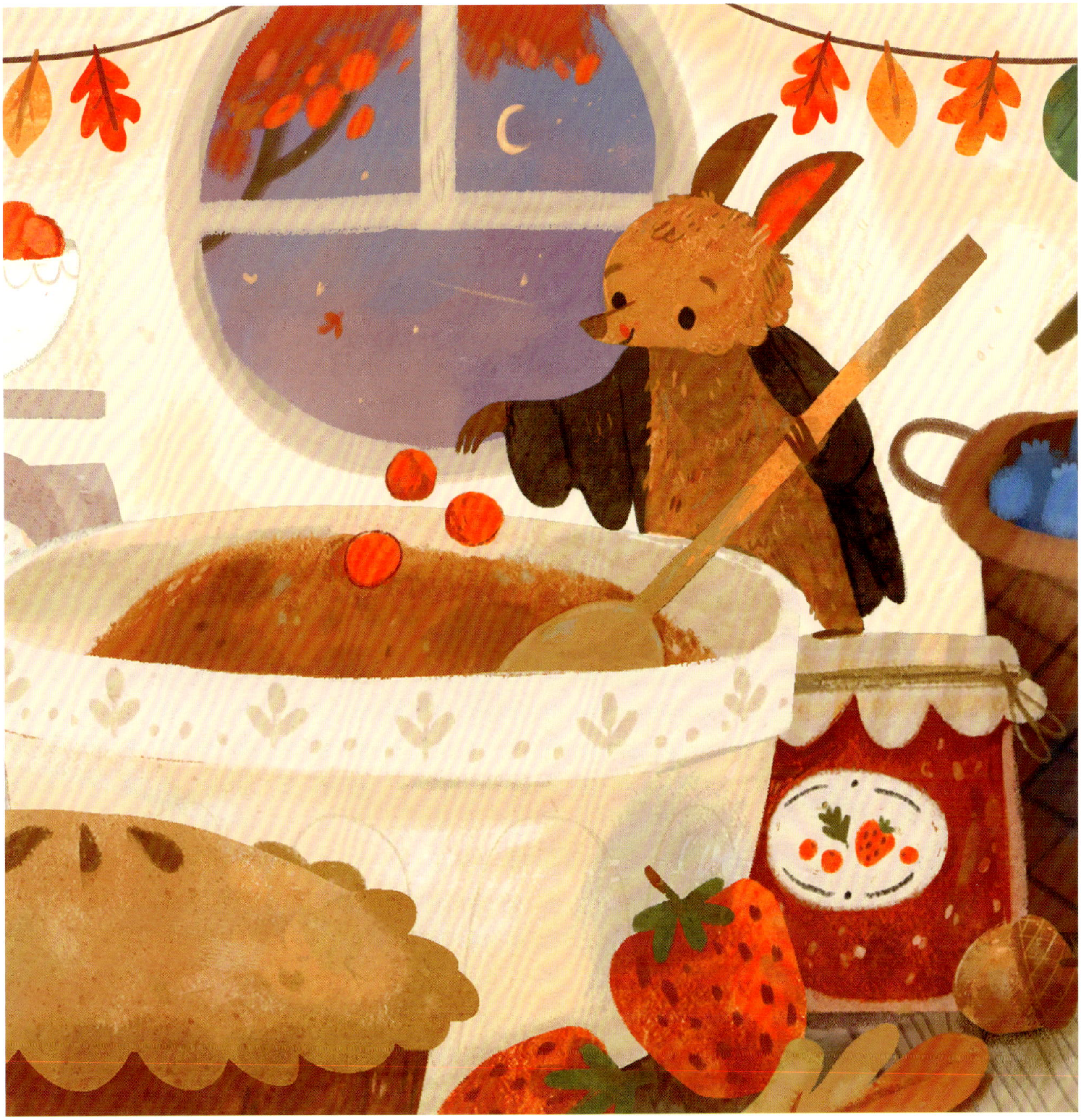

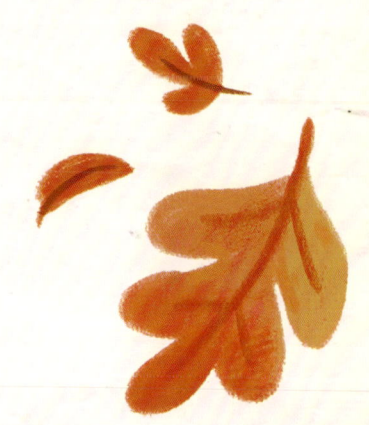

BRING IT ALL TOGETHER

Once you've got to know your character, their personality, and their appearance, you can go one step further. Drop them into a scene and show them interacting with their world. You can include some possessions or have them engaging in their favourite hobby to truly bring them to life.

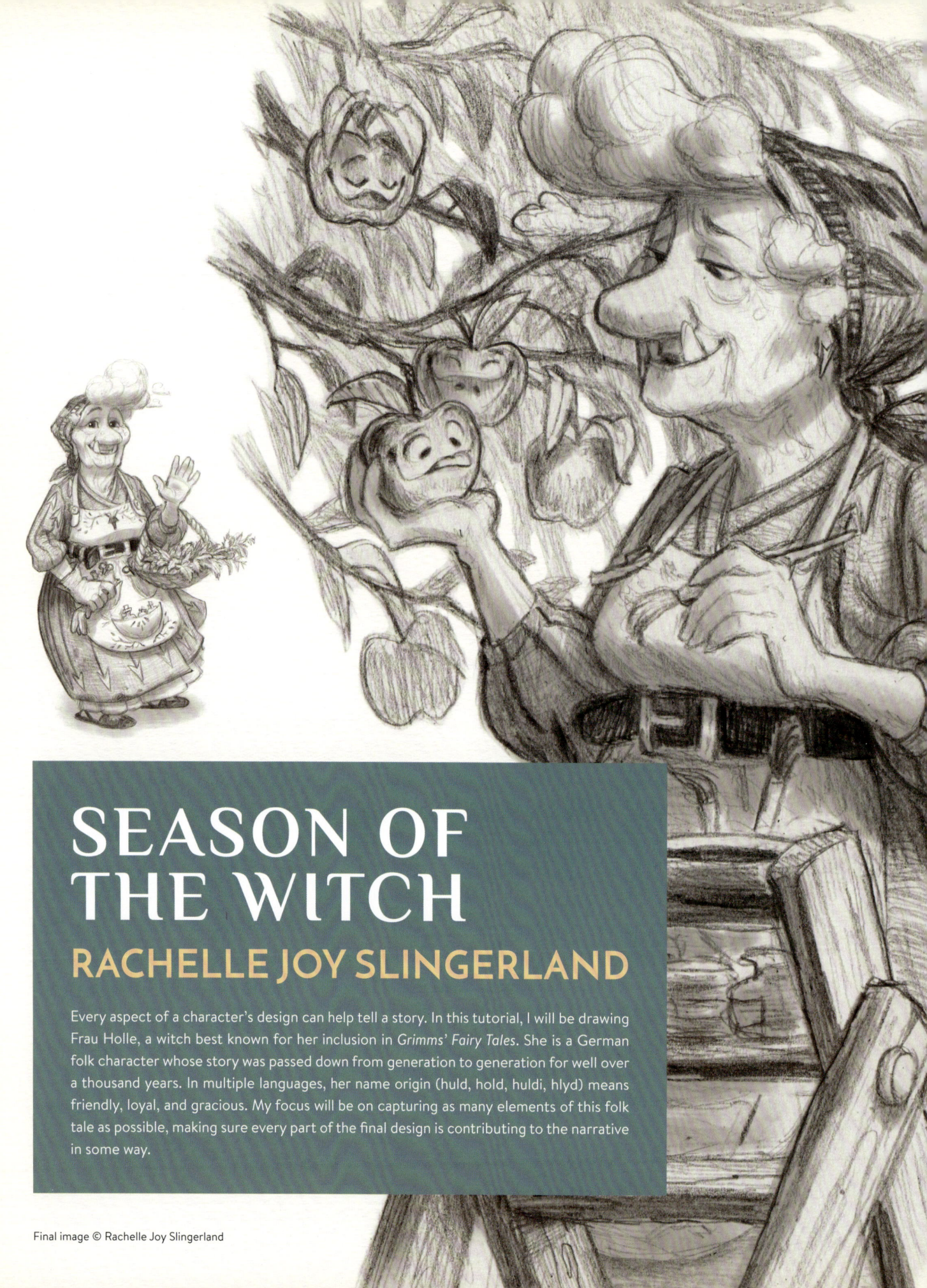

SEASON OF THE WITCH

RACHELLE JOY SLINGERLAND

Every aspect of a character's design can help tell a story. In this tutorial, I will be drawing Frau Holle, a witch best known for her inclusion in *Grimms' Fairy Tales*. She is a German folk character whose story was passed down from generation to generation for well over a thousand years. In multiple languages, her name origin (huld, hold, huldi, hlyd) means friendly, loyal, and gracious. My focus will be on capturing as many elements of this folk tale as possible, making sure every part of the final design is contributing to the narrative in some way.

Final image © Rachelle Joy Slingerland

HUNTING SEASON

For this piece, the narrative is incredibly important, so I start by considering the myth of Frau Holle and what elements I want to bring to her design. Frau Holle and her two daughters loved hunting, so much so they refused to ascend to heaven as hunting there is forbidden. To punish her for her disobedience, the other gods cursed the Frau's daughters, turning them into dogs.

The curse didn't work on Frau Holle, like it had on her daughters. While she didn't turn into a dog, her teeth changed to match theirs – big, ugly teeth. They may scare off visitors at first sight, but her kind nature quickly wins them over, as does her baking! These are all features of the narrative I want to include in my design.

SPINNING A YARN

Frau Holle spends her time spinning fabric. Her speciality is creating a thick, warm fabric from the nettles that surround her home. Not only do the nettles have healing properties, they also make a cracking cup of tea!

TALKING FOOD

In Frau Holle's magical forest, it's never quiet. In the orchard, chattering apples greet visitors, asking to be picked, and fresh loaves call out from the bakery, waiting to be taken from the hot oven. It's all part of the Frau's test for her visitors, to see if they're hard workers and selfless, or lazy and selfish.

UP IN THE CLOUDS

As Frau Holle's cottage sits high in the clouds, a traditional pointy witch's hat wouldn't stand up to the wind, so a simple scarf will suffice. The final ingredient is Frau's command of the weather, the snow she creates by shaking out her blanket. The feathers that escape from her bedsheets form beautiful snowflakes, covering whatever surface she flies above.

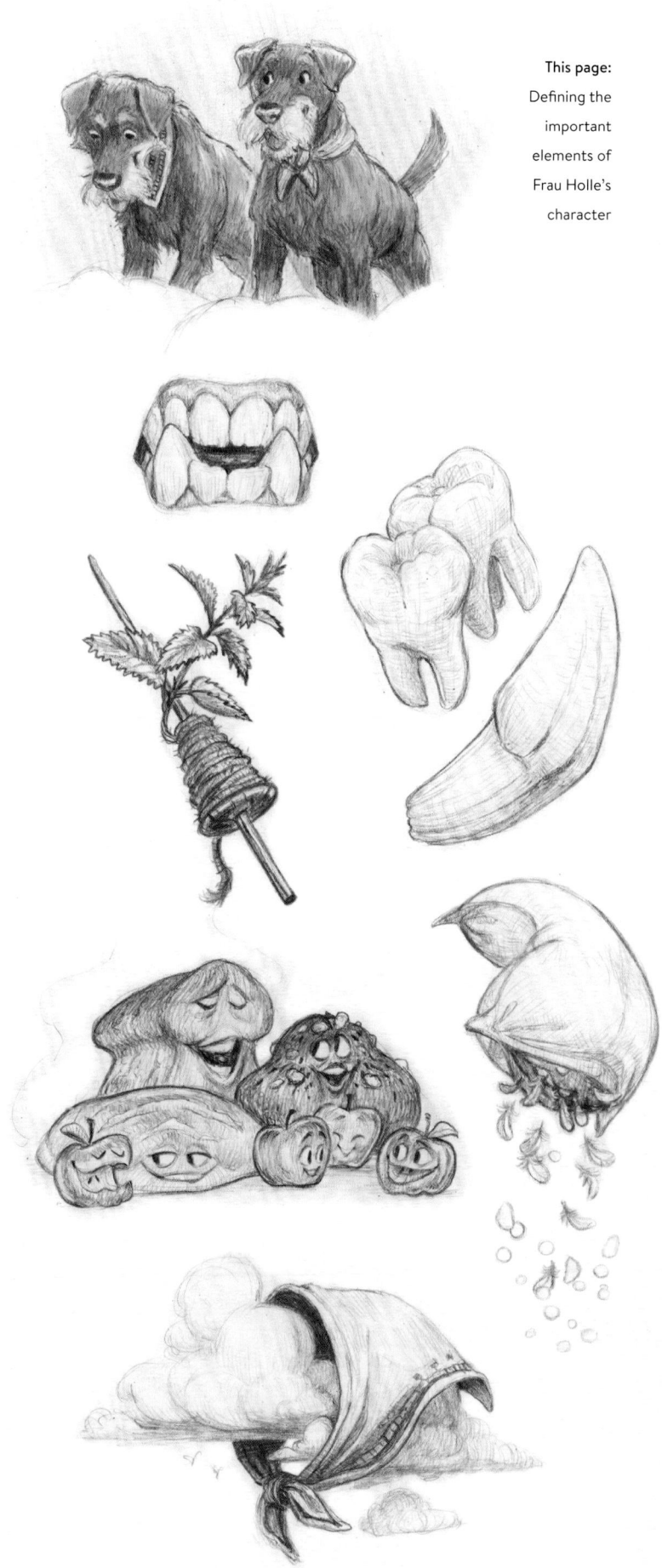

This page: Defining the important elements of Frau Holle's character

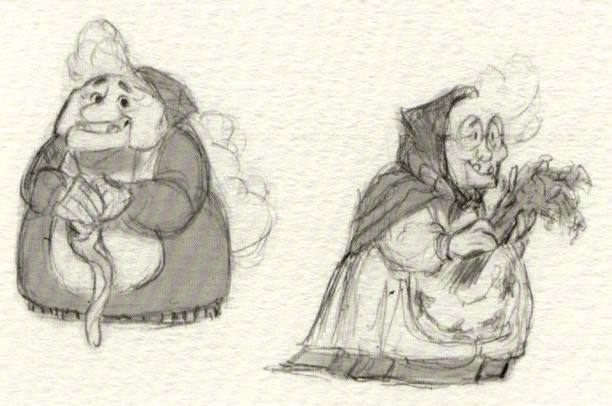
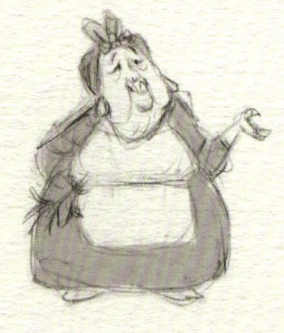
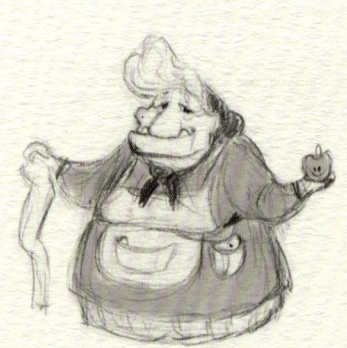

THE FIRST DESIGNS

What makes our lovely Holle holler? Now we've chosen our ingredients, we can start cooking and see what does and doesn't work. I draw four thumbnails based on the research I've done so far – but which one to move forward with? Frau Holle's love for hunting suggests she is active, even though she is ancient – these thumbnails seem too old and 'fluffy'. They embody the kind old grandma part of her personality, but they don't quite mesh with the other details.

DEVELOPING THE FRAU

I continue sketching thumbnails, trying to find the right design. Thumbnails 1, 2, and 3 seem a little too youthful and give off vibes of a 'cute' housewife. Thumbnail 4 is lacking a bit of power, probably due to the pose. 5 and 6 are closest to the sort of look I'm after. The only thing I think I will take from the other thumbnails is the cloudy looking hair. Long, flowing locks don't seem very practical when living in the clouds. The face of thumbnail 6 is exactly what I'm looking for: the big, witchy nose and big teeth, but a soft expression, and many pockets to hide her crafty equipment.

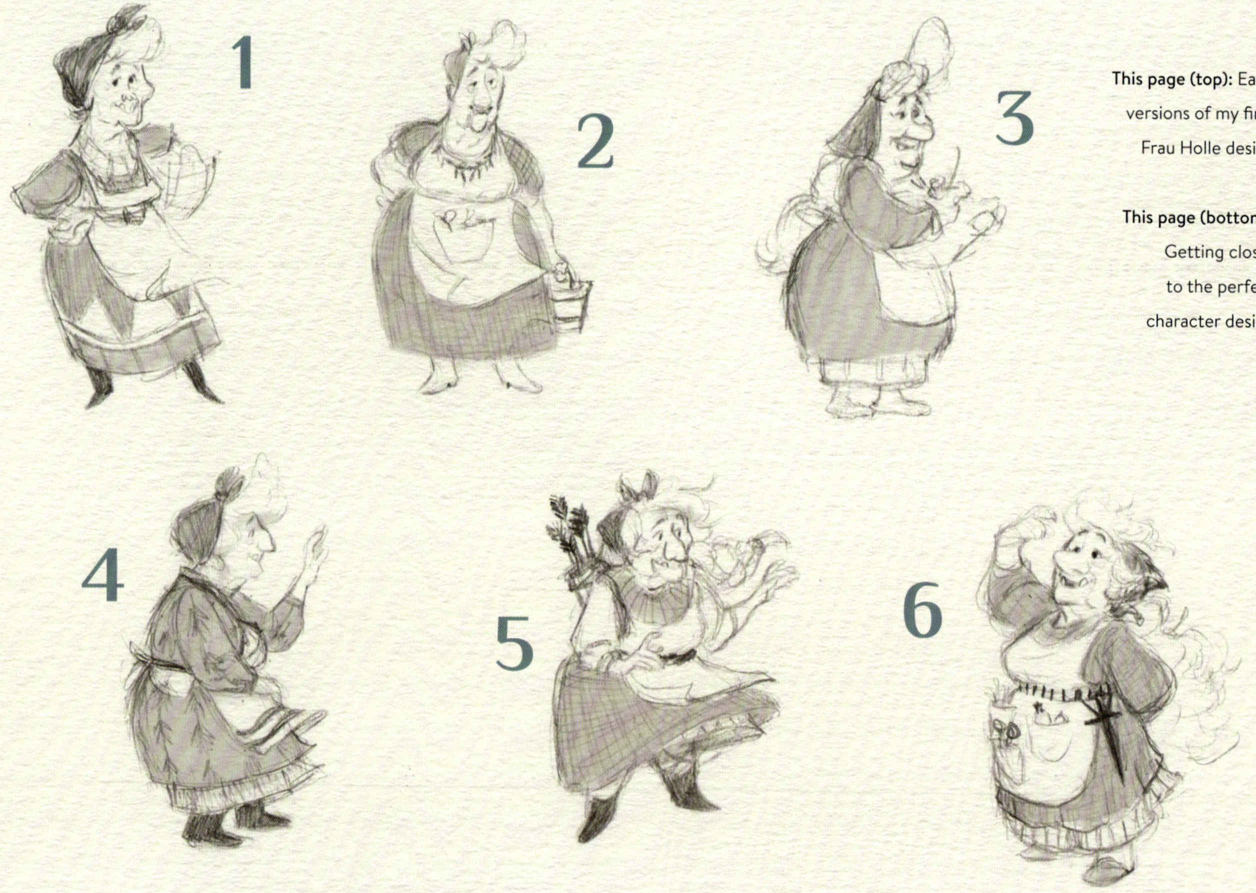

1

2

3

This page (top): Early versions of my final Frau Holle design

This page (bottom): Getting closer to the perfect character design

4

5

6

A CRAFTY GRANDMA

Our happy, retired goddess is finally taking shape. First, I sketch Frau Holle from the front, where her soft, crafty side is mostly on display. Her fluffy, cloudy hair adds that extra bit of magic, so you can tell she's not just any old granny. I draw her clothes as though they are made from nettles, creating a sturdy and warm fabric, perfect for embroidery. I can then detail her clothing with arrows, stags, and branches, showing her love for hunting and craft. These details soften the impact of her fanged teeth.

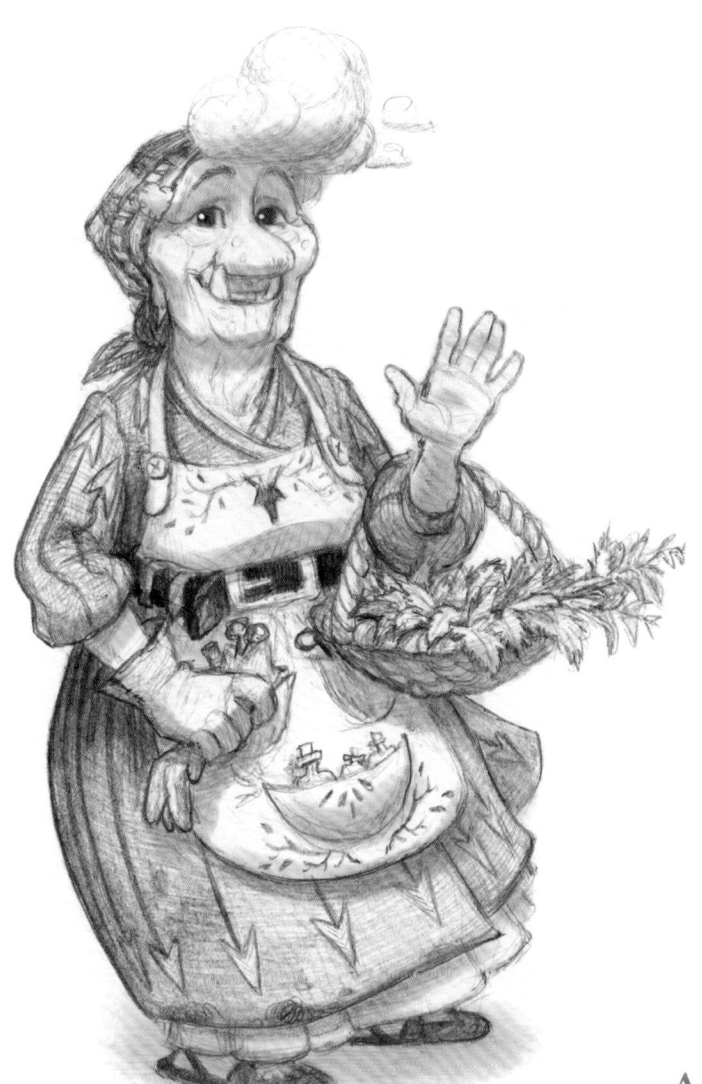

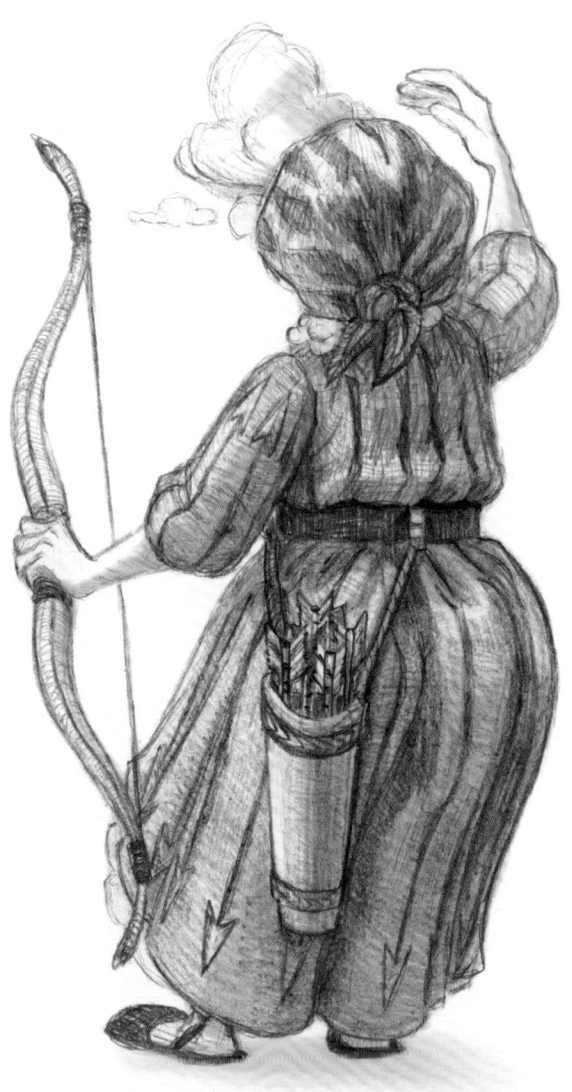

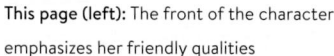

This page (left): The front of the character emphasizes her friendly qualities

This page (right): The back shows she is still a fierce hunter

A SKILLED HUNTER

Next, I sketch the reverse of the character, showing more of her tougher, hunter side. With her trusty bow and a quiver of arrows hung from her belt, she's just as ready to hunt the birds that fly overhead as she is to bake a perfect loaf of bread. The design I settled on is versatile enough to show both sides of her character without needing a costume change – especially as her lovely canine daughters will be running to gather any prey!

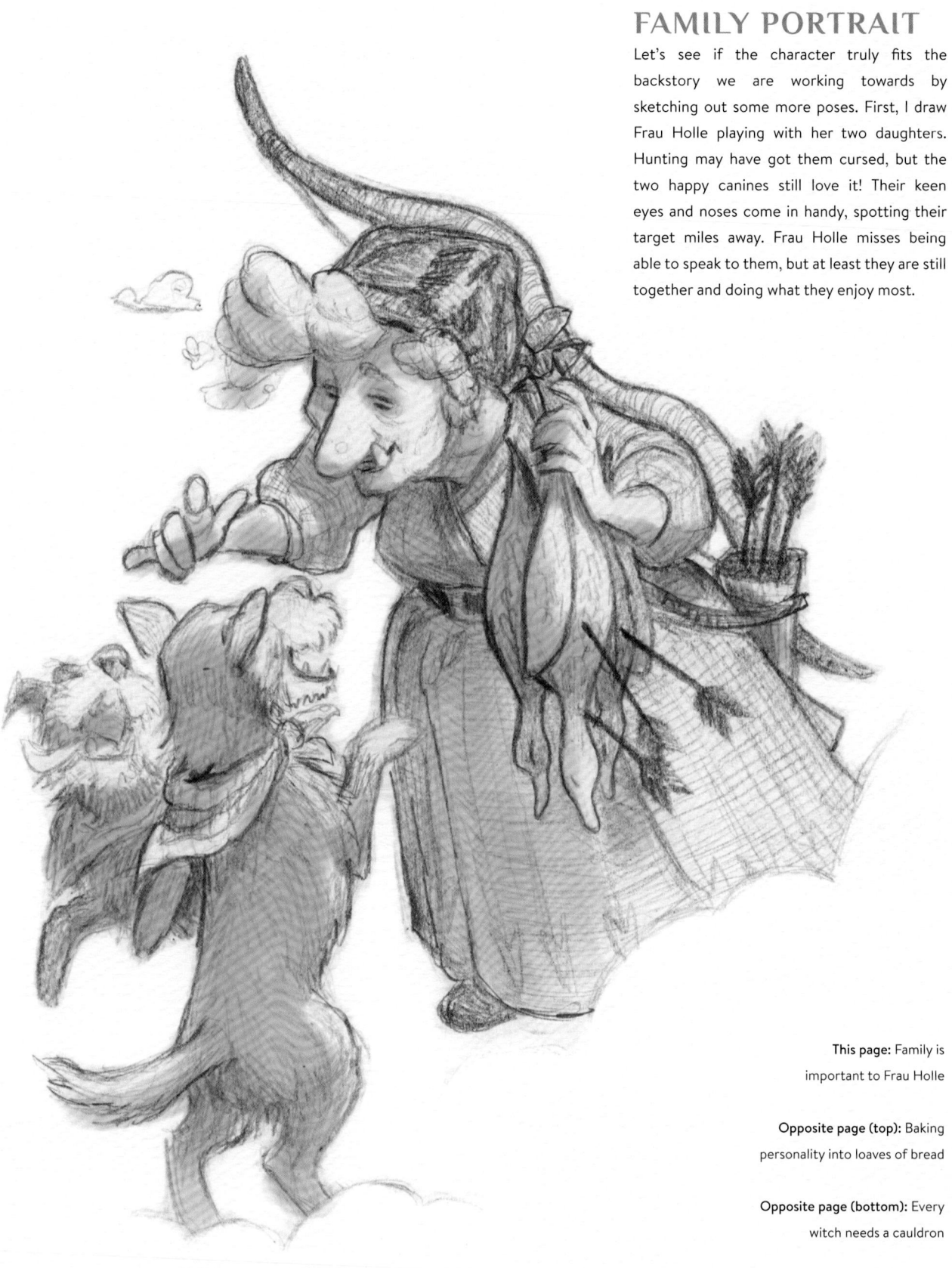

FAMILY PORTRAIT

Let's see if the character truly fits the backstory we are working towards by sketching out some more poses. First, I draw Frau Holle playing with her two daughters. Hunting may have got them cursed, but the two happy canines still love it! Their keen eyes and noses come in handy, spotting their target miles away. Frau Holle misses being able to speak to them, but at least they are still together and doing what they enjoy most.

This page: Family is important to Frau Holle

Opposite page (top): Baking personality into loaves of bread

Opposite page (bottom): Every witch needs a cauldron

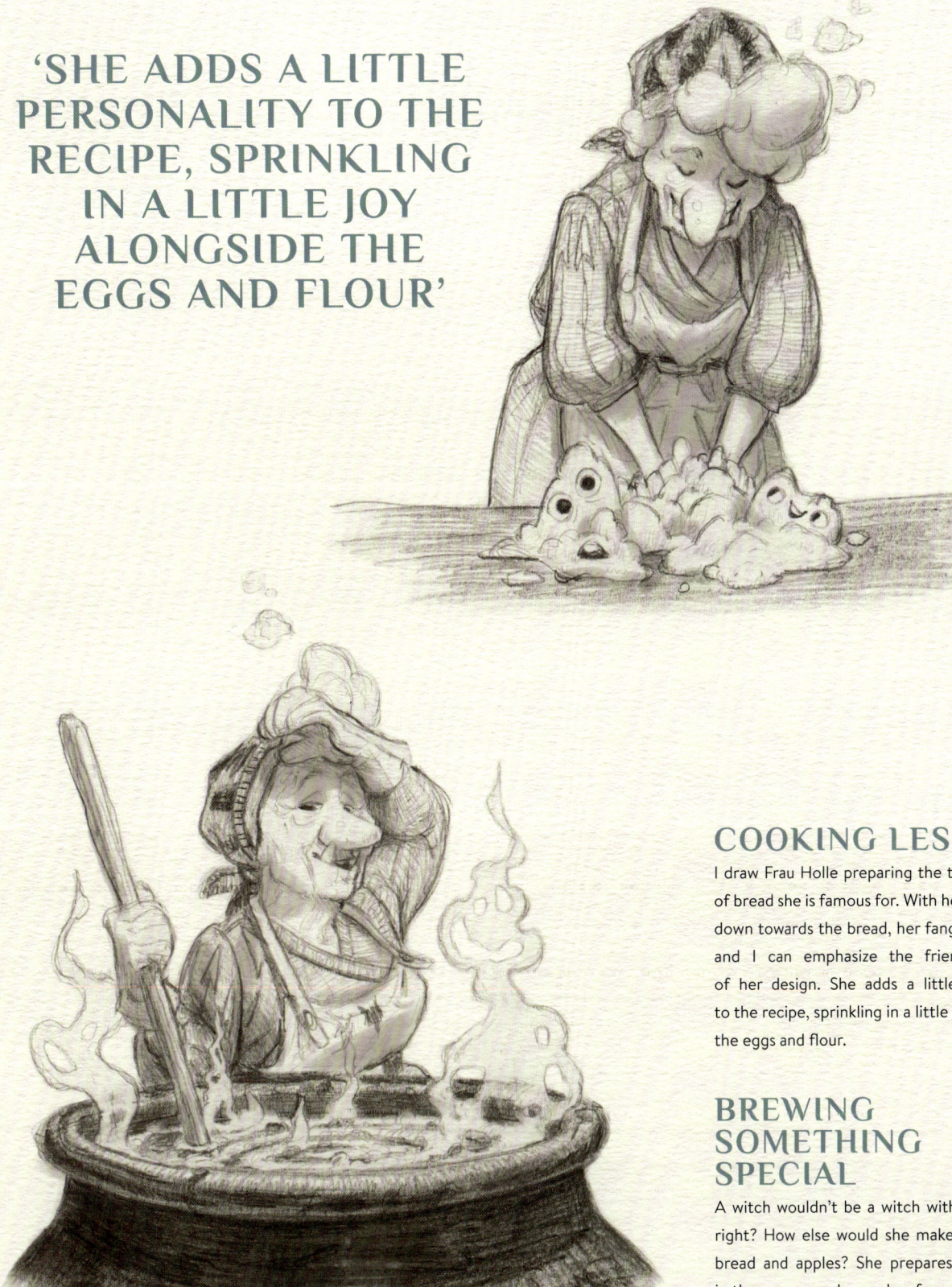

'SHE ADDS A LITTLE PERSONALITY TO THE RECIPE, SPRINKLING IN A LITTLE JOY ALONGSIDE THE EGGS AND FLOUR'

COOKING LESSONS

I draw Frau Holle preparing the talking loaves of bread she is famous for. With her head tilted down towards the bread, her fangs are hidden and I can emphasize the friendly aspects of her design. She adds a little personality to the recipe, sprinkling in a little joy alongside the eggs and flour.

BREWING SOMETHING SPECIAL

A witch wouldn't be a witch without potions, right? How else would she make her magical bread and apples? She prepares her potions in the summer, when only a few mountaintops down below need to be sprinkled with snow from her blankets.

This page: Frau Holle paints the apples to bring them to life

Opposite page: Ready to blanket the world below in snow

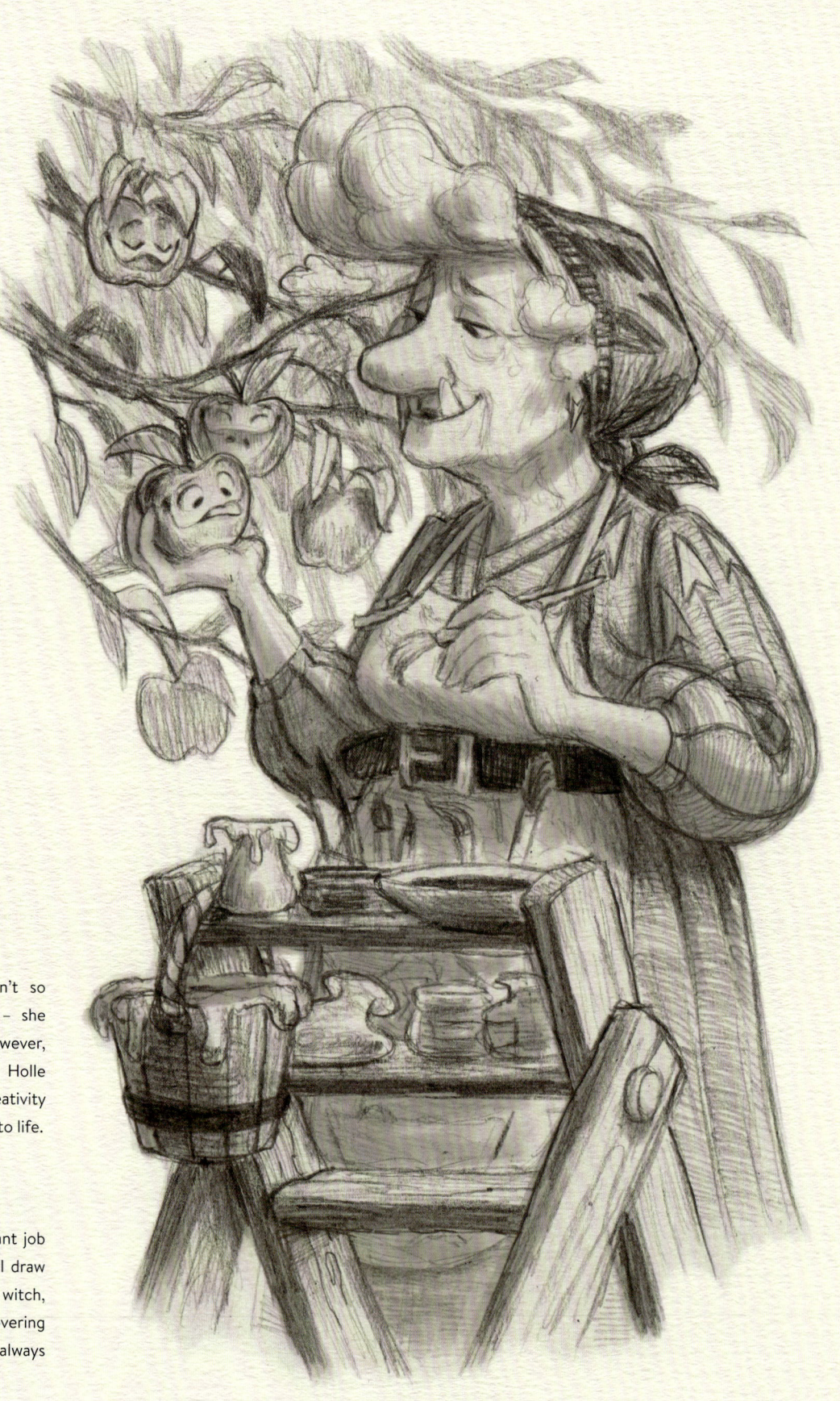

OUT IN THE GARDEN

Our happily retired goddess isn't so different to regular pensioners – she loves gardening and painting. However, as she is no mere mortal, Frau Holle combines the two, using all her creativity to bring the apples in her orchard to life.

LET IT SNOW

Finally, Frau Holle's most important job of all: making a blanket of snow. I draw the blanket much larger than the witch, to show what a mammoth task covering the world with snow is. Guests are always welcome to take over the task!

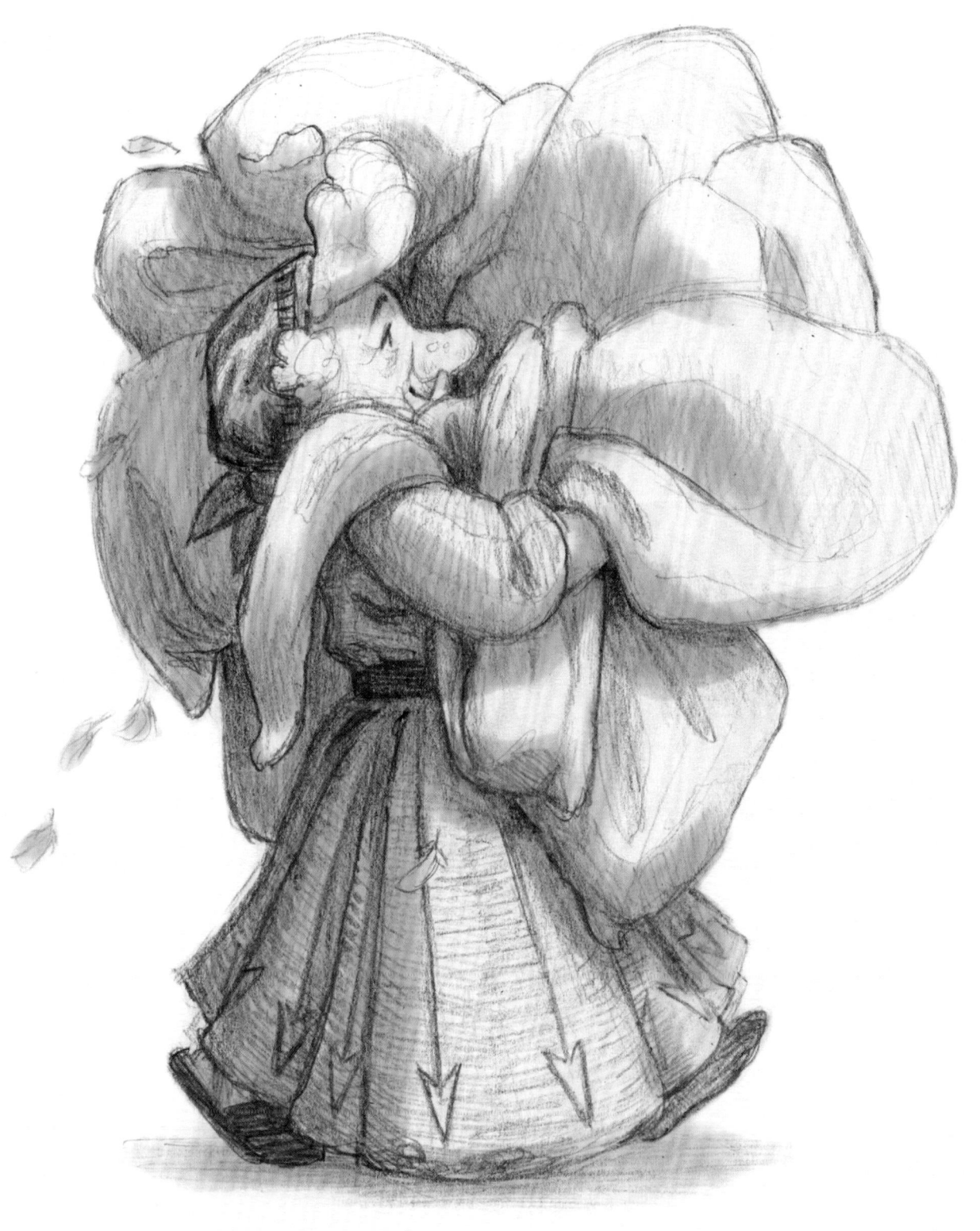

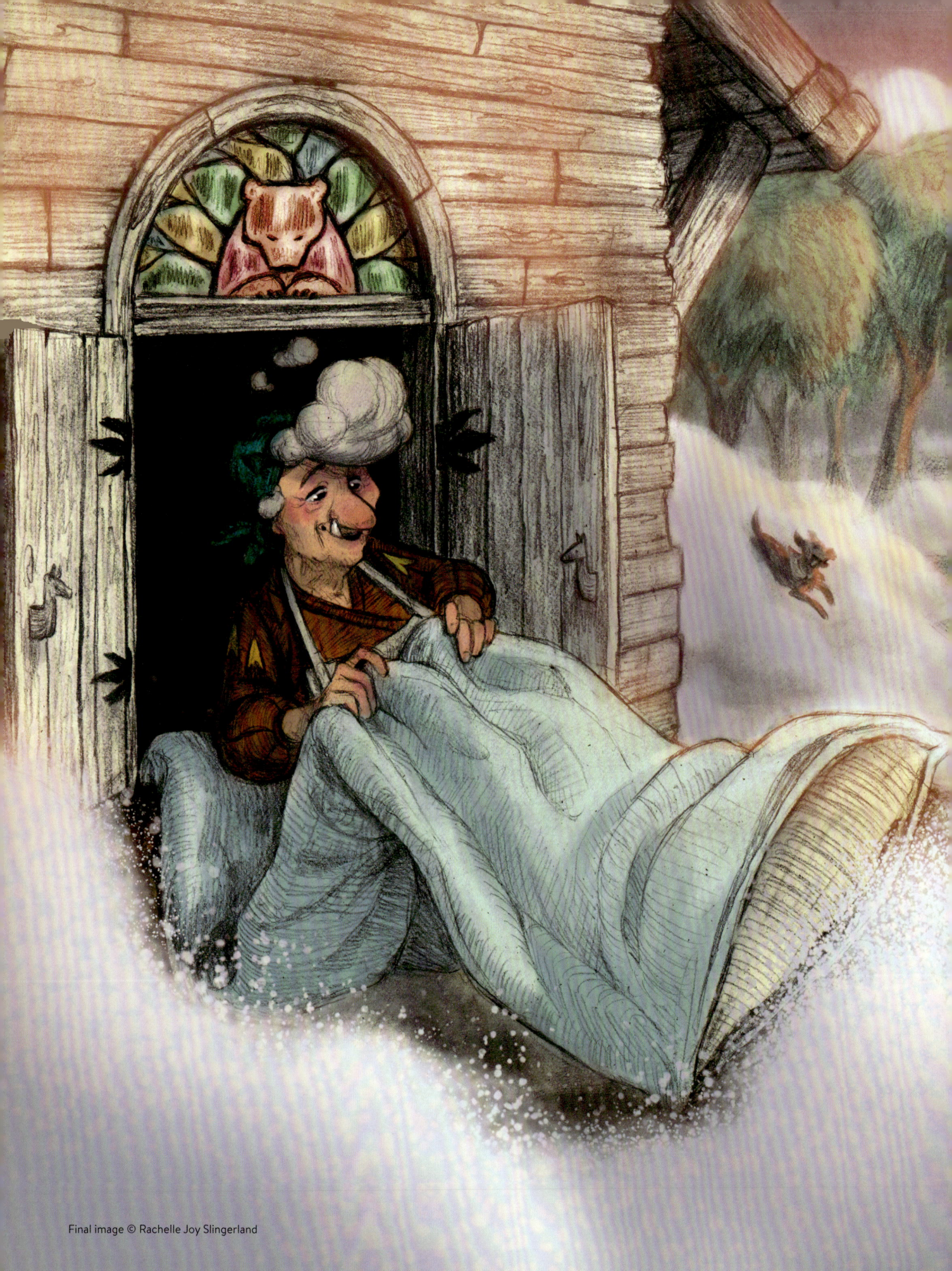

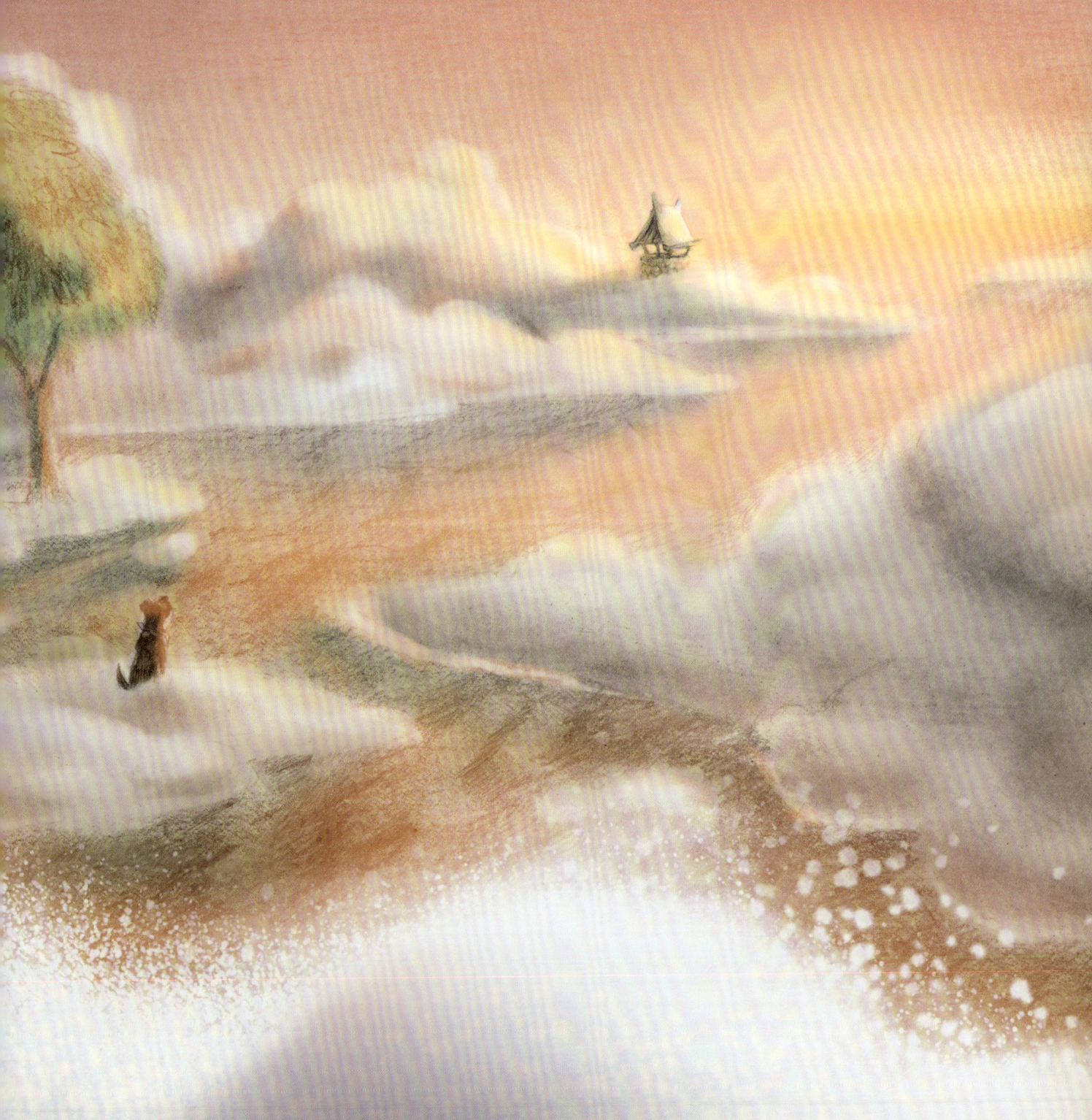

THE WITCHING HOUR

And the picture is complete! Up in the sky on a thick layer of clouds there is a beautiful field with wildflowers. There stands a single well, which serves as a portal to the mortals 'downstairs'. At the edge of the field, behind the apple orchard and the bakery, you can find Frau Holle's cosy cottage. The house stands on the edge of the clouds, with a large window facing outwards. She has plenty of room to shake out her blanket and cover the world in snow, and enjoy the amazing view of the lands below.

ARTIST CATCH-UP:

SARA PAZ

Sara Paz is a freelance graphic designer and illustrator from Portugal, whose wonderfully warm characters have earned a huge following on social media. We spoke to Sara about how her early days creating vector art influenced her style, how music continues to inspire her, and how she manages the pressures of being an artist on social media.

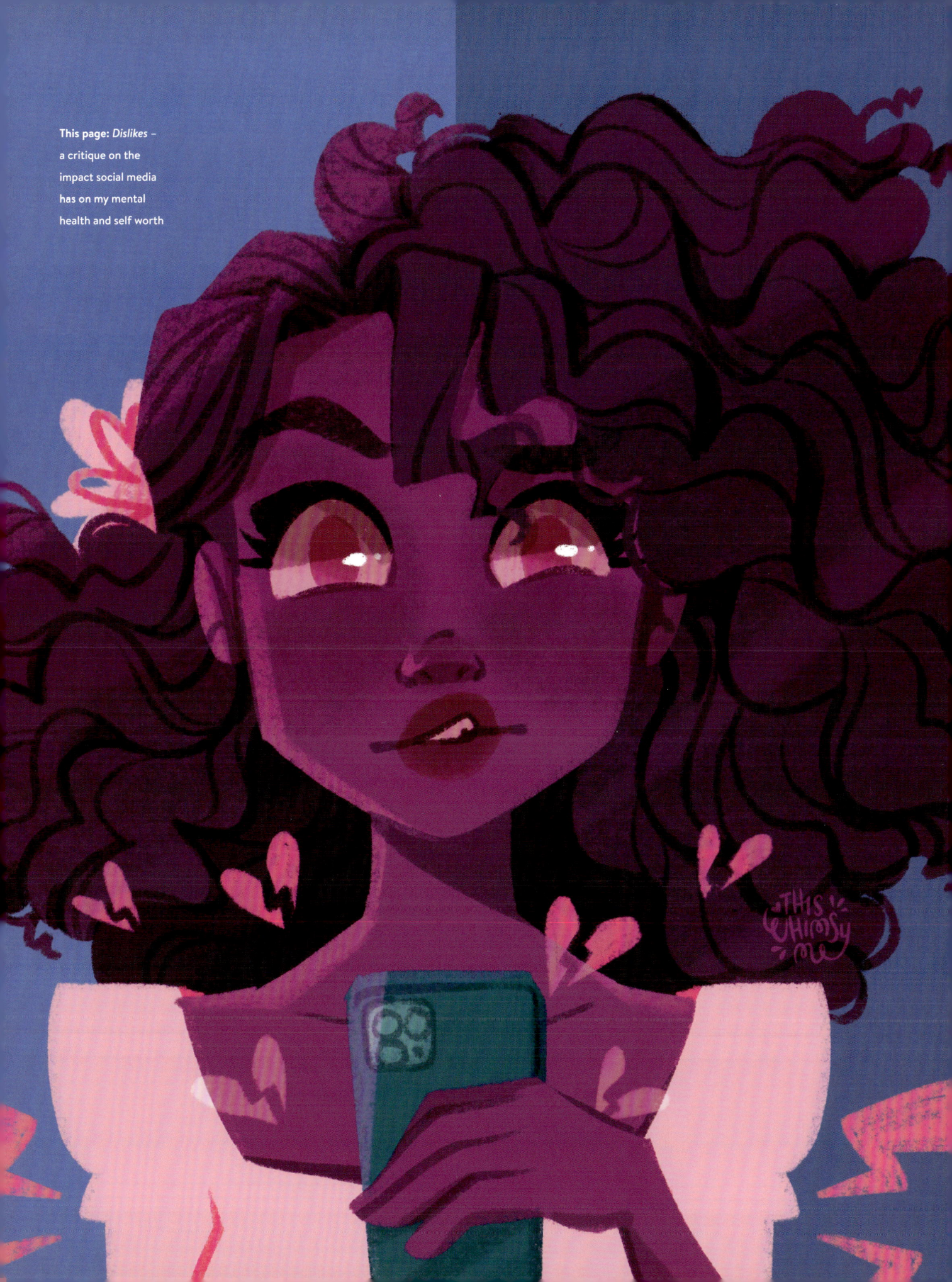

This page: *Dislikes* – a critique on the impact social media has on my mental health and self worth

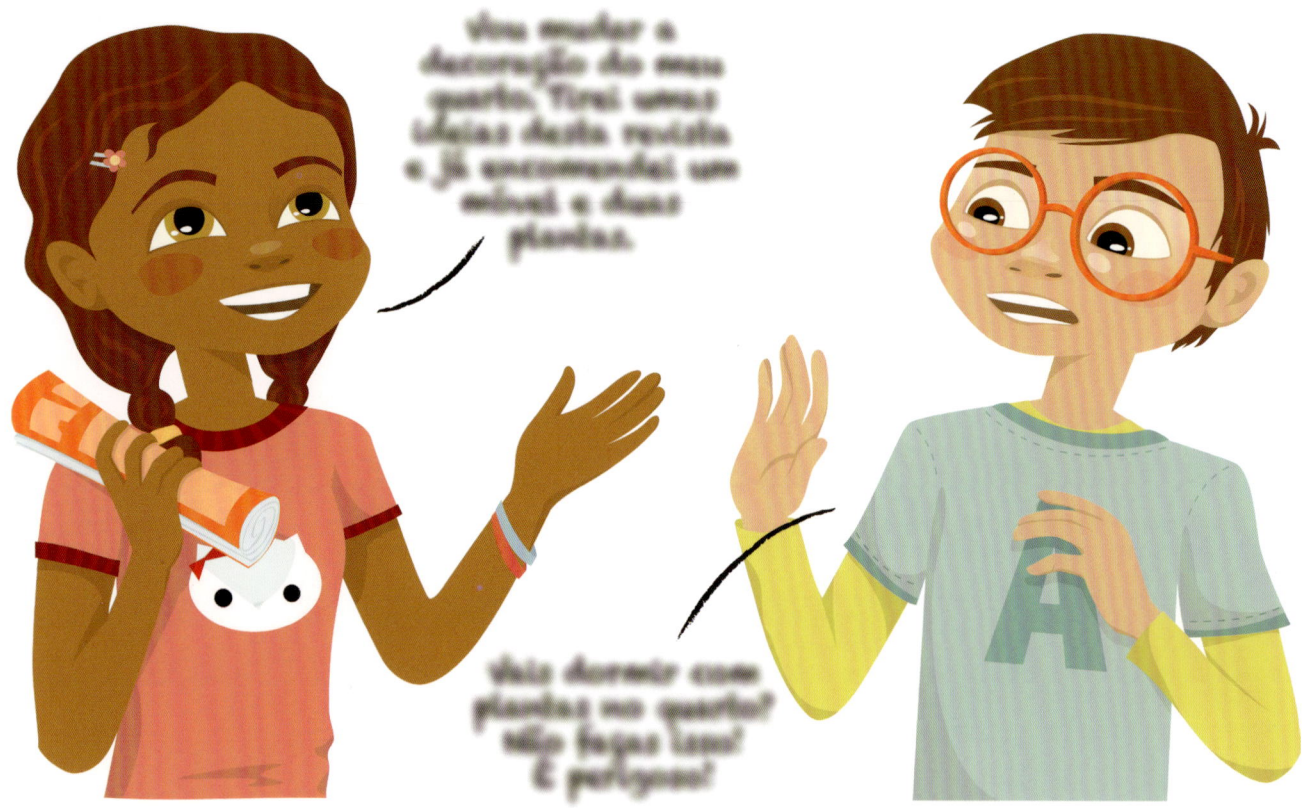

Hi Sara, welcome back to *CDQ*! Could you start by letting our readers know a little about your background and career so far?

Hi guys! I guess I would say I became an illustrator without noticing! Like most artists, I have been drawing since I could hold a pencil. While at high school, I started thinking about a career and fell in love with graphic design. I was obsessed with making alternative book and CD covers for those I didn't like and loved making my own designs to print on shirts. And so, back in 1999 I enrolled in graphic design at IADE, here in Portugal. I loved every part of my degree and after graduation ended up interning for a few companies. Back then, my drawing was on hold – I was designing medicine labels and perfume advertisements. That lasted for a couple of years and then I applied for a position designing infographics – something I had never thought about or had any experience

with – and that's when I started creating digital vector drawings. It wasn't exactly art, since I drew mostly maps and pie charts, but I started drawing infographics for kid's textbooks and loved it. I worked in this role freelance for quite some time and gradually publishers noticed my drawing skills and gave me opportunities to do more illustration and less infographics. And that's how, without planning it, I became an illustrator!

Were there skills learned from drawing vector art and infographics that are still useful with the drawings you do today?

I would say that those skills undoubtedly played a leading role in my art and what it has become today. The clean, simple, and lineless shape style was a conscious choice I made while exploring vector art. When I was still in college, my parents took me on a trip to

London – that's where I first took notice of the vector-art trend that started blooming around that time – all the big brands were doing it. I remember buying lots of prints at Portobello Road market and hanging them on my bedroom wall. They were definitely an inspiration for my first digital art creations which gave me the confidence to take the infographics job that further developed my illustration skills. It was a butterfly effect thing, right? Little, young, aspiring designer me flapped her wings back in London 20 years ago and here I am now, doing more – *way* more – illustration than design.

This page: *Ghost of art's past* – illustration from 2010 when I still just drew vector art, an ancestor of my current style

Opposite page: My first steps into art, back in 2013, still showing a lot of my infographic roots

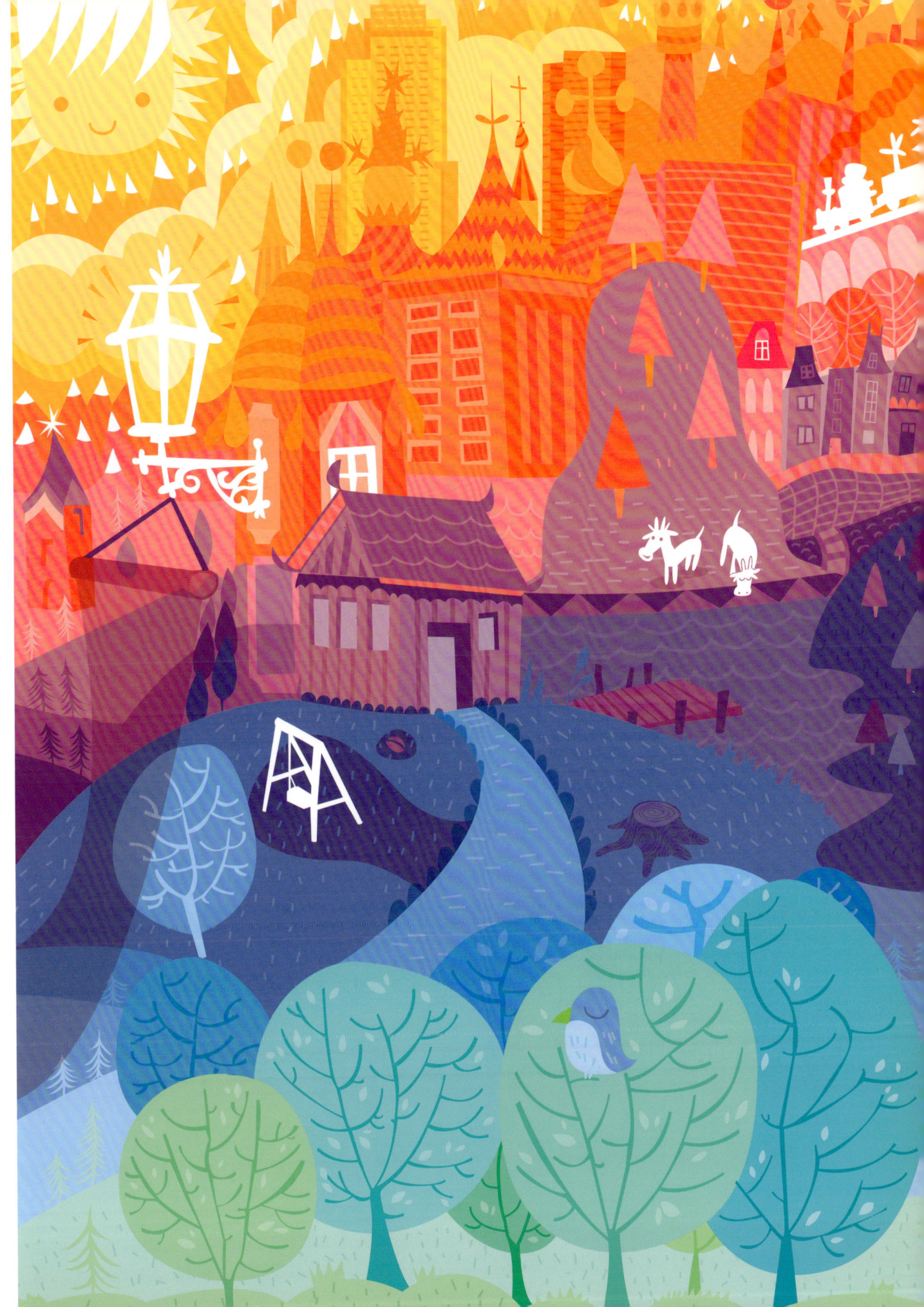

This page: *Blue Girl* – one of three from a series of happy girls, all exploring monochromatic palettes

Opposite page: *Tutorial girl* – floating heads are my absolute speciality; this one is part of a tutorial posted on my Instagram feed

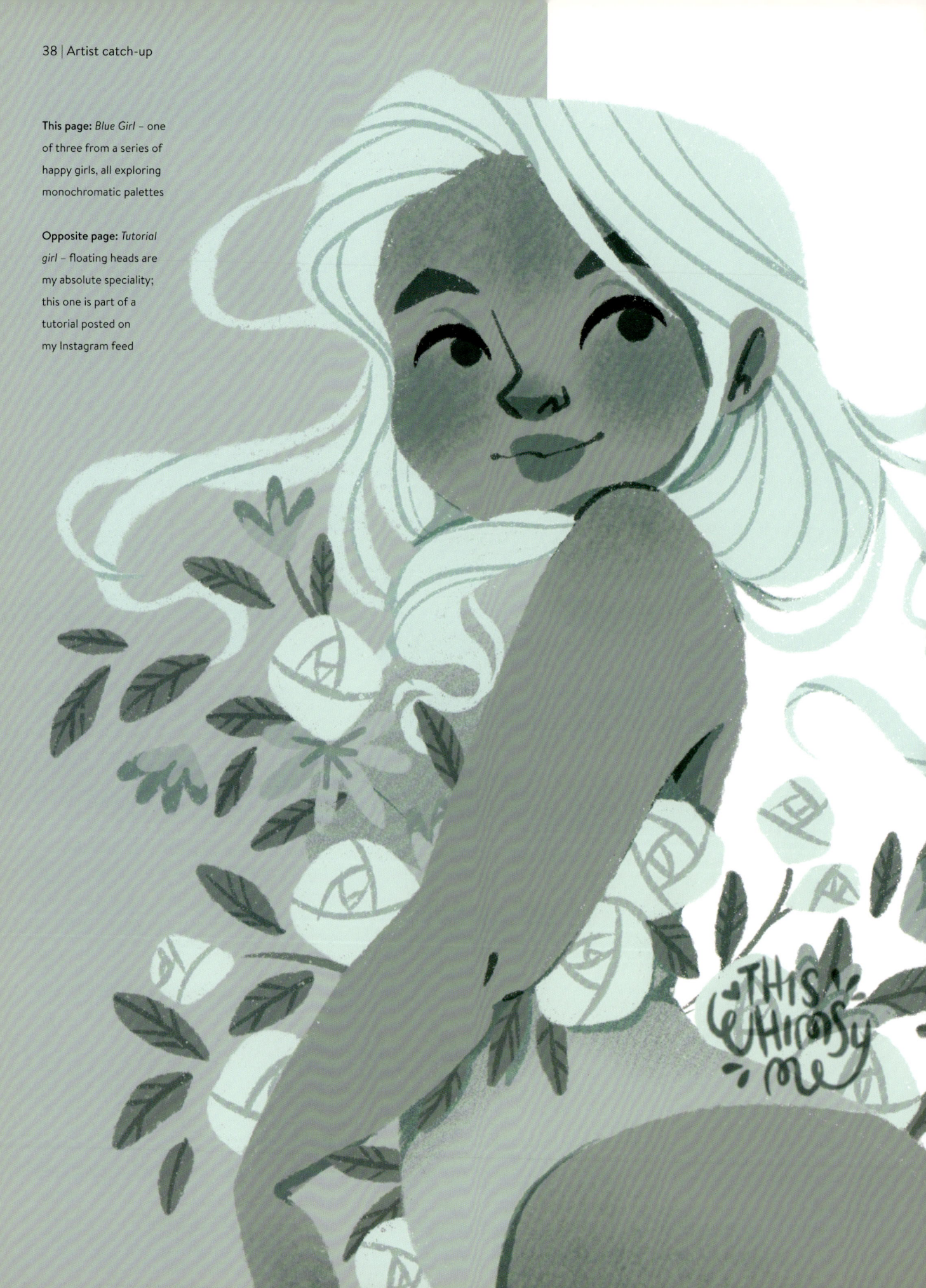

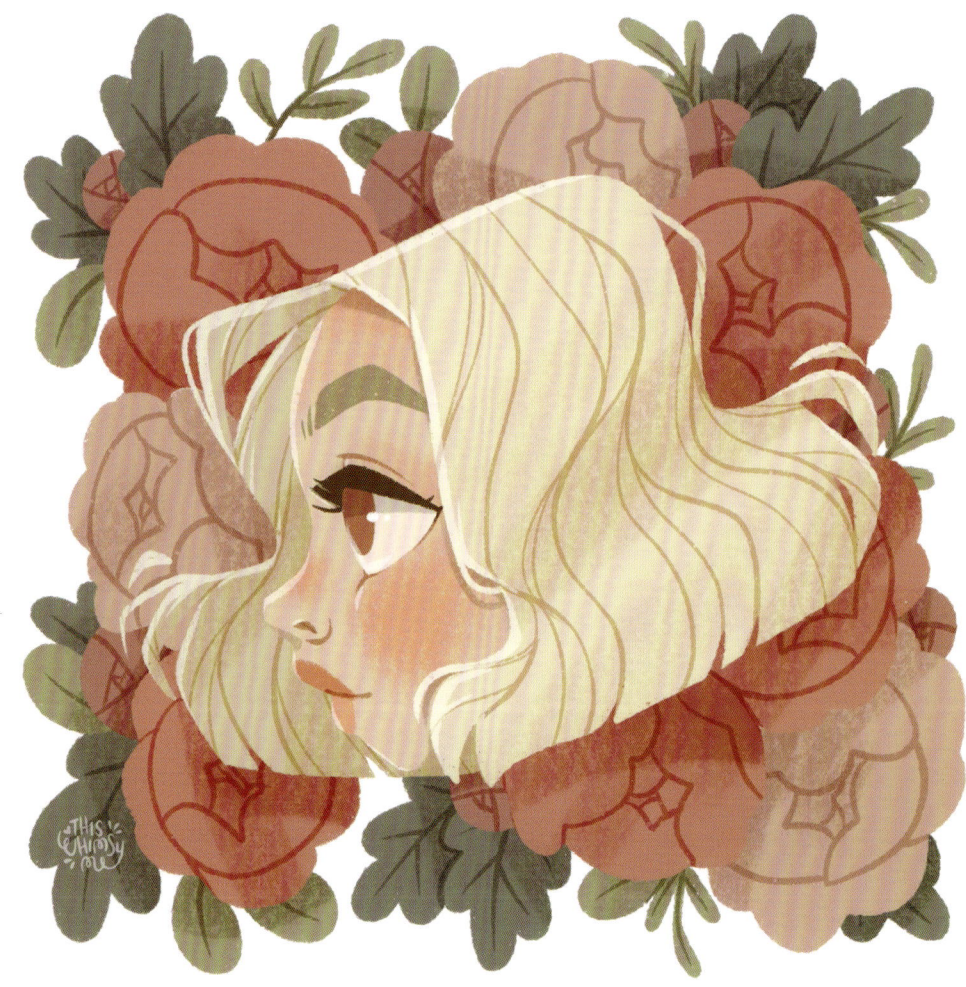

You have a strong following on social media. How important are things like Instagram and TikTok for an artist these days?

Social media definitely has a great impact on an artist's life nowadays. It has pushed people like me to work harder to evolve in their craft and into finding their own voice more than ever. Creating an art account has definitely made me exercise both my crafty and creative mind much harder than before. But, most of all, social media helped me find my peers: people that understood my growing pains, people that inspired me, and people I could bounce ideas off. These people have unquestionably been the best part of the experience. I worked hard (maybe too hard) online to get noticed, but I know it came with a lot of luck, too. Although I find those platforms great vehicles for getting your art known, I still think it's possible to find success without them — I know I have.

How do you step away from the grind of updating the feed all the time?

When I started my art account, I always felt so sad that some artists would let the pressure of posting get into their heads. There are so many undoubtedly amazing artists who doubt their abilities and I thought 'that's not me, I'll never be that insecure'. Boy, was I wrong!

Sometimes, the pressure gets to me, too – what I find helps is to not compare your journey with others. Likes, followers, number of posts, it's all an illusion. So, I guess my only advice is: create from the heart. Do what you love, regardless of likes. Post only when you feel like doing so and expect nothing in return but the joy of sending something you wholeheartedly made out into the world. Art shouldn't exist to make a number go up, art should mean something — if we create just for the sake of feeding our social media, then how are we different from soulless AI art?

Where do you find inspiration for your work?

I find most of my inspiration through music. Since I was a little girl, I've had this deep connection to sound. For the longest time I wanted to be a singer. Music made my heart beat faster and my feelings surface in a way nothing else did, and I found that that's what I wanted for my art: to convey, provoke, and surface feelings the way music does to me. And so, I look for inspiration in the way certain music makes me feel. If I close my eyes, I can see it: the mood, the colours, the elements. In a more direct way, my biggest influences when it comes to art are definitely Mucha and the entire Art Nouveau movement, for the dynamism and the curved lines. I'm also a big fan of Klimt and his pattern-driven compositions and warm tones. And, of course, I'm inspired by so many fellow artists on Instagram, each and every day.

The link between music and art is fascinating, and the synaesthetic ability to translate one into the other. If you look at other's work, do you find yourself 'hearing' music in their designs, too?

Yes, definitely! Sometimes, while scrolling through my feed, I find myself humming a certain song that art has evoked. Of course, with the ability to add actual music to posts artists can now explicitly build that bridge between art and music and show us exactly what they mean. I kind of like to leave my art up to interpration, to let the viewer's own perspective and references frame what they see. How my art makes you feel should ultimately only be up to you.

What do you find most enjoyable about character design?

When designing a character, I ask myself three questions. First, who are they? I like to do a small psychological profile about the character: their profession, age, the period in which they live (I love to create period-themed characters), and their dreams and aspirations. Next, I consider how they're feeling. I love using emotions to give characters depth. For instance, they could be a fun, bubbly character who, in that moment, is feeling sad. What can I do that will show that on the page? And finally, I think about colours, shapes, poses, hair, and so on. So, I'd say that imprinting a personality and a mood onto an illustration is what I like most – and also what scares me most – about character design.

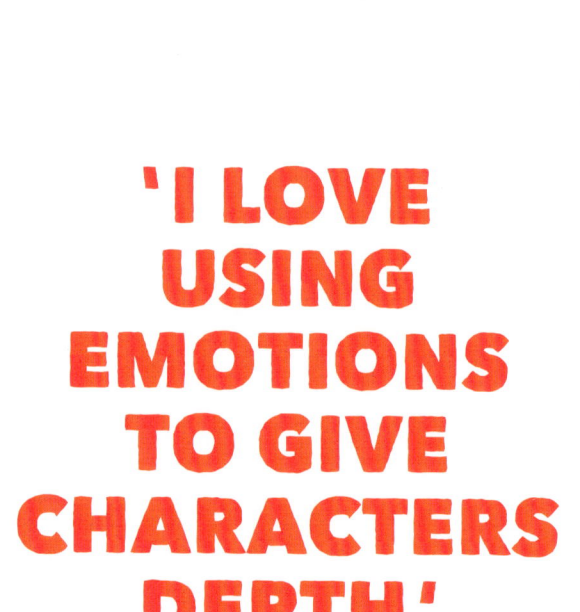

'I LOVE USING EMOTIONS TO GIVE CHARACTERS DEPTH'

This page: *Cup of Christmas* – I couldn't talk about teacups and not add one of my own. This is Coco, the hot chocolate elf, because I'm a chocolate addict!

Opposite page: *Summer mermaid* – the second (and last) of the 'four seasons' set that never got to see the light of day

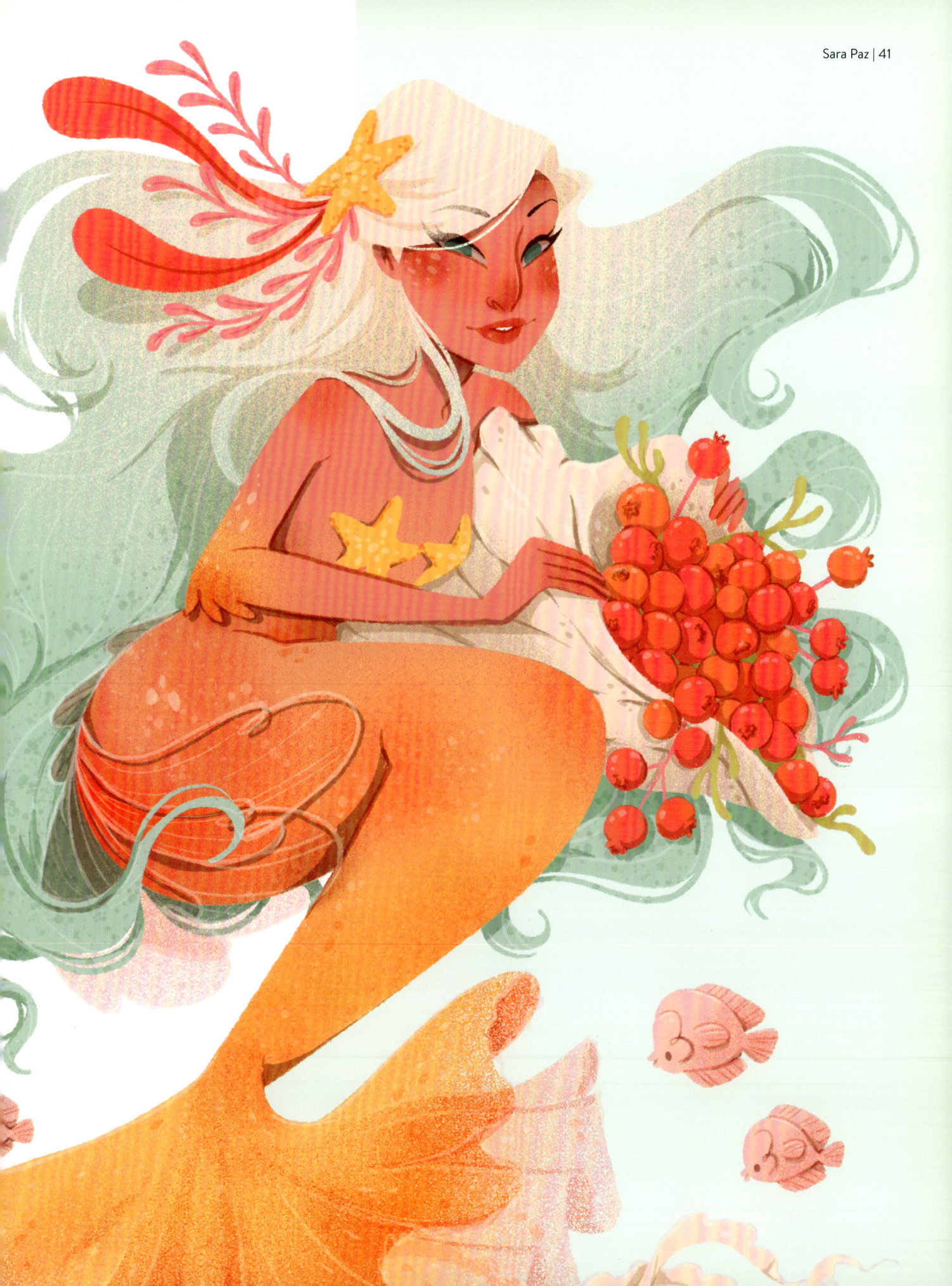

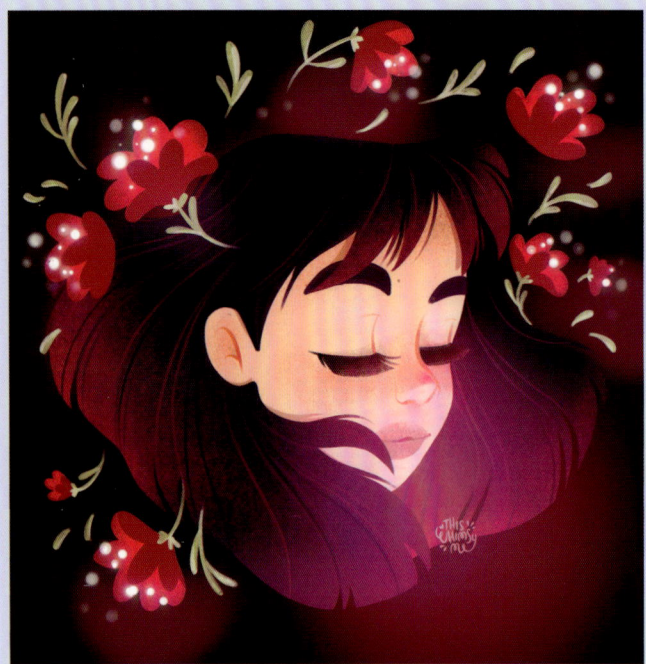

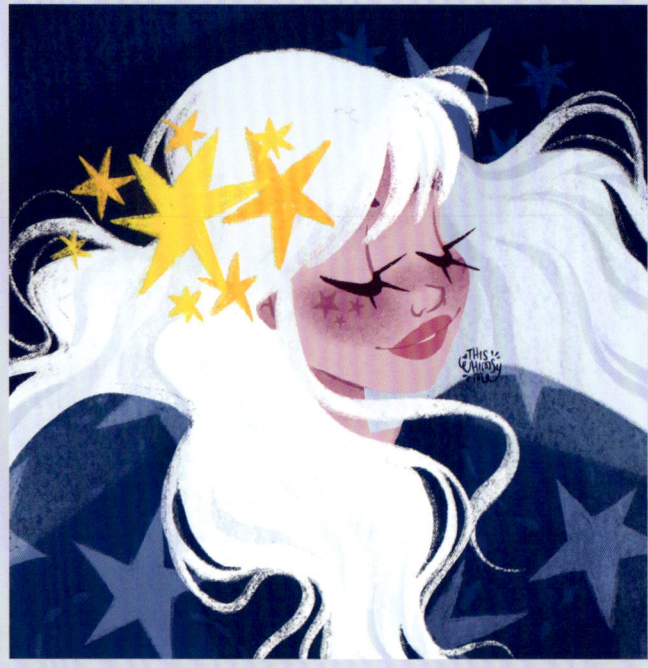

Do you have any advice for artists struggling to think of original designs?

I feel like my advice is always the same: draw a lot! It helps to join a prompt list that is out of your comfort zone. I know, I know, I don't like to leave my nest either, but it's a great way to make you draw things you wouldn't otherwise explore and widen your horizons. Imagine you're doing a 30-day teacup art challenge – by day five you probably exhausted all your great teacup ideas – that's when the magic happens! That's when you get to go outside of your 'box' and the goofy, strange, out of character ideas that flow from your brain after that are an exercise in creativity. A fun twist on this exercise is to pick a random word and create something based on it. Take the word rose, for instance. It can serve just as an inspiration (its smell, delicacy, fluidity, or shape), a detail of your design (like a girl with a rose in her hair), or be your entire drawing. The options are endless.

Your illustrations have such well-defined and coherent colour palettes. Do you have any tips for choosing the right colours to work together?

This is one of my favourite parts of creating an illustration. Colour is probably the most effective tool for conveying emotions, but getting it right can also be one of the most time-consuming parts of the process. For the longest time, I just went for what made sense to me, choosing my colours on the fly, but in time I've built a few go-to colour palettes to help me expedite the process. However, they aren't 'set in stone' palettes; I use them as a base to create a custom palette for each and every one of my creations. As I love warm colours, I tend to warm up all my palettes (even blues and purples). As for tips I can give: look up and study 'colour theory' and define and limit your palette based on what you're trying to convey, but don't be too rigid about it — a 'stray from the palette' colour in the right place can add the right 'pop' to the artwork. Always separate your colour layers so you can easily adjust them later. And last but not least, experiment and have fun!

Thanks for talking with us, Sara! Is there anything coming up from you we should be looking out for?

Right now I'm mainly focusing on client work. I illustrate a pretty successful series by a Portuguese author, which is what I'm doing right now. I'm also drawing a lot for a chain of amusement parks which has kept me very busy and has also rekindled my love for vector art. On the backburner, I have lots of ideas for children's books – my husband writes wonderful stories and 'kidlit' is a style I'm very interested in further developing. I've also been wanting to create my own art fanzine and finally set up an online store — let's hope this is the year!

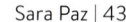

Opposite page (left): *Floating flowers* – my breakthrough illustration, the one that made me say 'I found my style'. I was so proud

Opposite page (right): *Star girl* – this illustration is the perfect example of how social media can mess with my head — I love how it turned out but I'm afraid to post it and see it shredded by the evil algorithm

This page: *My boy* – every year I go back to my kidlit roots and draw my kids on their birthdays; this one is from when Pedro turned four

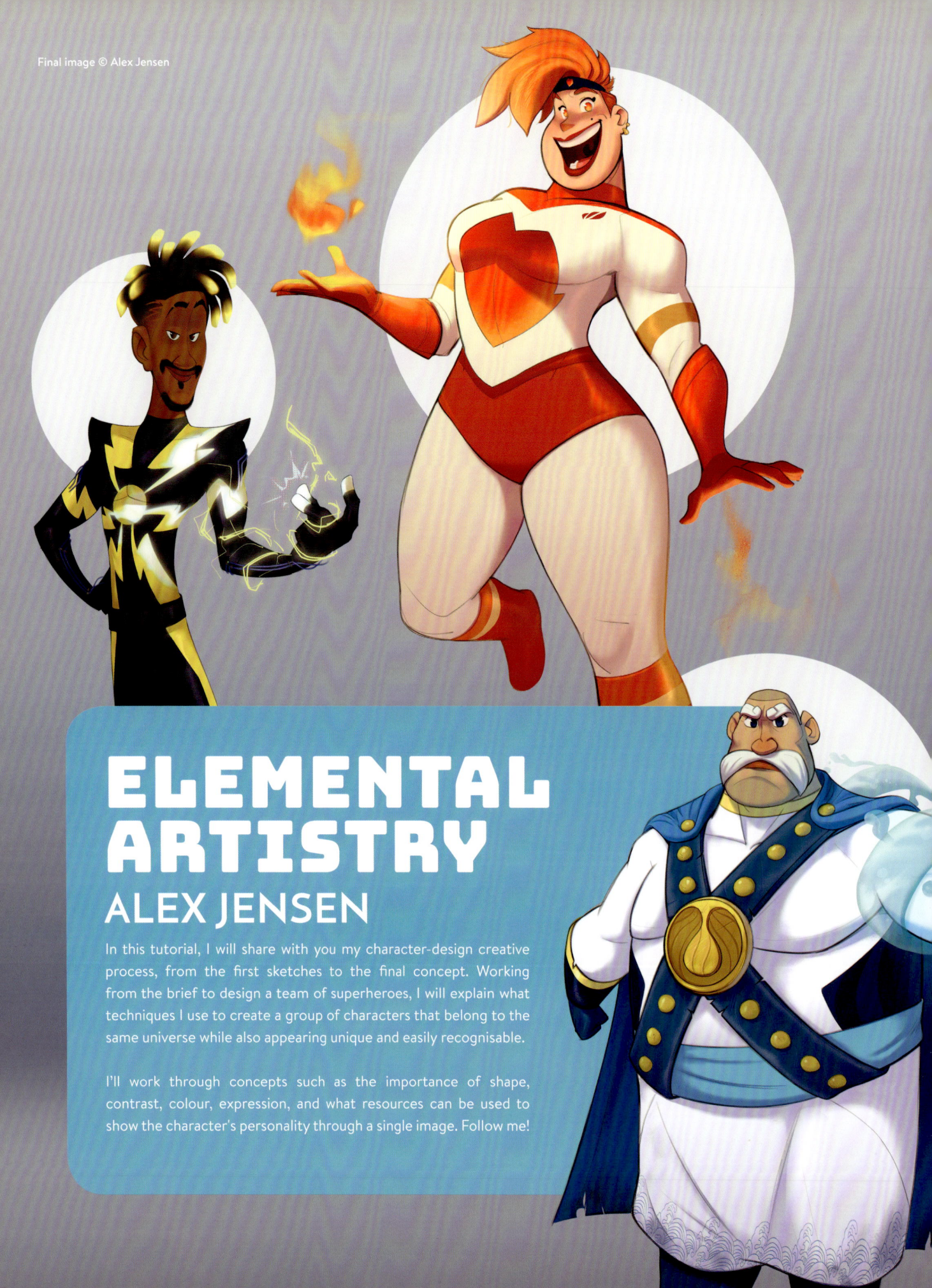

ELEMENTAL ARTISTRY

ALEX JENSEN

In this tutorial, I will share with you my character-design creative process, from the first sketches to the final concept. Working from the brief to design a team of superheroes, I will explain what techniques I use to create a group of characters that belong to the same universe while also appearing unique and easily recognisable.

I'll work through concepts such as the importance of shape, contrast, colour, expression, and what resources can be used to show the character's personality through a single image. Follow me!

IDEAS TAKE SHAPE

Contrast is essential when we have a set of characters – it's what allows us to differentiate them from one another at first sight. A very useful tool that I often use is to think in basic shapes as a starting point, associating each character with a different shape. I consider how these early design choices might affect a character's personality and what ideas I can add to create further contrast between each design.

FIRST EXPLORATIONS

Once you have a clear idea of where to go, it's time to draw! This step is really fun, because you can try all kinds of sketches without paying much attention to detail, blurting out all kinds of ideas, no matter how crazy they may seem. This process is usually accompanied by a search for references.

I use a larger brush size than usual and draw elements as though I am looking at the characters from a distance. This prevents me from adding too much detail too soon. Don't just stick with black for these sketches – I find using a variety of colours makes it easier for me to let go and for the creative process to take over.

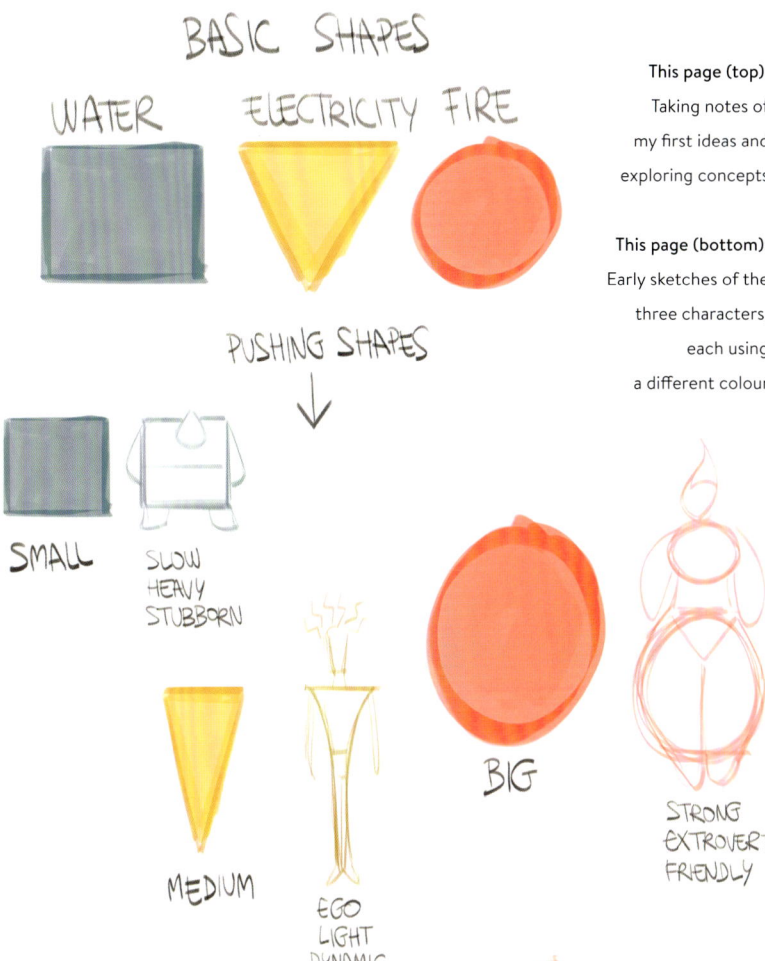

BASIC SHAPES

WATER ELECTRICITY FIRE

PUSHING SHAPES

SMALL

SLOW HEAVY STUBBORN

MEDIUM

EGO LIGHT DYNAMIC

BIG

STRONG EXTROVERT FRIENDLY

This page (top):
Taking notes of my first ideas and exploring concepts

This page (bottom):
Early sketches of the three characters, each using a different colour

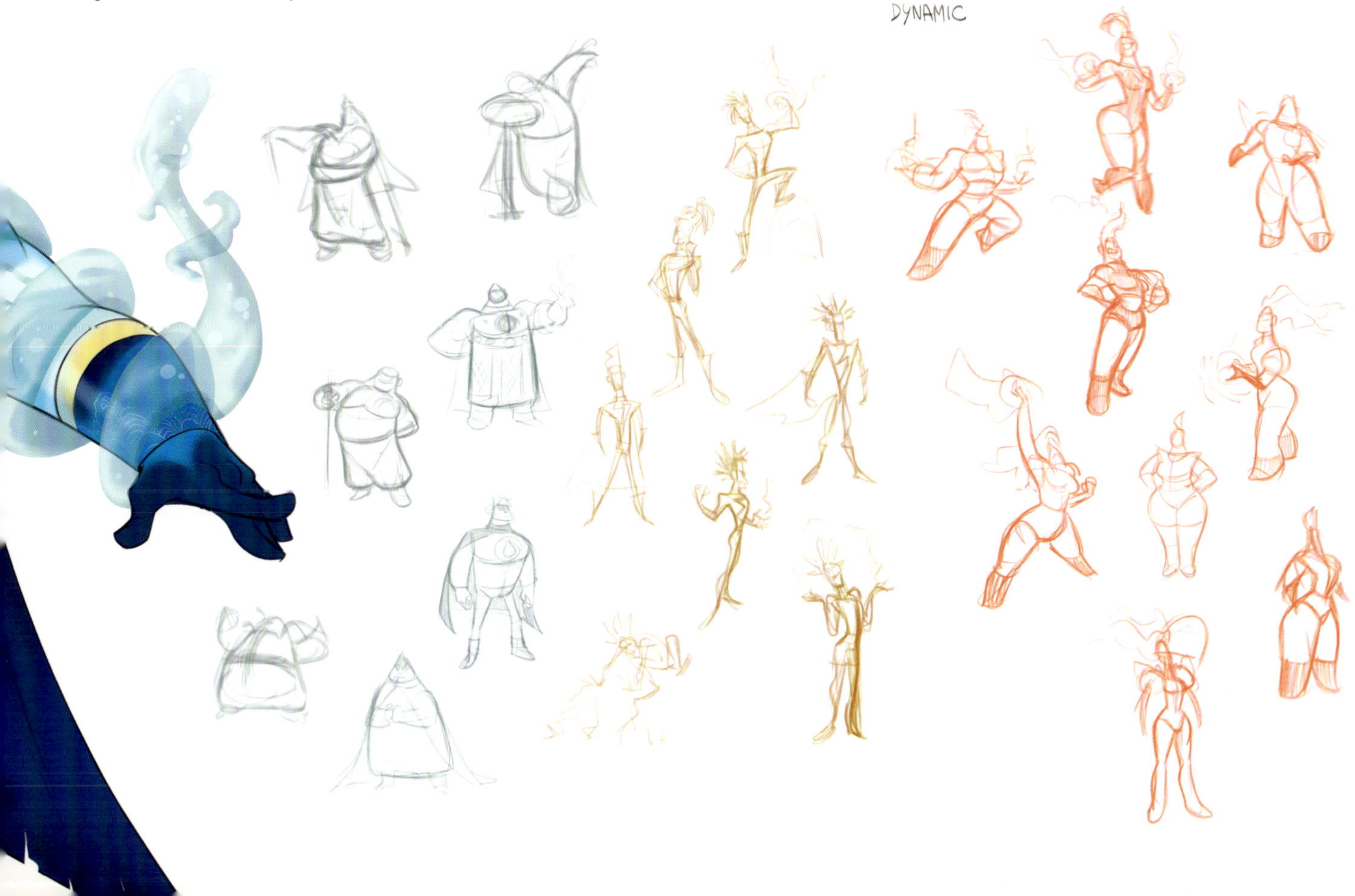

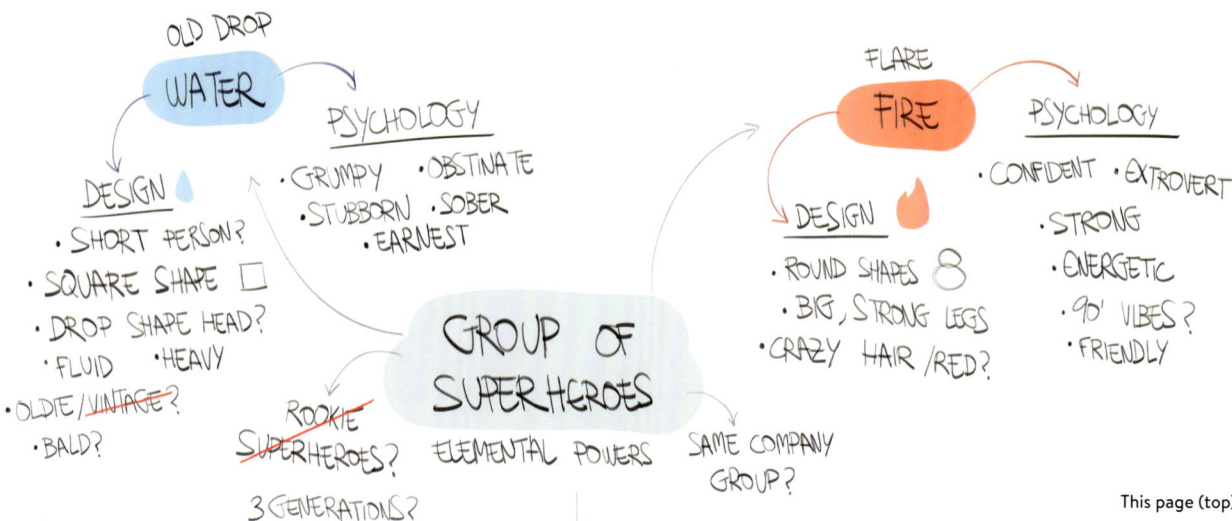

OLD DROP
WATER

PSYCHOLOGY
• GRUMPY • OBSTINATE
• STUBBORN • SOBER
• EARNEST

DESIGN
• SHORT PERSON?
• SQUARE SHAPE □
• DROP SHAPE HEAD?
• FLUID • HEAVY
• OLDIE/VINTAGE?
• BALD?

GROUP OF SUPERHEROES

ROOKIE
SUPERHEROES?
3 GENERATIONS?

ELEMENTAL POWERS

SAME COMPANY
GROUP?

FLARE
FIRE

PSYCHOLOGY
• CONFIDENT • EXTROVERT
• STRONG
• ENERGETIC
• 90' VIBES?
• FRIENDLY

DESIGN
• ROUND SHAPES
• BIG, STRONG LEGS
• CRAZY HAIR /RED?

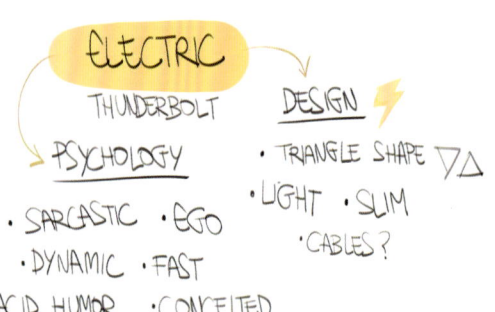

ELECTRIC
THUNDERBOLT

PSYCHOLOGY
• SARCASTIC • EGO
• DYNAMIC • FAST
• ACID HUMOR • CONCEITED

DESIGN
• TRIANGLE SHAPE ▽△
• LIGHT • SLIM
• CABLES?

DEFINING THE CHARACTERS

While going through the process of deciding what ideas I want to go forward with, I collect all the concepts in a single image so I have a clear idea what I'm aiming for. At this stage, I want to be clear what concepts I'm moving forward with and which I'm ruling out.

I create a diagram with references to use as a summary. Usually, I will add this to a mood board for the project I'm working on. In production, you may have a detailed briefing or a script that describes the narrative of the project, but even then writing down your ideas will help you go deeper and always keep in mind the character you're working on.

SHAPING FACES

I always like to start designing a character with the face, as I consider that the most important part! I start with the design of my water hero, Old Drop. Beginning with simple shapes, I play with distances and sizes to create variety and contrast. Refer back to your word diagram and think about how to incorporate your concepts into the designs. For instance, how can I make the hair look like a wave or the head look like a water droplet? These questions will help add more unique and interesting features to your character.

This page (top):
The collected ideas which will form the basis of the designs going forward

This page (bottom):
Face explorations for my character Old Drop

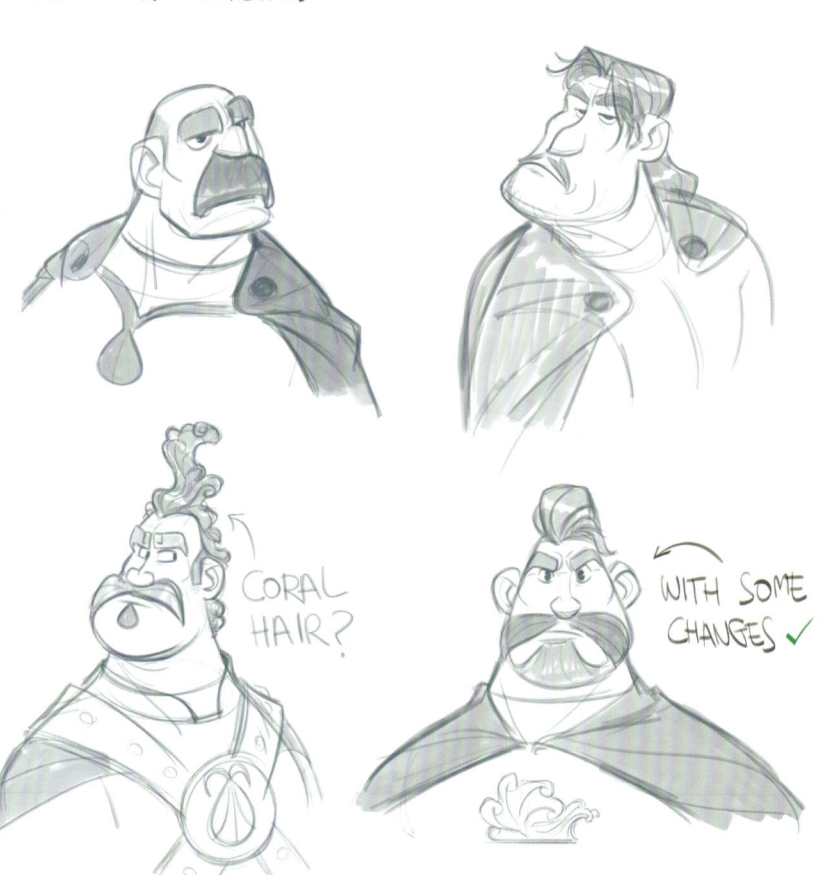

CORAL HAIR?

WITH SOME CHANGES ✓

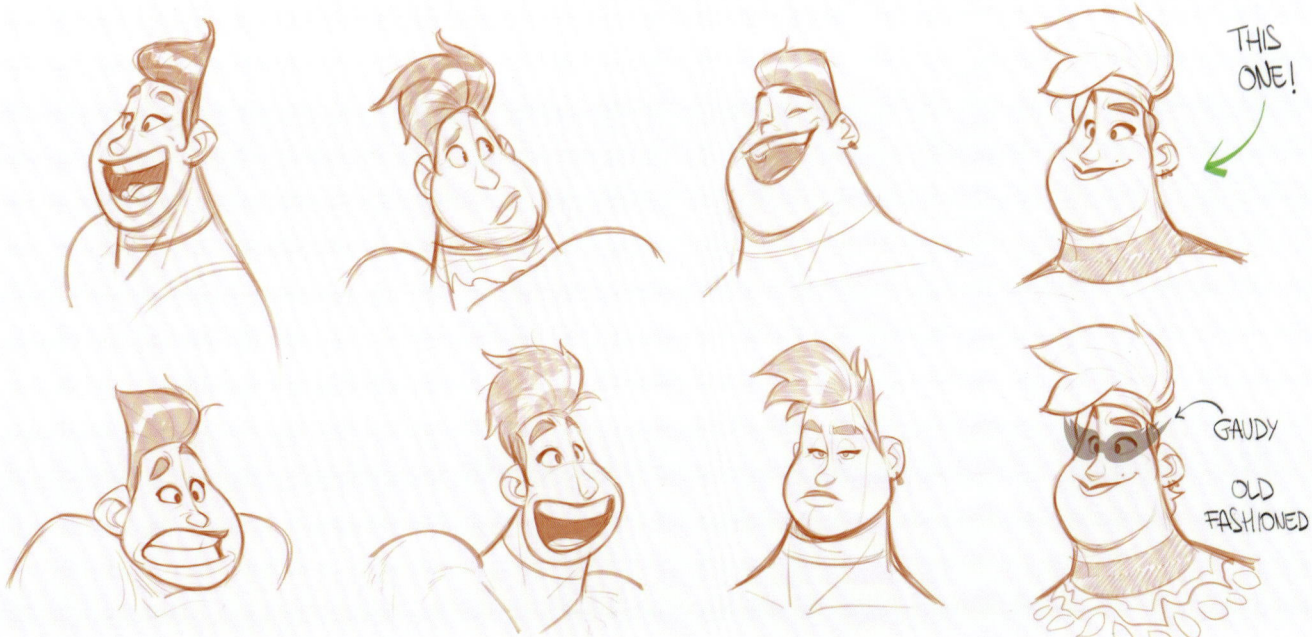

PERSONALITY TEST

I move on to designing the face for my fire-based superhero, Flare. I work with the volumes and masses of the character, exploring personality through facial expressions. Consider how your character smiles when they're happy, or how they scowl when they're angry – it all adds up to a deeper understanding of who they truly are.

In Flare's case, I use soft and round shapes for the face, gradually becoming more energetic and direct through her hairstyle. I want to show that she's a friendly extrovert who is also strong and powerful. Use visual elements that support the character's personality whenever you can.

HAIR-RAISING TALES

My third hero is Thunderbolt, a lightning-based character. For this design, I explore how to show personality and mood through his hair. Since he's a stylish character, he always has a trendy hairstyle. As this is an important part of his personality, maybe when he is angry, his hair reacts to his emotions? I add some lightning bolt designs on the side of his head, reinforcing his character. Finally, I decide on elegant dreadlocks that generate electricity when he activates his powers.

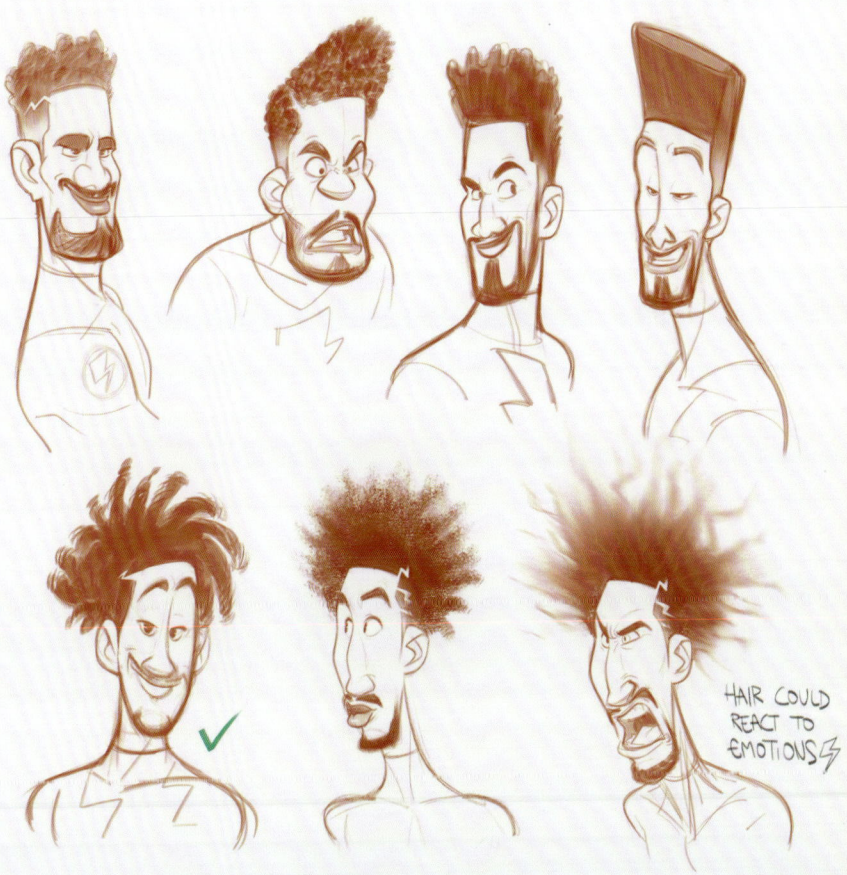

This page (top): Exploring Flare's personality, from basic forms to solid expressions

This page (bottom): Explorations for Thunderbolt, playing with his hair and emotions

BODY POSITIVE

Next, let's draw some bodies! A helpful tip to get started designing and posing your character is to draw from the outside towards the middle. For example, start by drawing a rectangular shape for the body and then add more detail when you have a clearer idea of the character you're working on. When you're drawing the whole pose, put the face to one side, initially, and focus on how the overall design will look.

For my first character, Old Drop, I want to make him look bulky and heavy – slow, but robust. I also add curved shapes to reflect his water powers and give the character some contrast.

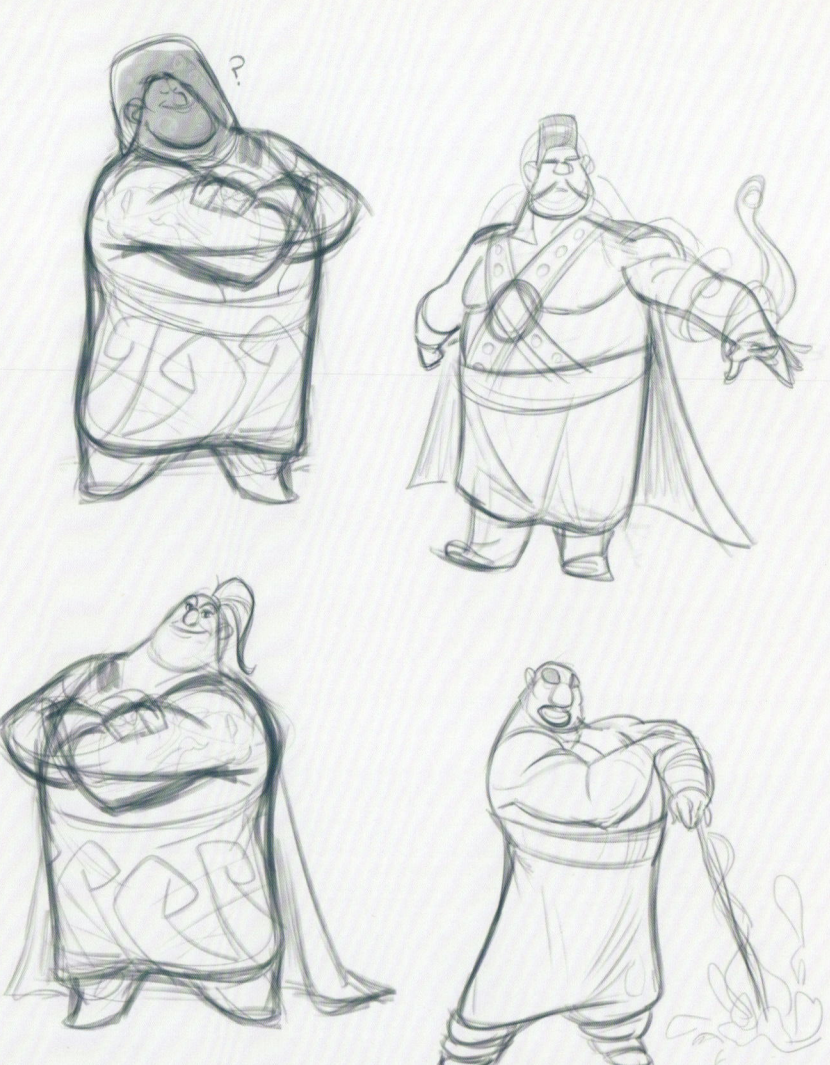

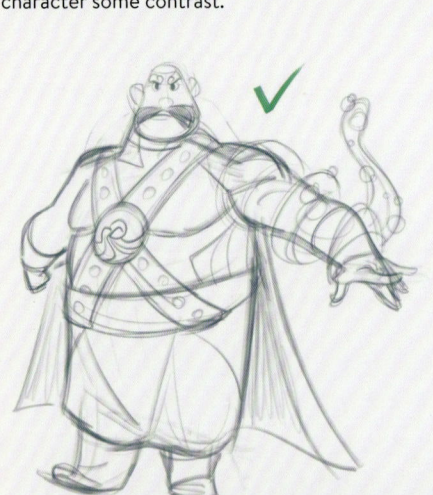

IDEA TRASH CAN

At some point, an idea occurred to me: what if superheroes' professions were associated with their powers? I created some tests of a plumber with water powers, but discarded it in the end as I thought it wouldn't be recognizable enough. Trying new things midway through the process helps you reaffirm whether your idea is working or whether you should change things before it becomes too complicated.

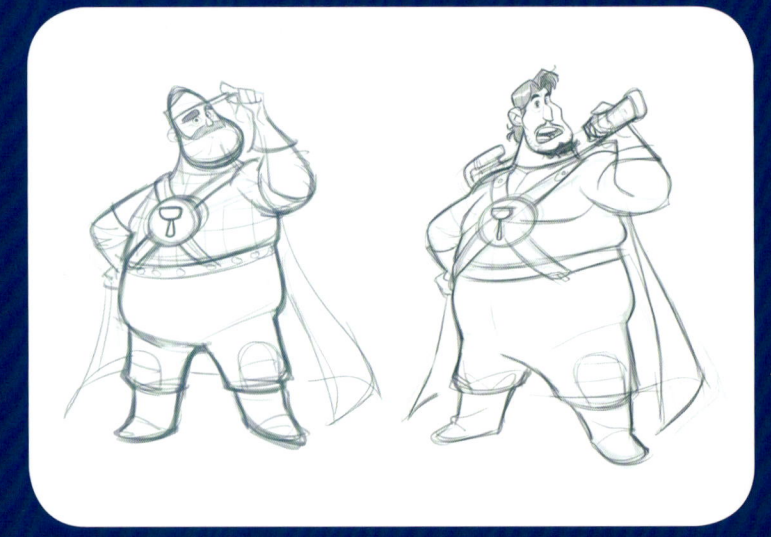

THE HERO POSE

The concept of the hero pose is usually used to present a character to the audience. For this iconic look, ask yourself what are the most important elements of your character that can be captured in a single image? In this instance, I need to find a balance between a pose that looks unique and impactful, and at the same time works well within the group.

I create a series of poses for Thunderbolt. Many of these examples have a lot of action and dynamism that might work better on a separate character pose sheet. When introducing a character, think about what elements reinforce their shape and personality, so people can quickly recognise all the development work you've done. Remember, simple is better!

THE ATTITUDE PROBLEM

For Flare, I want her pose to reflect her energy. I think about what hobbies she might have: sports, aerobics, dance, and running. I explore different ways to show her energy through her arms and legs, and take the chance to explore some 90s inspired aerobic outfits, which are very trendy again now.

Whenever you can, go back and forth between your characters to check how these explorations fit with the rest of the ensemble and avoid possible conflicts in the final design of the group.

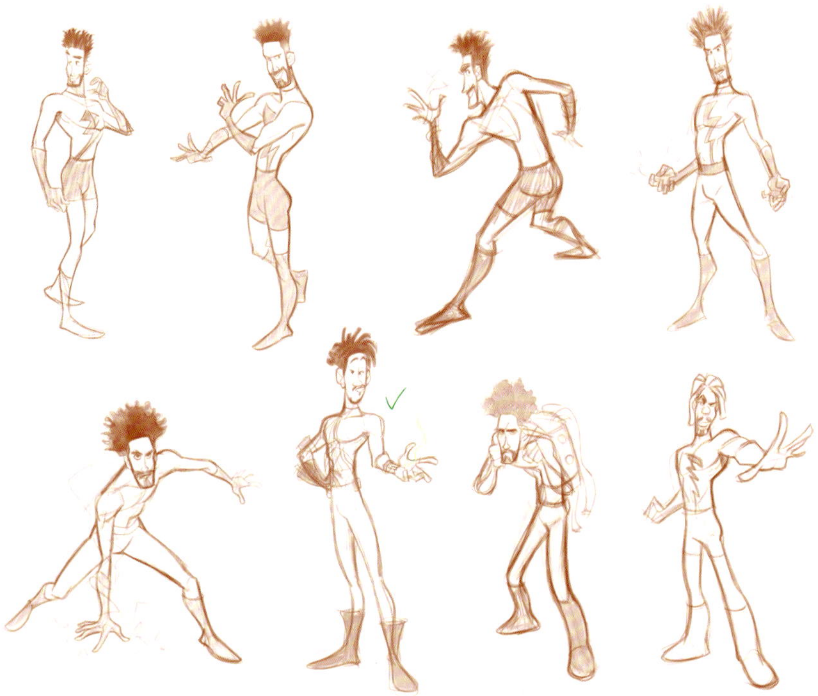

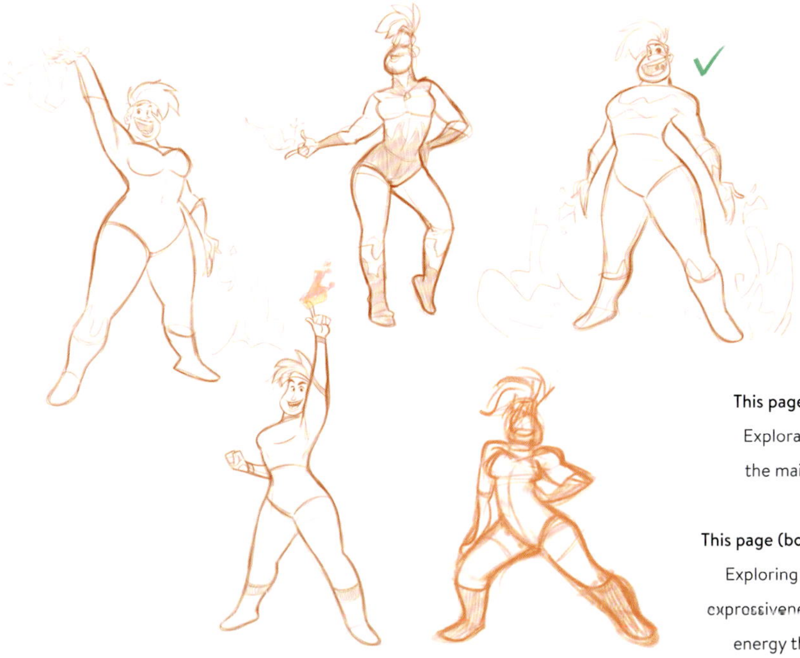

This page (top):
Exploration of the main pose

This page (bottom):
Exploring Flare's expressiveness and energy through her pose

AVOIDING SYMMETRY

While drawing, you might get stuck following a purely mechanical process and forget to address some of the conceptual aspects of your design. Having symmetrical poses makes the character more boring and predictable. Breaking the symmetry in the design will make the character look more dynamic and interesting. Keep the older versions of your design so you can see how much your character has improved.

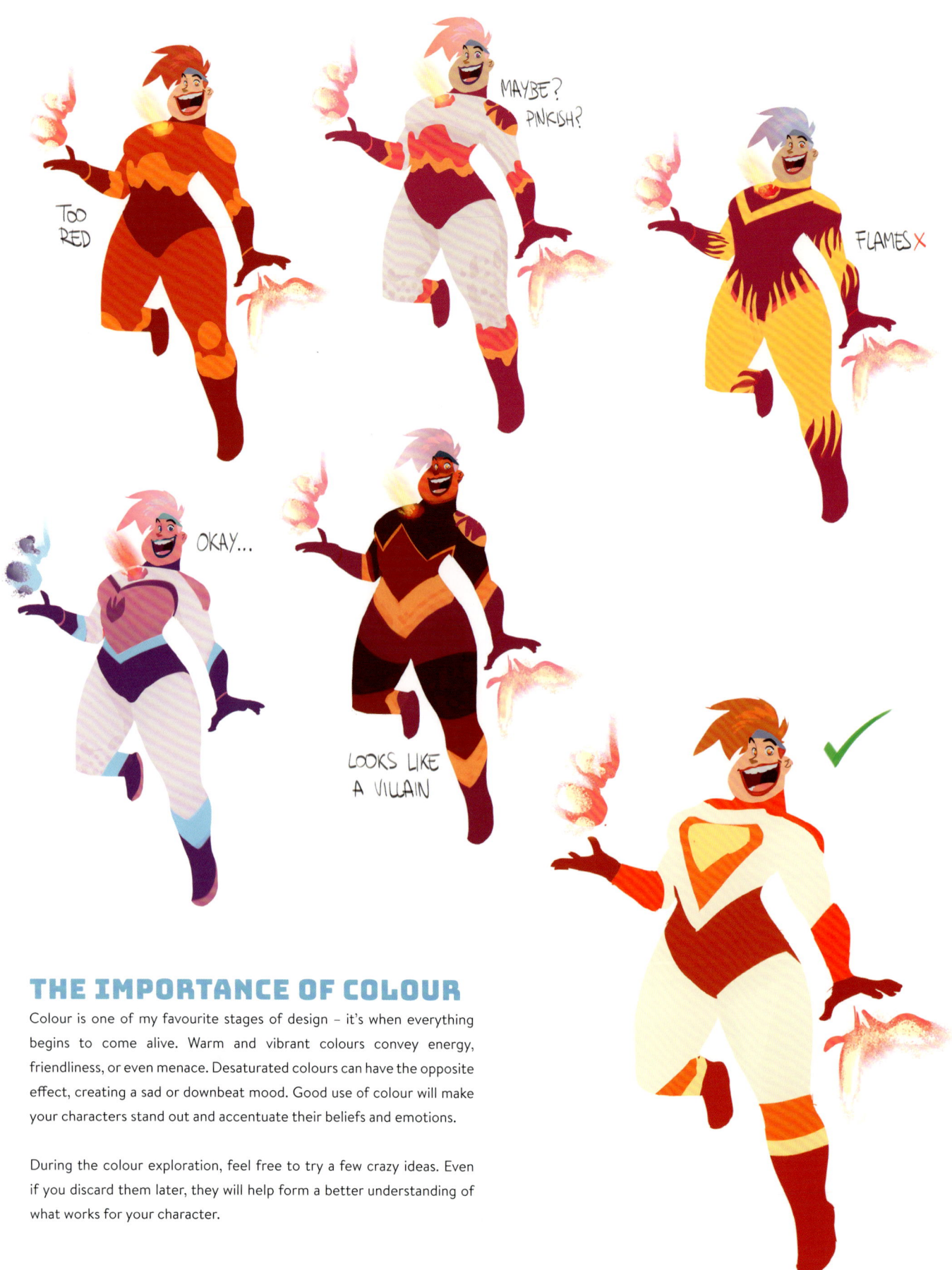

THE IMPORTANCE OF COLOUR

Colour is one of my favourite stages of design – it's when everything begins to come alive. Warm and vibrant colours convey energy, friendliness, or even menace. Desaturated colours can have the opposite effect, creating a sad or downbeat mood. Good use of colour will make your characters stand out and accentuate their beliefs and emotions.

During the colour exploration, feel free to try a few crazy ideas. Even if you discard them later, they will help form a better understanding of what works for your character.

'I TRY TO KEEP A CHARACTER'S PALETTE LIMITED TO JUST A FEW COLOURS THAT COMPLEMENT EACH OTHER WELL'

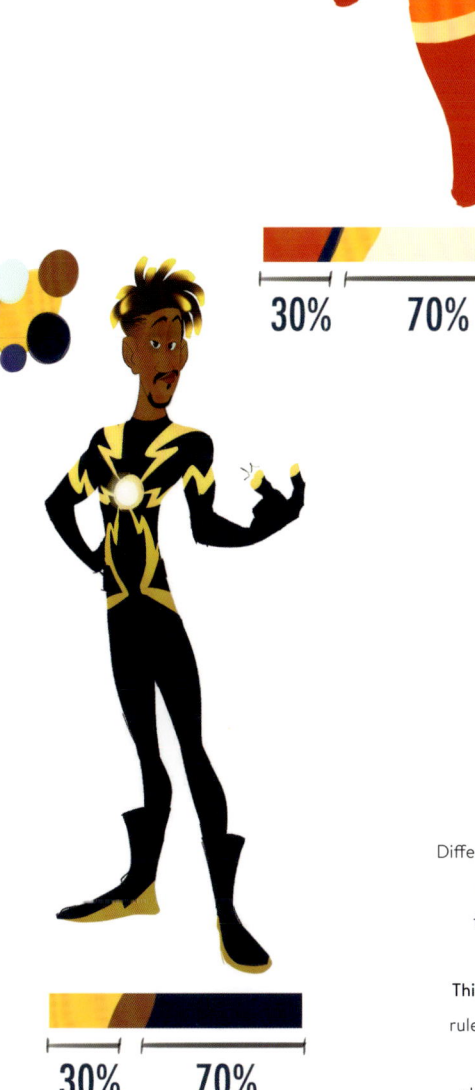

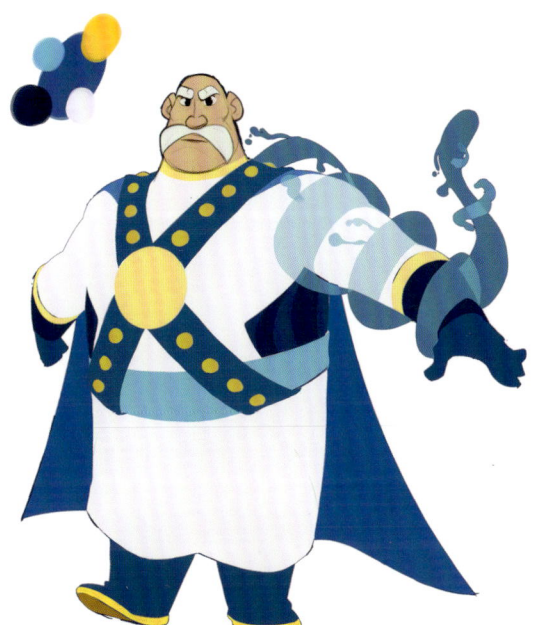

30% **70%**

30% **70%**

30% **70%**

SIMPLE IS BETTER

Using too many colours can make a design seem busy and unpleasant to look at. I try to keep a character's palette limited to just a few colours that complement each other well. Try to identify a character with a unique colour and then use a few more to highlight areas that interest you. I choose blue, yellow, and red as the main colours for my three heroes, and try to use other common hues throughout each design. A good rule to use is a 70/30 split – 70% of a character's colour is less intense background shades, and 30% is their primary colour.

Opposite page:
Different colour options
for Flare, trying to
find a good balance

This page: I use simple
rules to create variety,
but also cohesive
characters in a group

CHECKING SILHOUETTES

Before proceeding with the final step, it's important to check if the silhouette reads well or if you need to make any final adjustments. Make sure you do these checks before adding any more detail, otherwise making changes later will be a lot more complicated and time consuming.

To check the silhouette, lower the lightness of your design or simply fill it with black. Having a solid colour that contrasts with white allows you to identify what might need improving. Check that lines and shapes point to the face and don't distract attention from other things that aren't relevant.

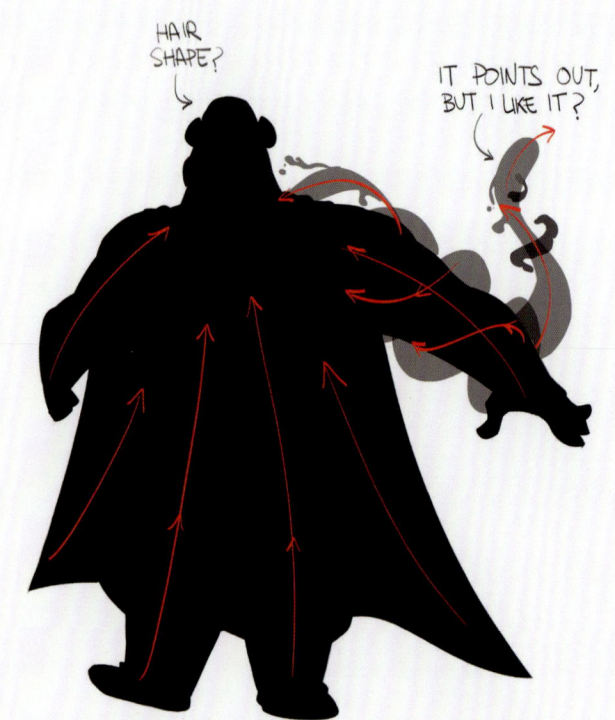

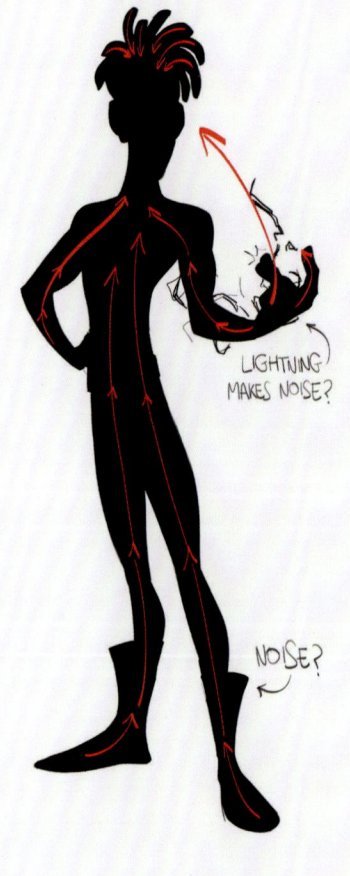

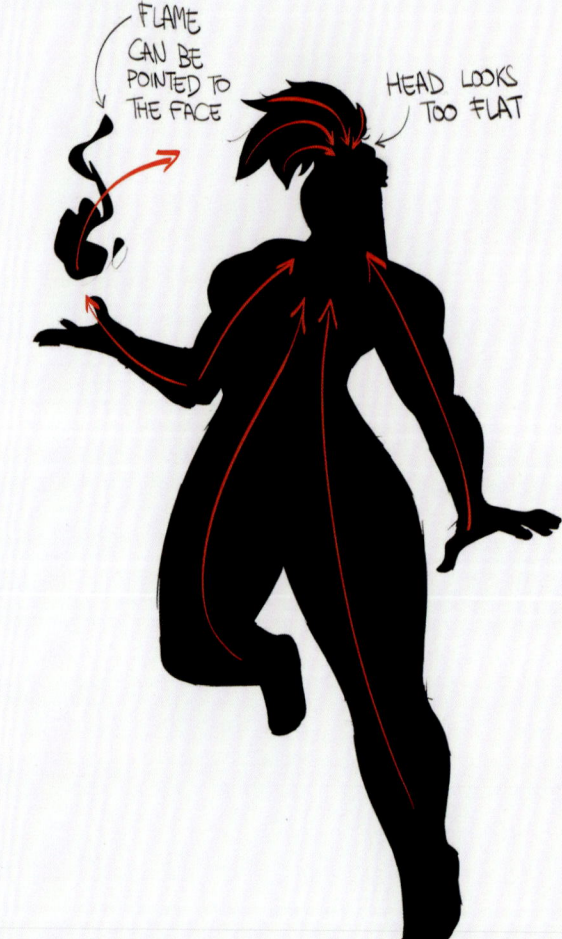

This page: Reviewing the silhouettes and checking if the shapes are oriented in a good direction

Opposite page: An example of my workflow when rendering a character

START RENDERING

Rendering gives you a more solid image of your character and makes it easier to judge the volumes of the design. It can also be useful for the modelling department (or client) to see what the character would look like in a 3D environment.

How I render is quite simple: I choose where the light comes from and then I add blending modes. I use a Multiply layer (set to around 30% to 45% opacity) to add shadows, and a Dodge Colour layer to add highlights and effects.

'RENDERING GIVES YOU A MORE SOLID IMAGE OF YOUR CHARACTER AND MAKES IT EASIER TO JUDGE THE VOLUMES OF THE DESIGN'

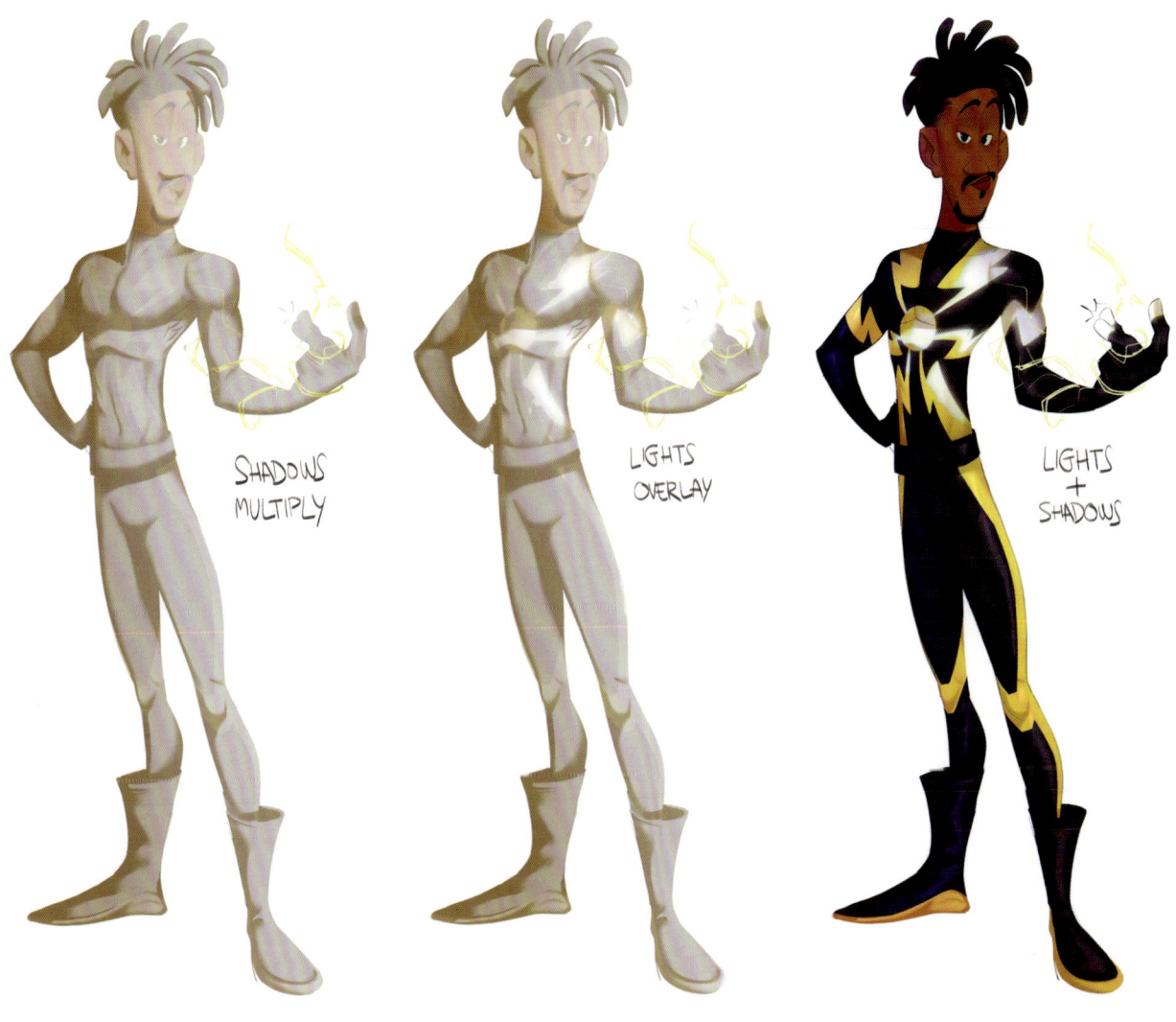

SHADOWS MULTIPLY

LIGHTS OVERLAY

LIGHTS + SHADOWS

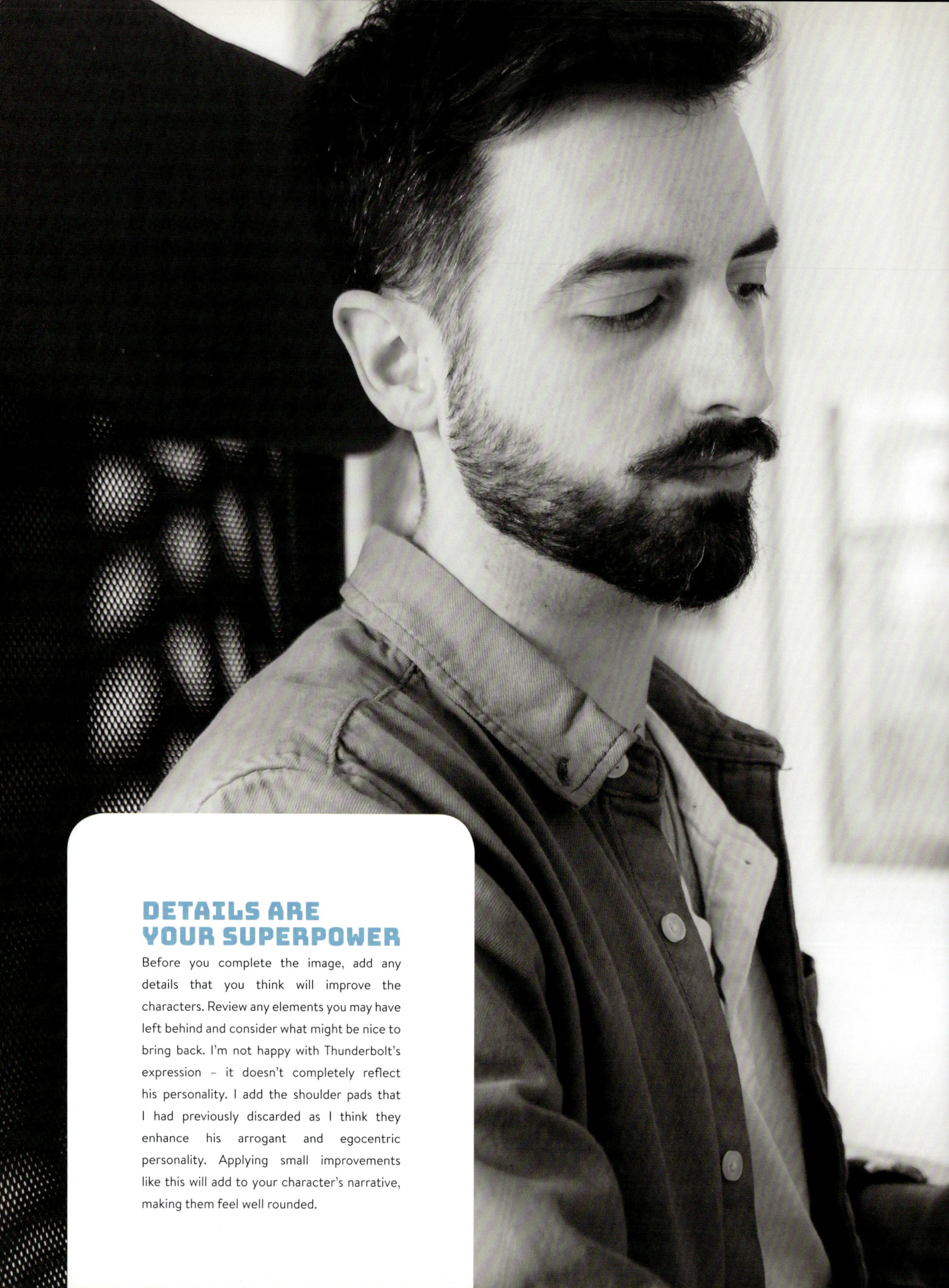

DETAILS ARE
YOUR SUPERPOWER

Before you complete the image, add any details that you think will improve the characters. Review any elements you may have left behind and consider what might be nice to bring back. I'm not happy with Thunderbolt's expression – it doesn't completely reflect his personality. I add the shoulder pads that I had previously discarded as I think they enhance his arrogant and egocentric personality. Applying small improvements like this will add to your character's narrative, making them feel well rounded.

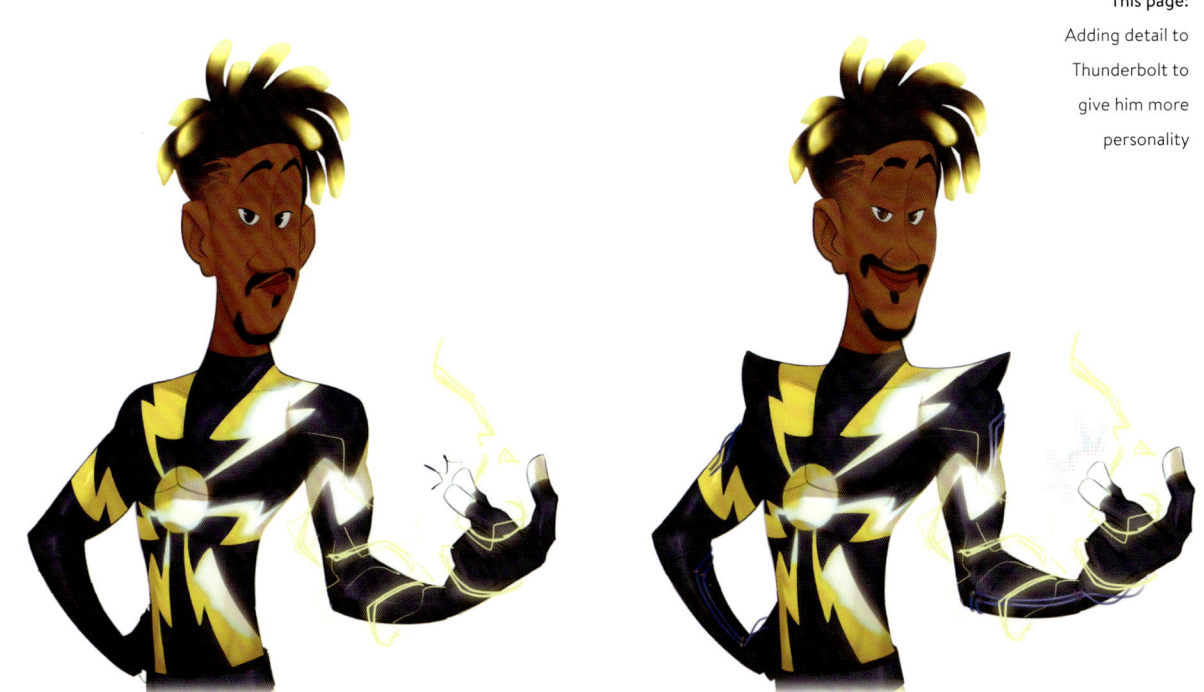

This page:
Adding detail to
Thunderbolt to
give him more
personality

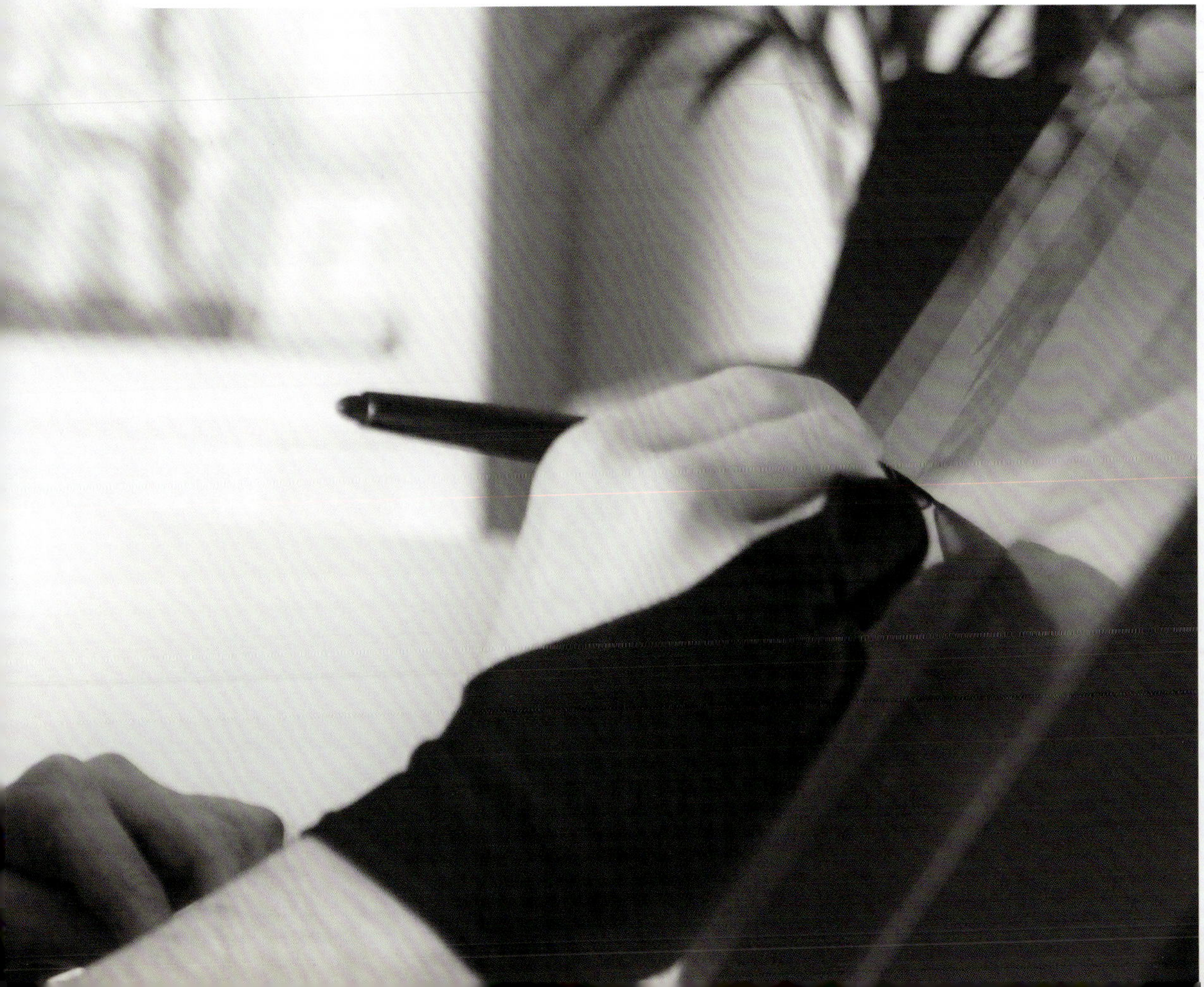

OUR SUPERHEROES ARE READY!

And that's all folks, the superheroes have assembled! Bearing in mind the limitations of telling a story with just one image, I'm happy with how the whole squad has turned out. It's an interesting group of characters that work both collectively and individually. I feel that many aspects of each character's narrative comes through in the design, which for me is the most important thing. I can imagine the three heroes working together, what kind of situations they may encounter, and how they would help each other to save the day.

Remember, enjoy the process and never settle for your first idea. The more fun you have, the more impactful the final result will be, and the more you explore your characters, the more complete they will feel.

These pages: Final render, with the full cast of characters in their heroic poses

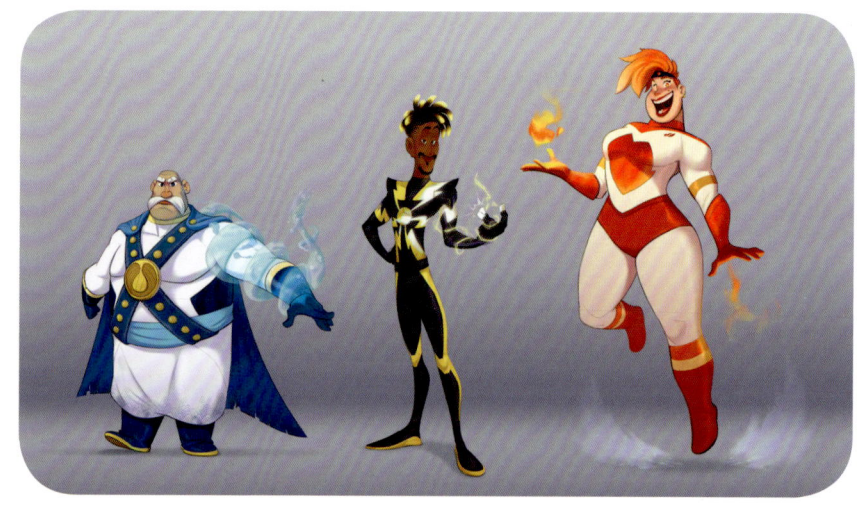

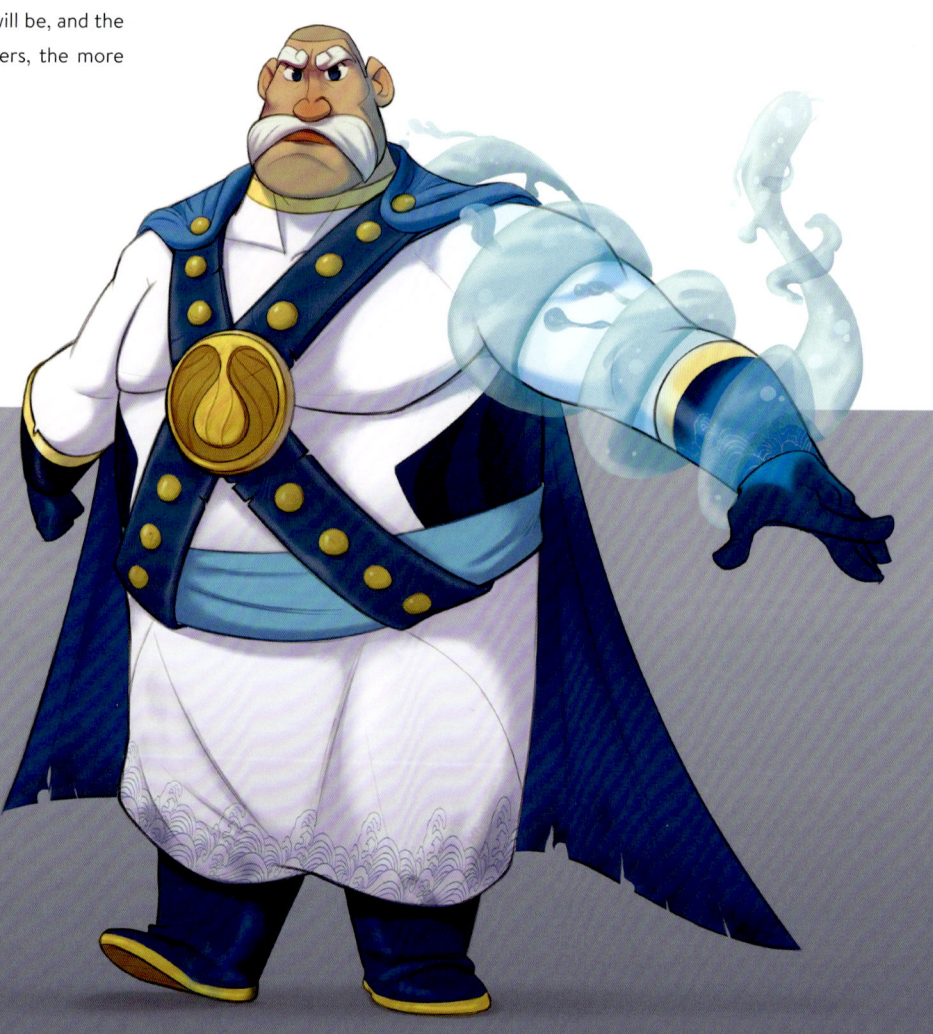

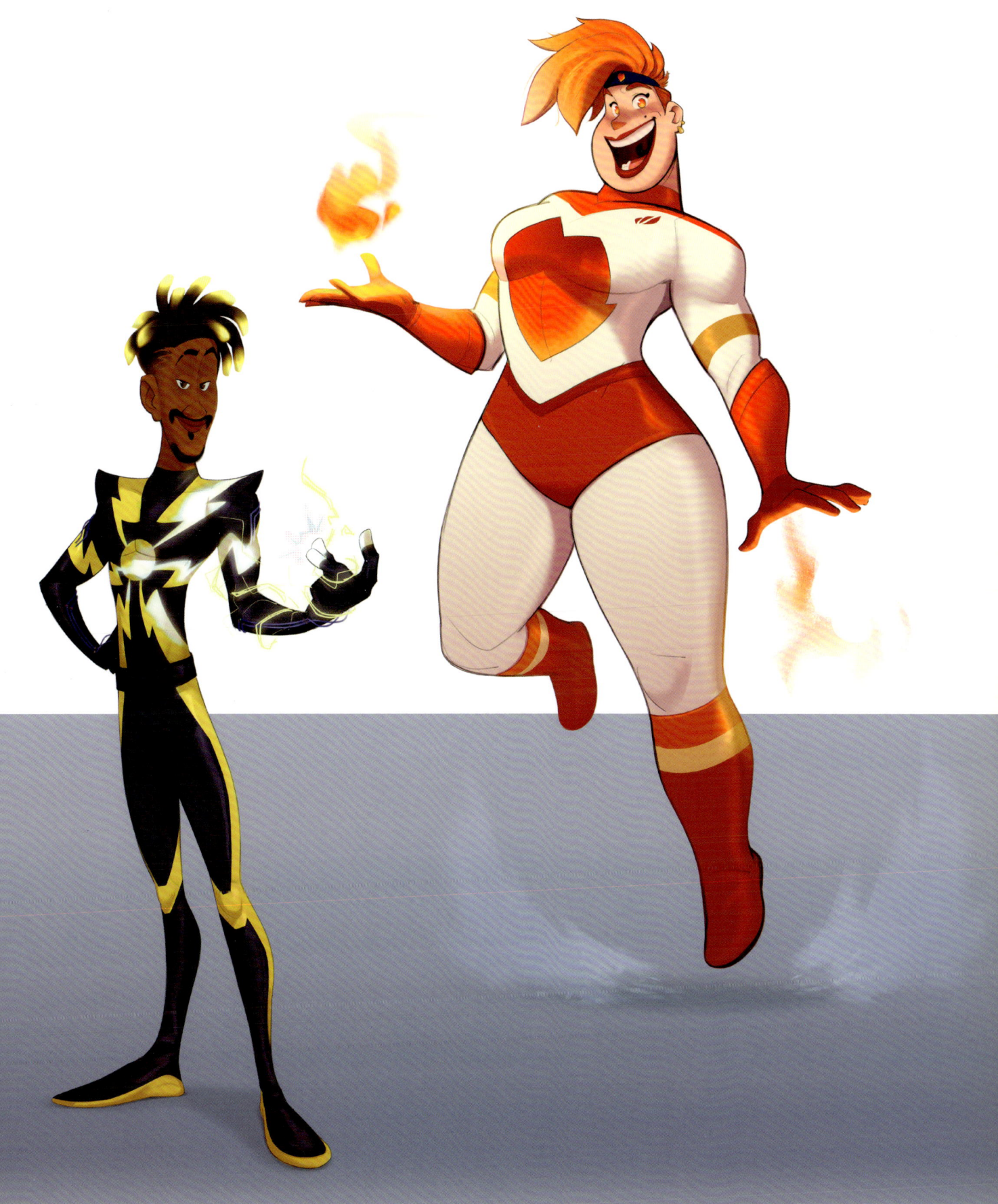

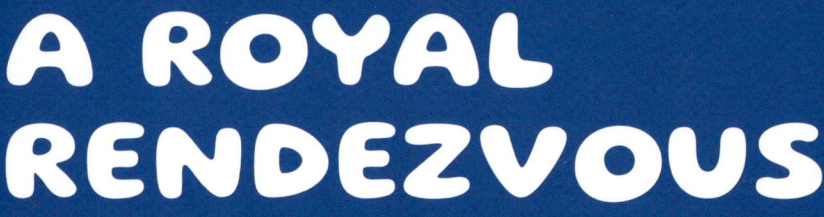

A ROYAL RENDEZVOUS

ABRAHAM REYES

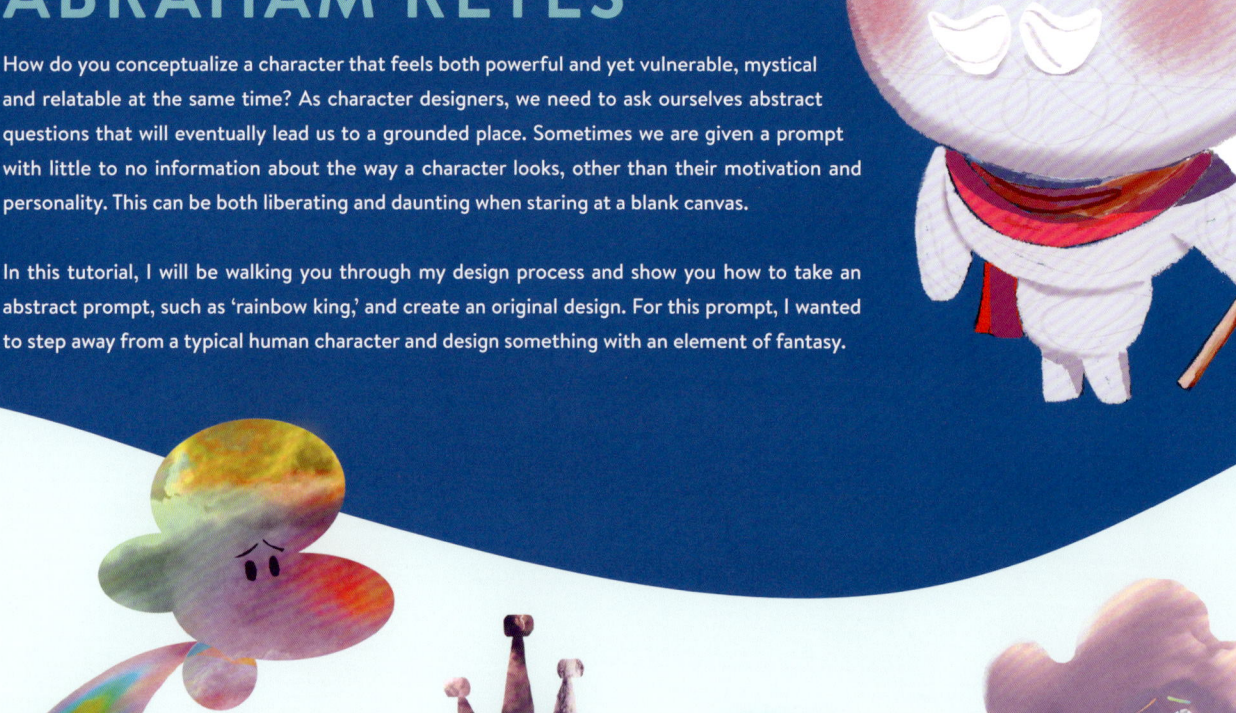

How do you conceptualize a character that feels both powerful and yet vulnerable, mystical and relatable at the same time? As character designers, we need to ask ourselves abstract questions that will eventually lead us to a grounded place. Sometimes we are given a prompt with little to no information about the way a character looks, other than their motivation and personality. This can be both liberating and daunting when staring at a blank canvas.

In this tutorial, I will be walking you through my design process and show you how to take an abstract prompt, such as 'rainbow king,' and create an original design. For this prompt, I wanted to step away from a typical human character and design something with an element of fantasy.

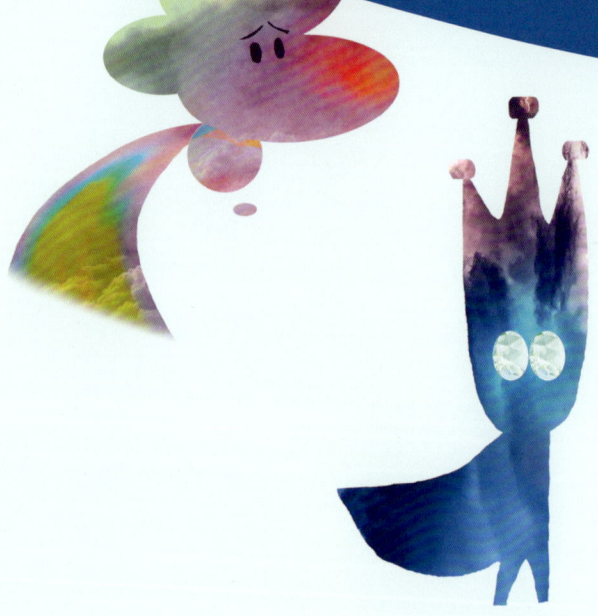

REGAL RESEARCHING

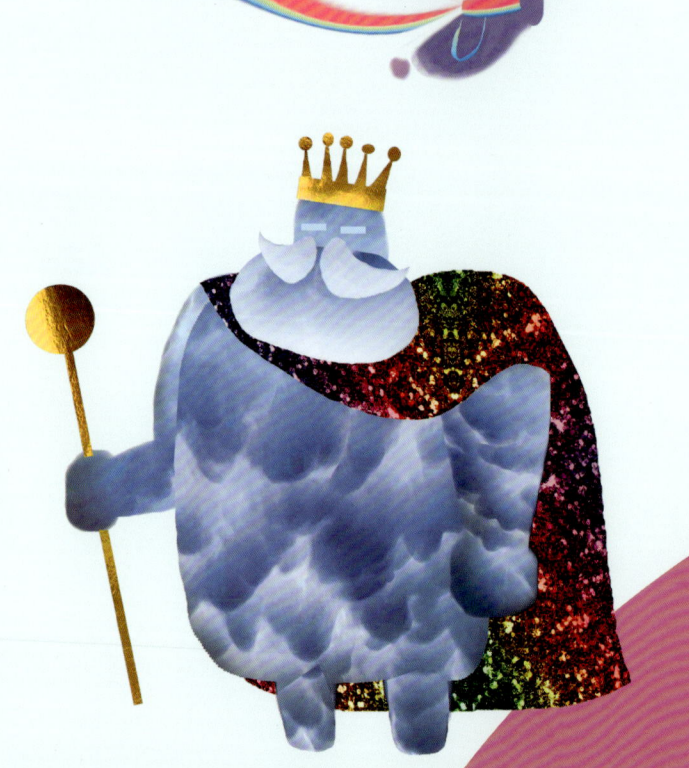

What if the Rainbow King was a cloud-like being that lived in the skies, watching over his kingdom and appearing within a rainbow after it rains? After brainstorming ideas for a backstory, research and gather as many references as you can. The key is to have intent behind your research. Before you begin sketching out your rough ideas, consider doing a photo collage first. This process will help you see the bigger picture and not get caught up with unnecessary details. Playing with shapes and textures during this stage will quickly help you establish the overall mood of your character.

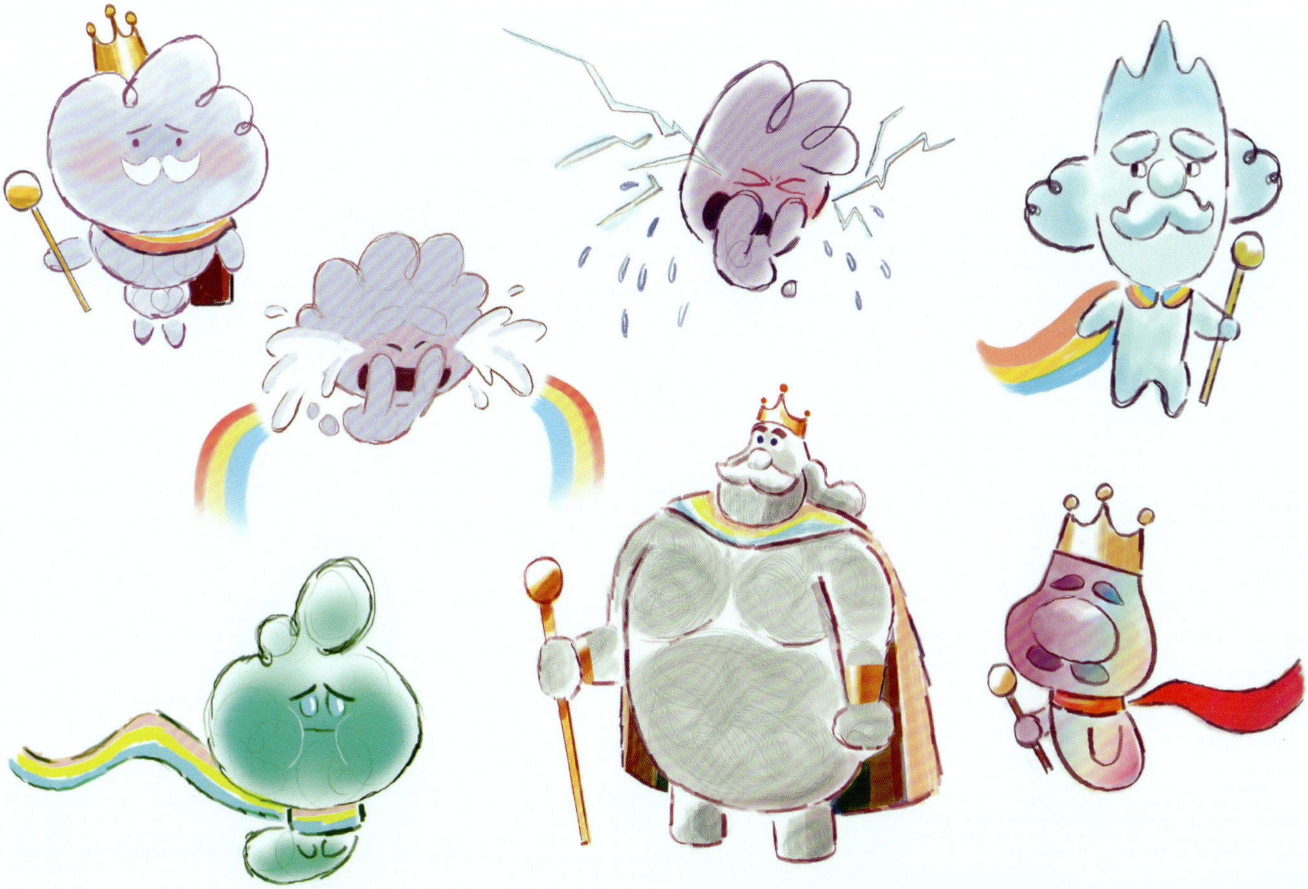

CHARACTER EXPLORATIONS

After developing a few collage designs, set those aside and use them as a source of inspiration. As you begin to sketch out your ideas, always keep in mind your character's personality type and motivation. Although colour isn't necessary for this stage, it's a tool you can use to help inform textures, props, and costume.

TURNAROUND AND AROUND

Once you have a design you are happy with, consider doing a turnaround. This process will not only help you envision your character in three-dimensional space, but also iron out some design kinks you may run into. Use different coloured lines to inform which elements of the design overlap your character's body, such as their costume, hair, and props.

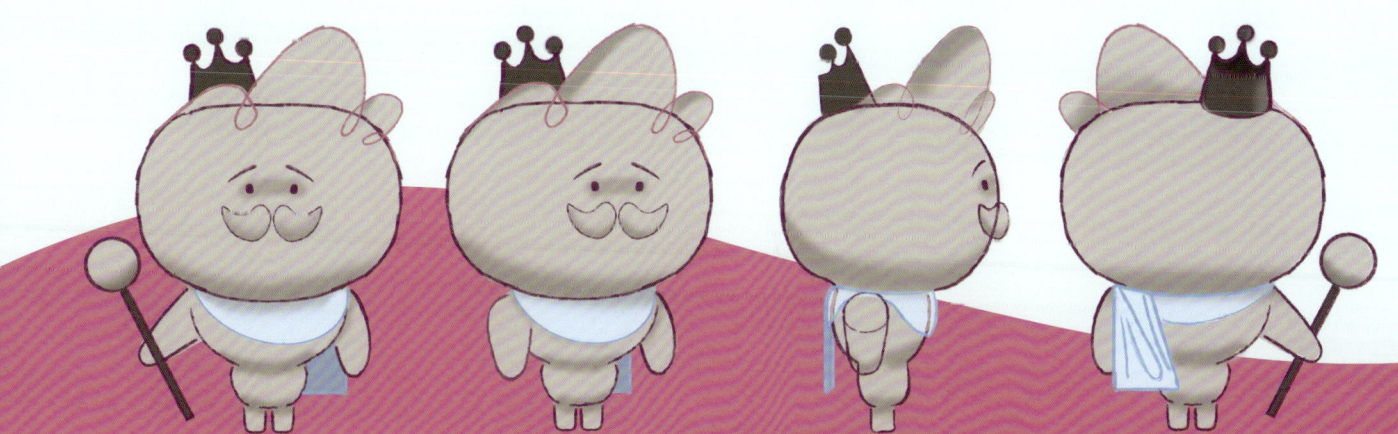

All images © Abraham Reyes

FEEL THE EMOTION

After you've established your character's proportions, work on examples of extreme facial expressions. Use the three-quarter view of your character as a base on which to draw. Ask yourself how your character would look if they expressed a certain emotion. Looking in the mirror and using your own face as a reference is always a good place to start.

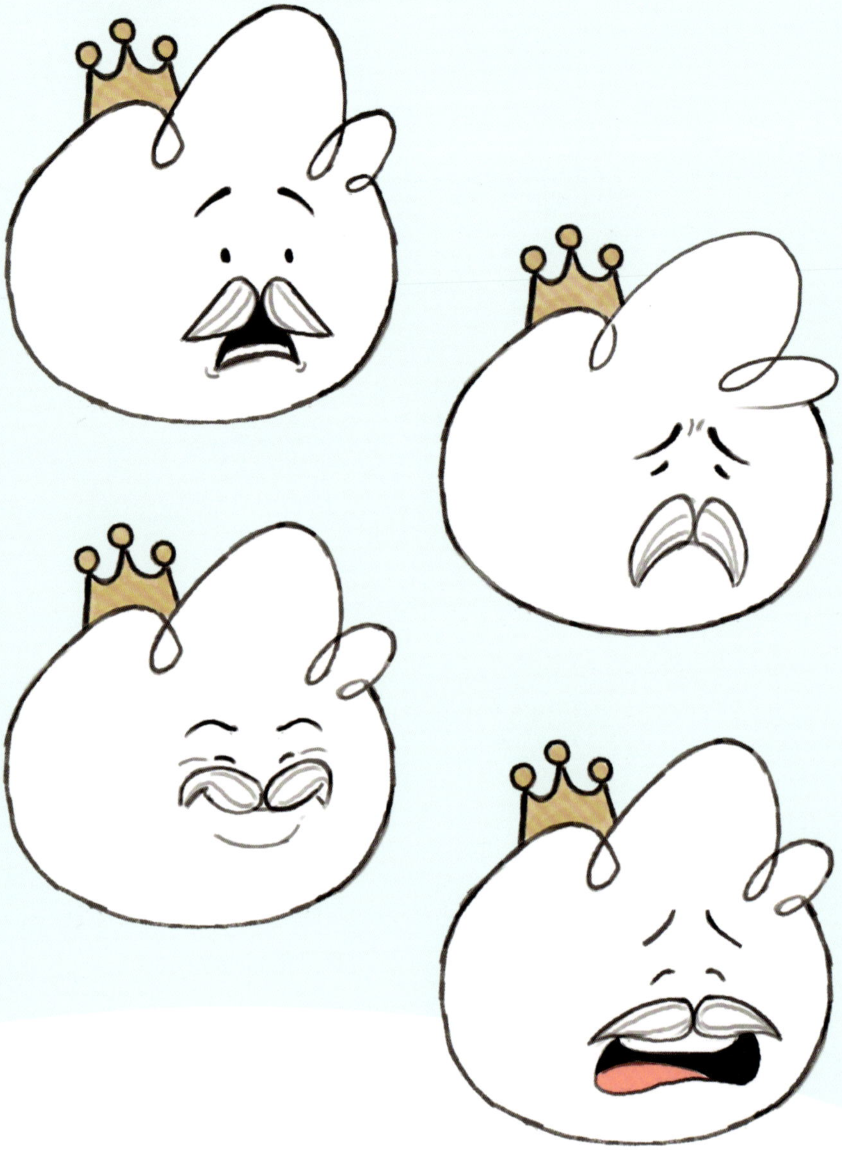

COLOURING THE KING

When working with clients, you may be asked to do a colour pass from time to time. Although you don't have to be a great colourist to be a great character designer, colour can help inform certain design choices within your character. Keep your overall palette consistent with either warm or cool tones. For the Rainbow King, I reduce the colours of the rainbow scarf down to three colours. This allows for a more simplified version that can be posed and understood with ease.

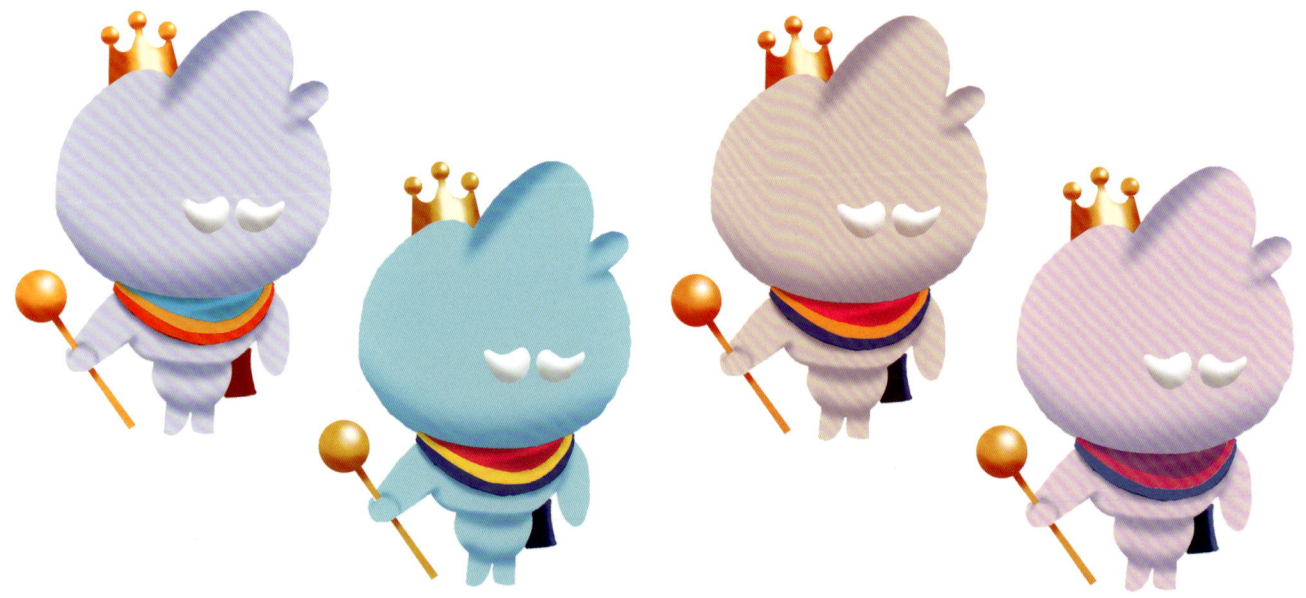

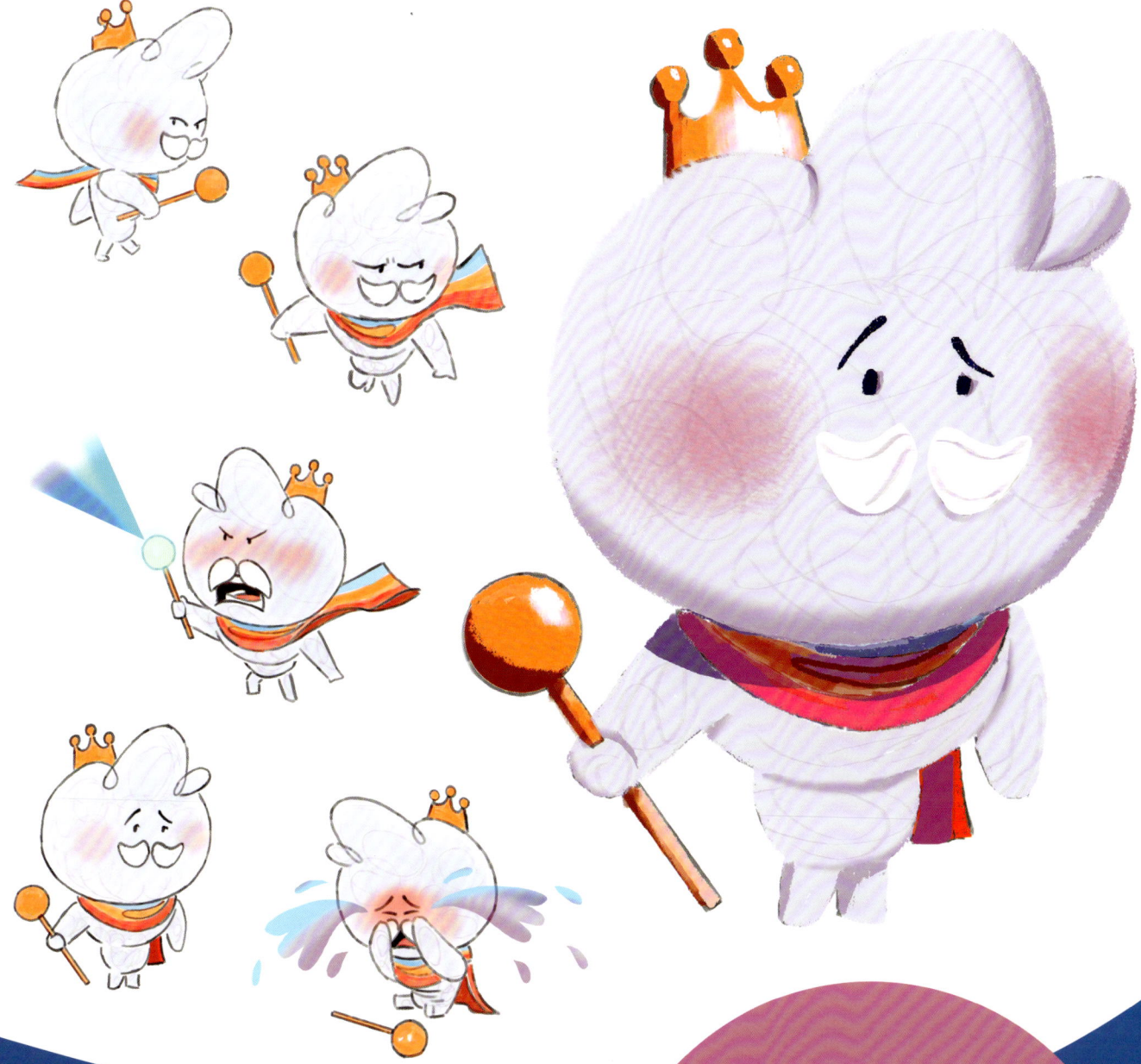

PUTTING ON A SHOW

After you've locked down your design and colour choices, it's time for your character to perform! Each pose should say something unique about the character's personality and the way they feel. Although it's important that you have great draftsmanship skills, this stage is less about drawing pretty pictures and more about showing who this character really is. Use your turnaround drawings as a foundation for your poses to keep your character on model. Research poses or photograph yourself as a reference.

BECOME A CASTING DIRECTOR

A great mentor of mine once told me 'When designing characters, think of yourself as a casting director looking to hire the right actor for the role.' This way of thinking helped influence the way I design characters for animated projects. As a character designer, I'm always searching for a design that is not only appealing and serves the script, but also evokes a familiar feeling that the audience can relate to.

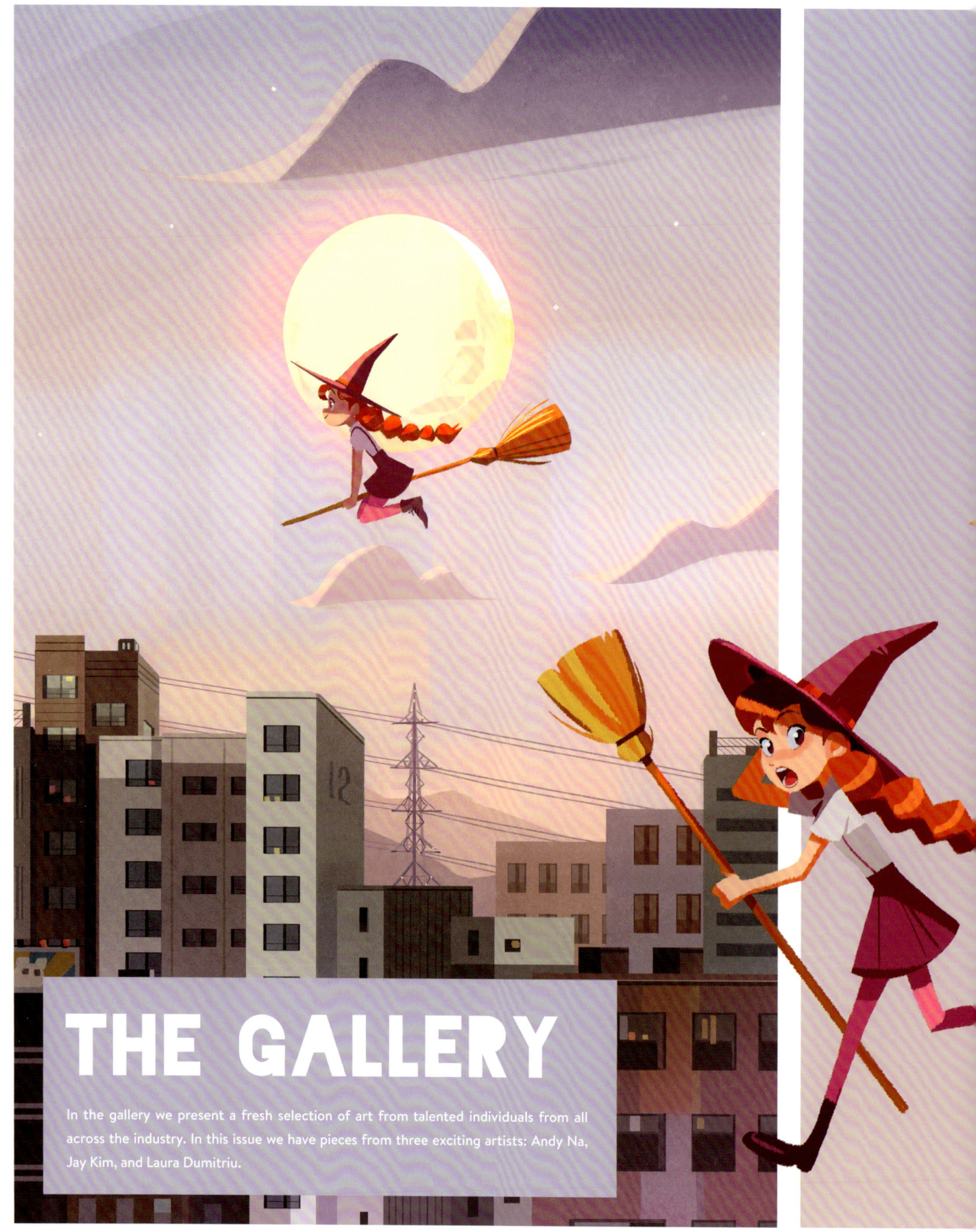

THE GALLERY

In the gallery we present a fresh selection of art from talented individuals from all across the industry. In this issue we have pieces from three exciting artists: Andy Na, Jay Kim, and Laura Dumitriu.

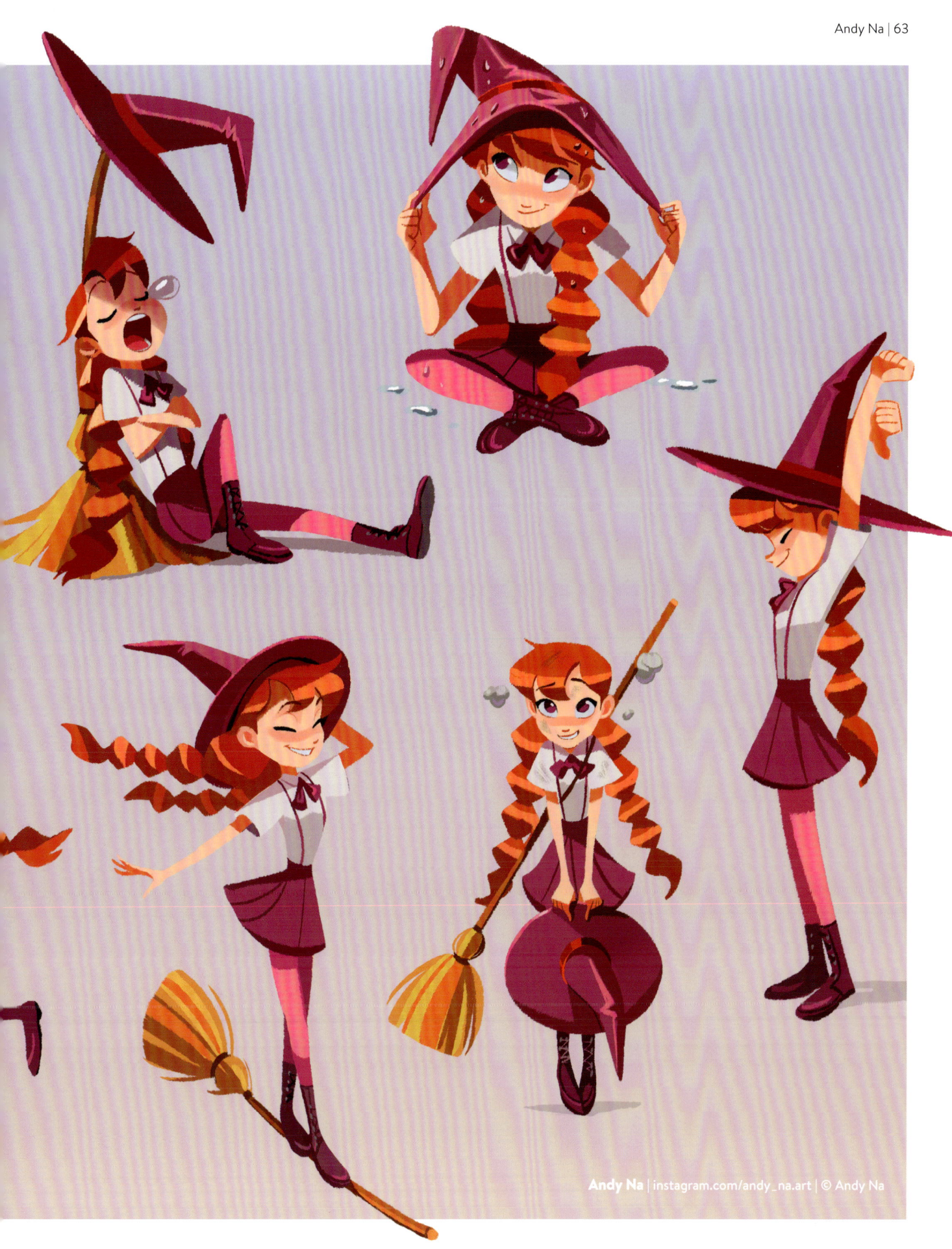

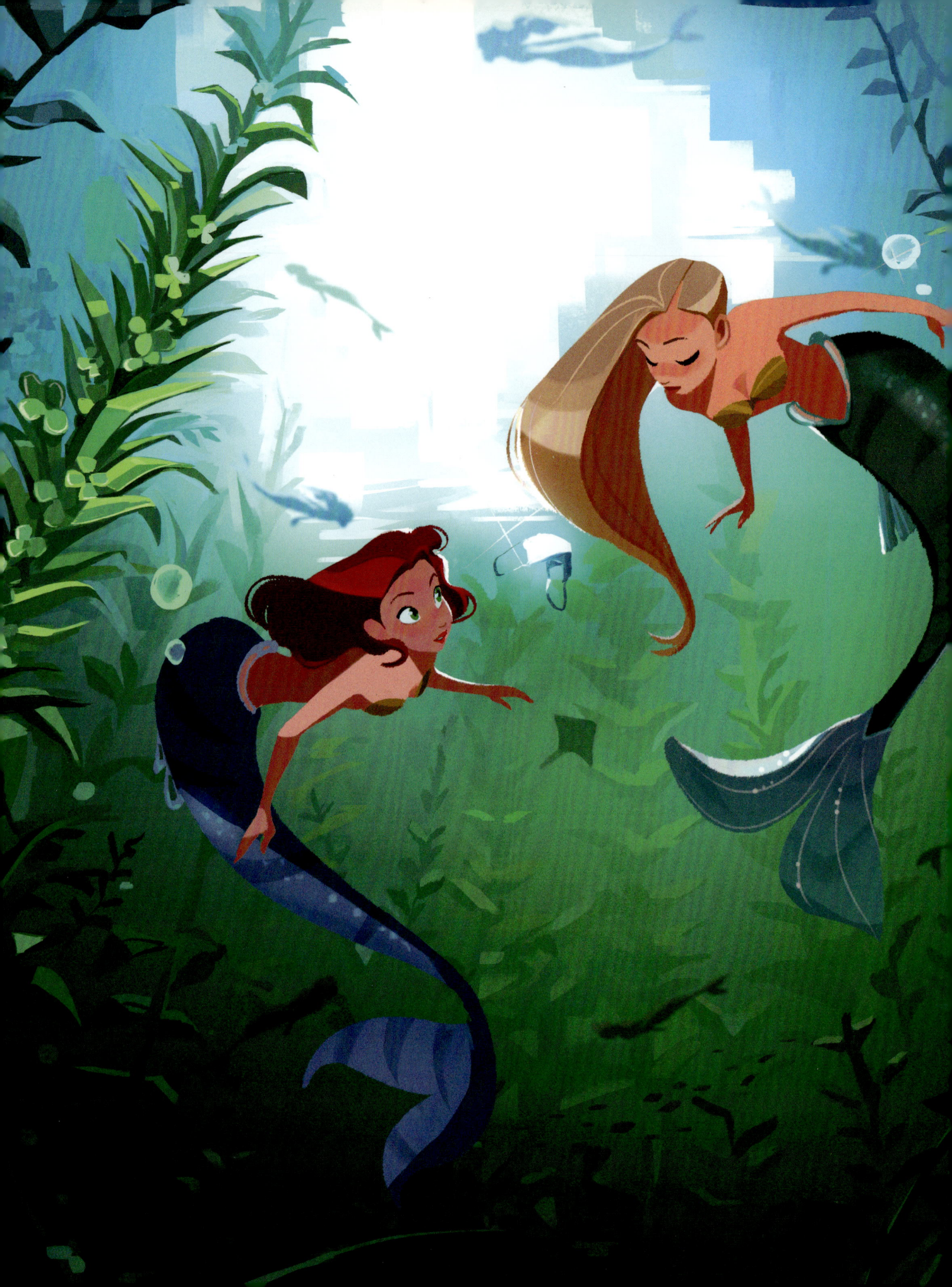

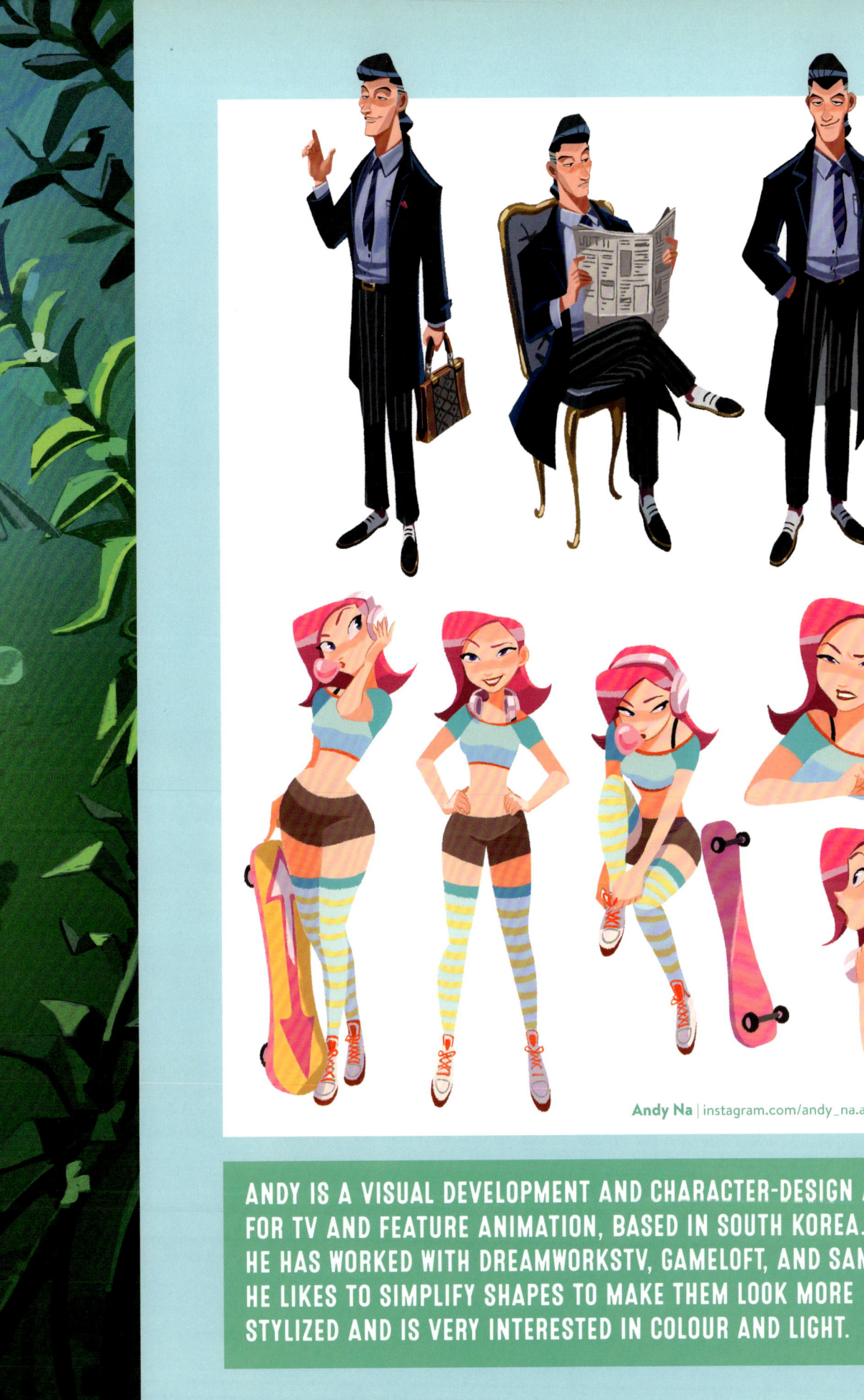

Andy Na | instagram.com/andy_na.art | © Andy Na

ANDY IS A VISUAL DEVELOPMENT AND CHARACTER-DESIGN ARTIST FOR TV AND FEATURE ANIMATION, BASED IN SOUTH KOREA. HE HAS WORKED WITH DREAMWORKSTV, GAMELOFT, AND SAMSUNG. HE LIKES TO SIMPLIFY SHAPES TO MAKE THEM LOOK MORE STYLIZED AND IS VERY INTERESTED IN COLOUR AND LIGHT.

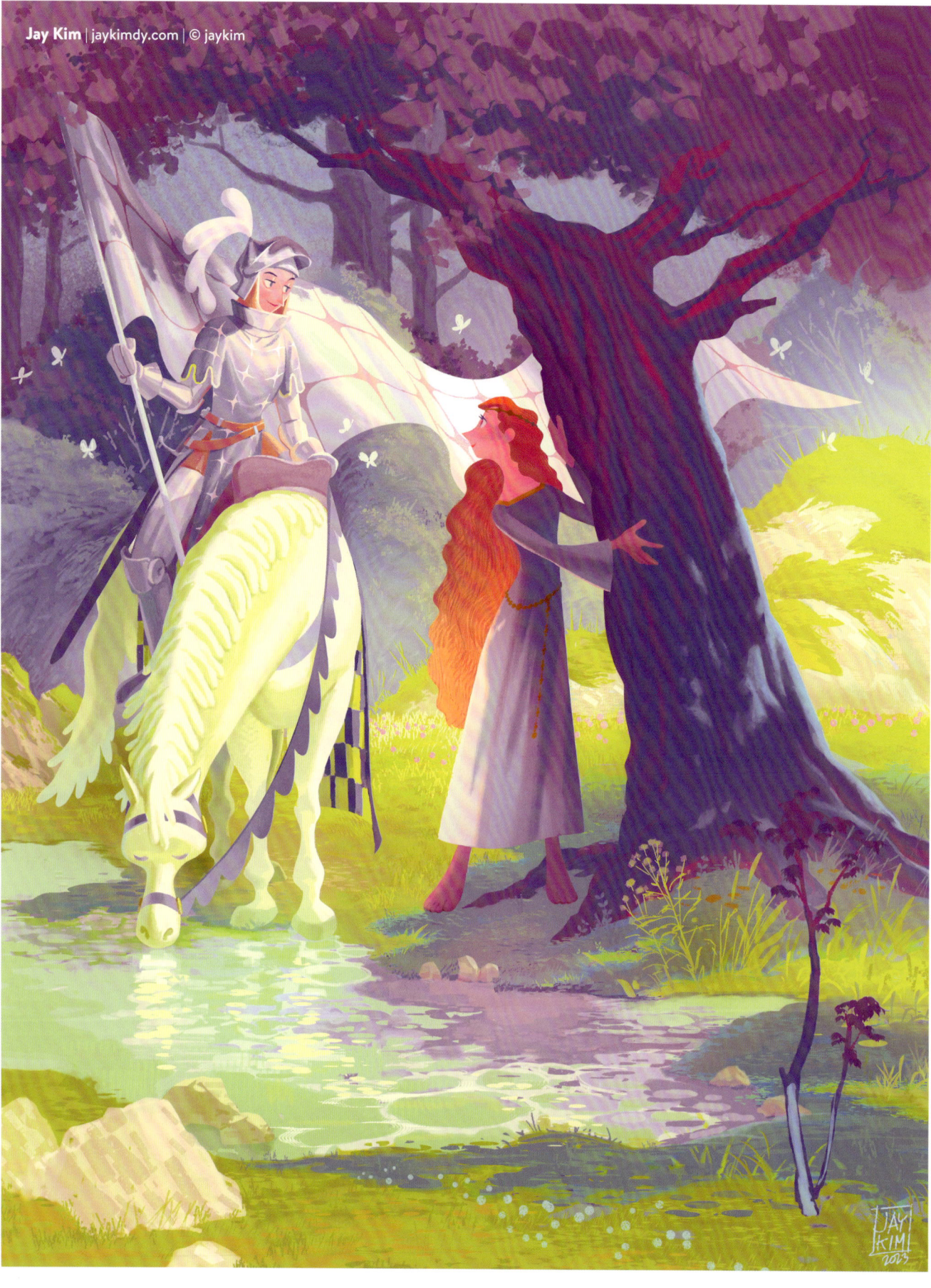

JAY KIM IS AN ARTIST FROM SOUTH KOREA WHO SPECIALIZES IN VISUAL DEVELOPMENT, CHARACTER DESIGN, AND ILLUSTRATION. HER PASSION LIES IN CREATING CHARACTERS THAT HAVE UNIQUE BACKSTORIES AND DISTINCTIVE FEATURES, MAKING EACH ONE OF THEM SPECIAL.

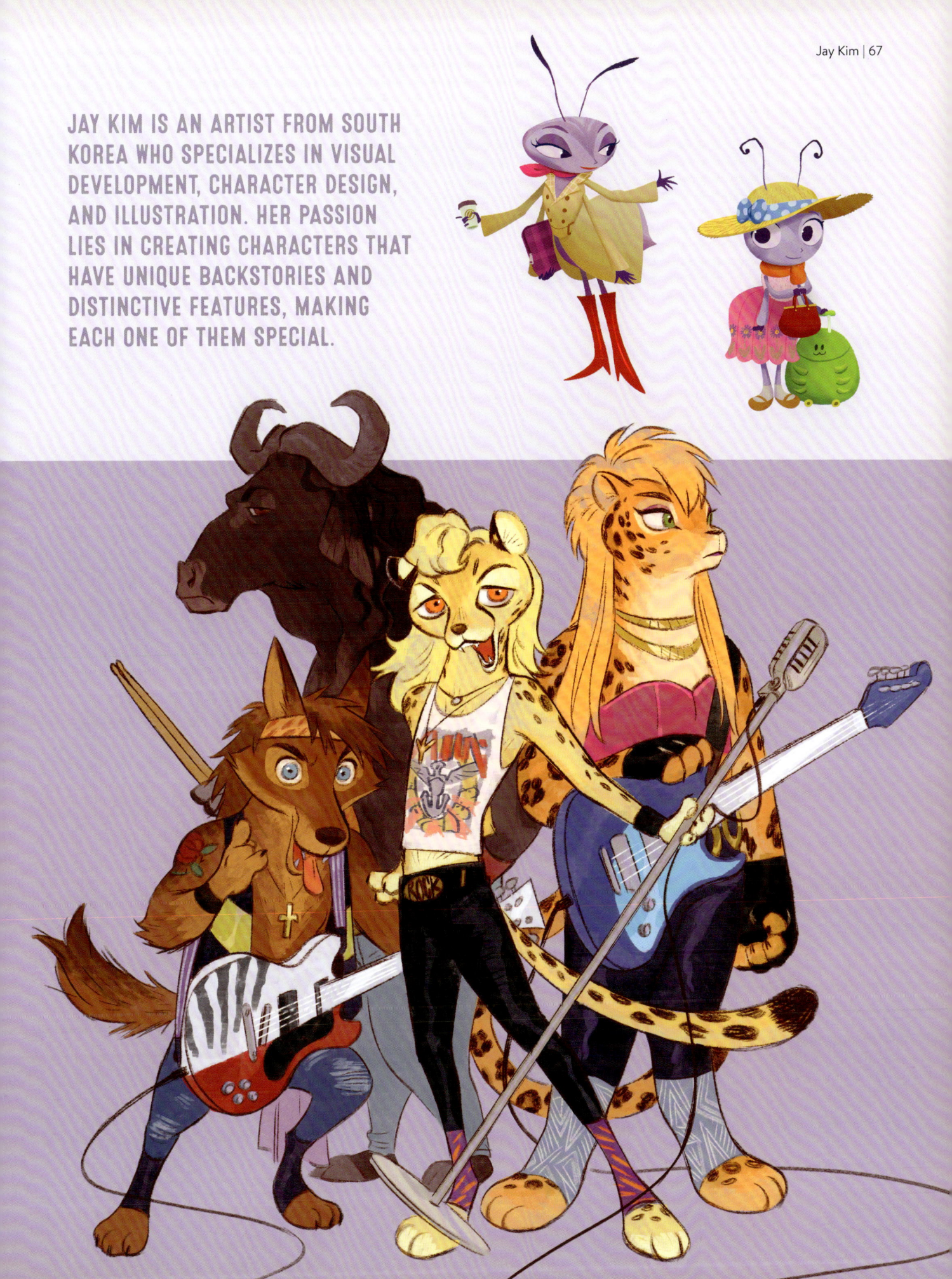

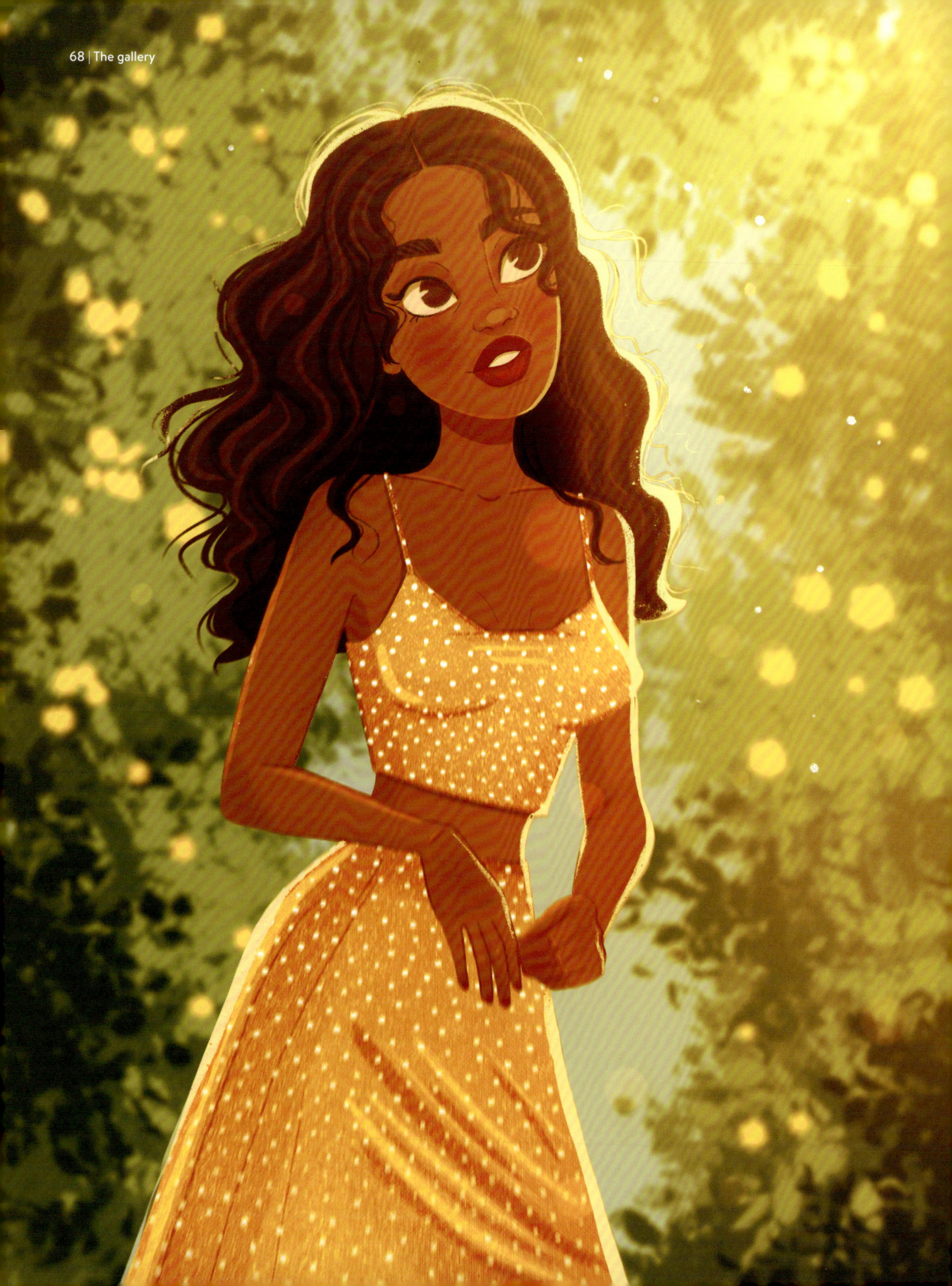

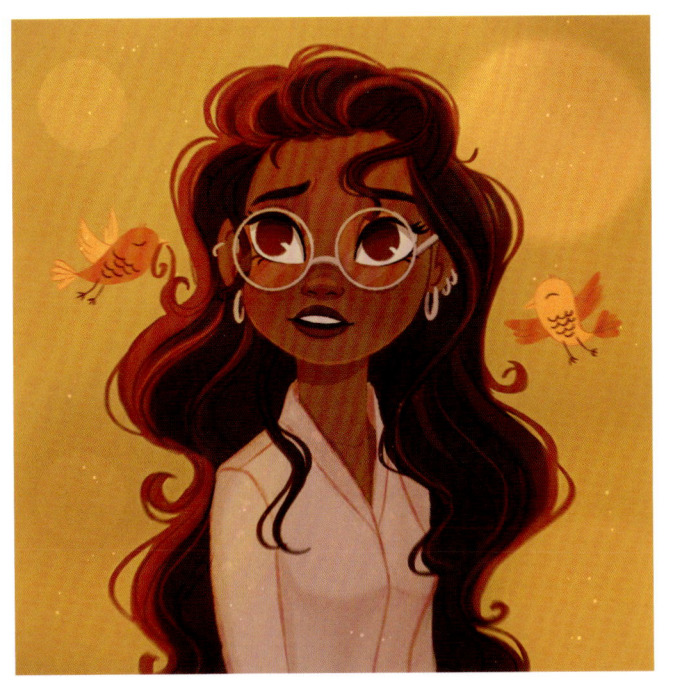

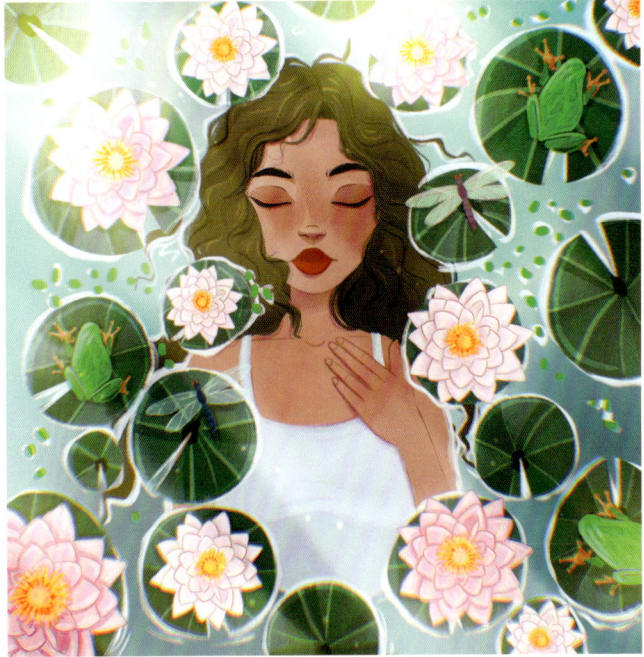

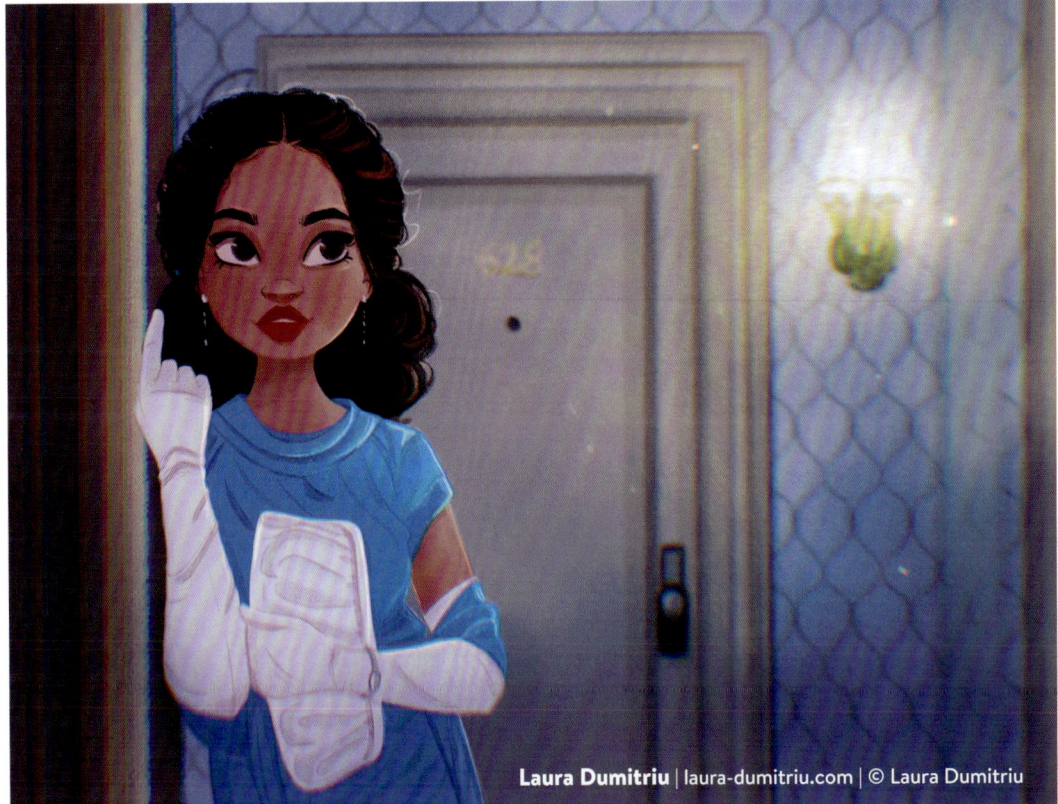

Laura Dumitriu | laura-dumitriu.com | © Laura Dumitriu

LAURA DUMITRIU IS AN ILLUSTRATOR, ORIGINALLY FROM ROMANIA, CURRENTLY BASED IN SUNNY BARCELONA, SPAIN. AFTER STUDYING ART IN HIGH SCHOOL AND UNIVERSITY, LAURA WORKED AS A GRAPHIC DESIGNER UNTIL 2019, WHEN SHE DECIDED TO FOCUS SOLELY ON ILLUSTRATION.

TRASH-CAN CRITTERS
SAULO NATE

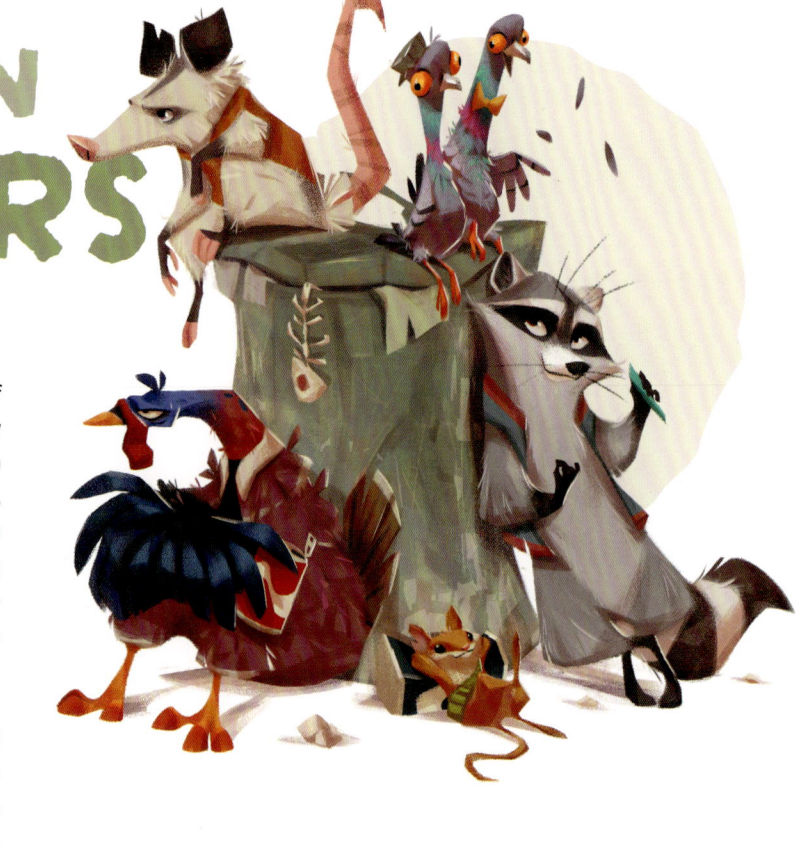

You might sometimes need to create a quick ensemble of characters that read as a team, and I'm going to show you how I do it. I've decided to create a trash gang that consists of a resourceful raccoon, two annoying pigeons, a cunning possum, a smart mouse, and a messed-up turkey! They forage through garbage cans and dumpsters, creating chaos and finding treasures in the urban jungle. I love giving a new perspective to urban wildlife – creatures have so much to communicate and so many ways to inspire us.

I will discuss how to tell a story (or at least a big part of one) within a single composition. Our goal here is to please the audience with an appealing narrative that won't take forever to work out. We'll start with thumbnails and balance, move on to refining the sketch, then proceed to colour-blocking, contrast, and finally texturing and emphasis. Let's get started!

'MAKE SURE YOU THINK ABOUT THE FOUNDATION AND WEIGHT OF THE COMPOSITION'

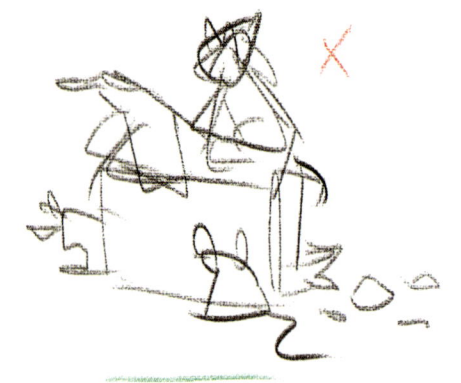

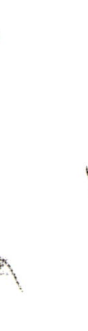

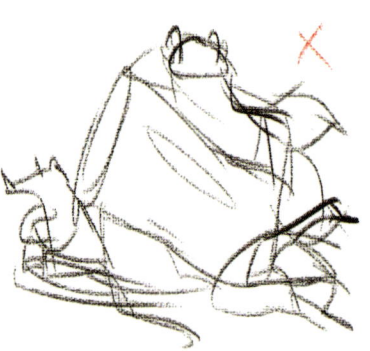

LAYING THE FOUNDATIONS

To start, make sure you think about the foundation and weight of the composition. Test for consistency and choose a balanced thumbnail for clarity. I want to use the principle of central alignment to focus the viewer's attention on the main subject, so the thumbnail with the characters gathered around the centre makes the most sense.

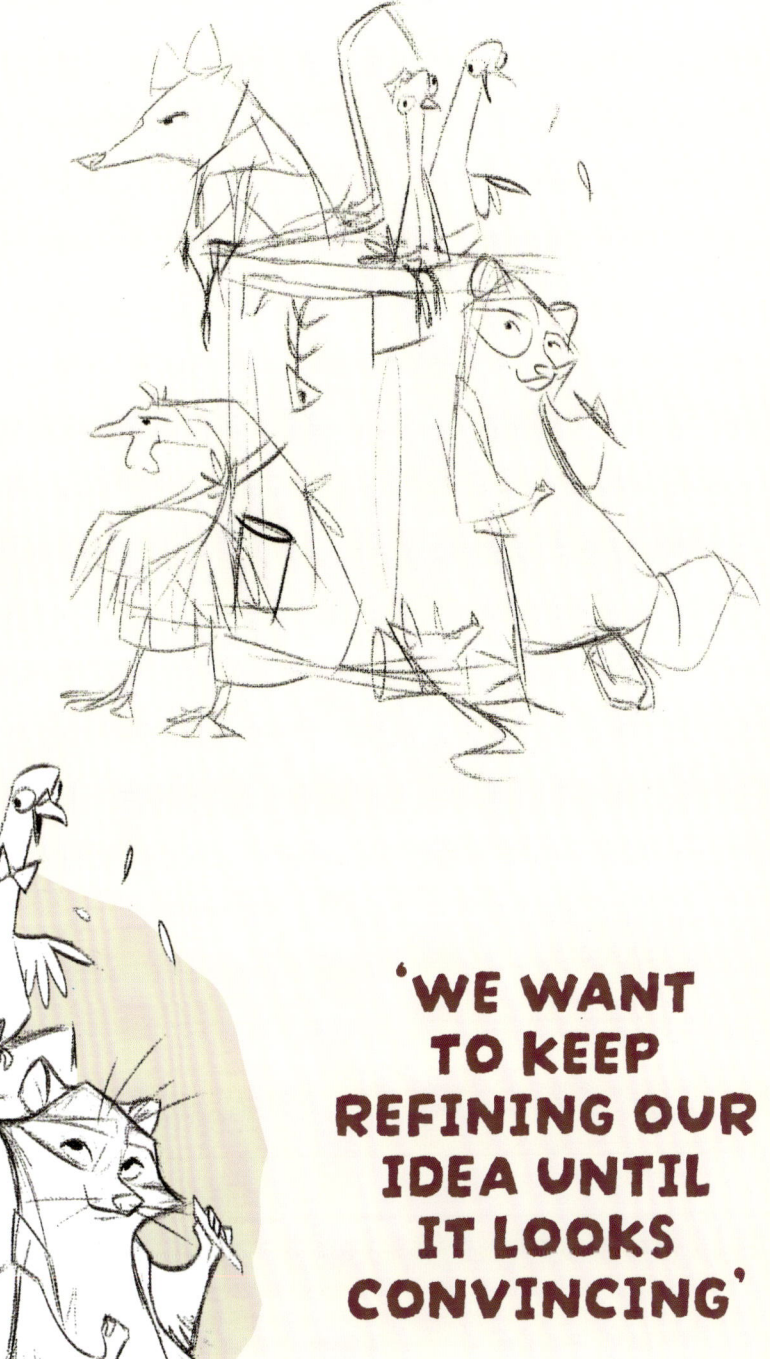

A BALANCING ACT

To achieve visual balance, the components and their varying visual weight must be distributed harmoniously throughout the composition. If the overall layout is symmetrical, be sure to add some asymmetrical elements, too. Overall, keep an eye on creating a sense of stability and unity in your characters.

REFINING THE DESIGN

Now, let's have some fun! For this step, we take our references, determine the correct mood, and make the most powerful and appealing design we can. Not happy with your first design? Don't be afraid to erase and start over. We want to keep refining our idea until it looks convincing – a 'half-baked' drawing won't do at this stage.

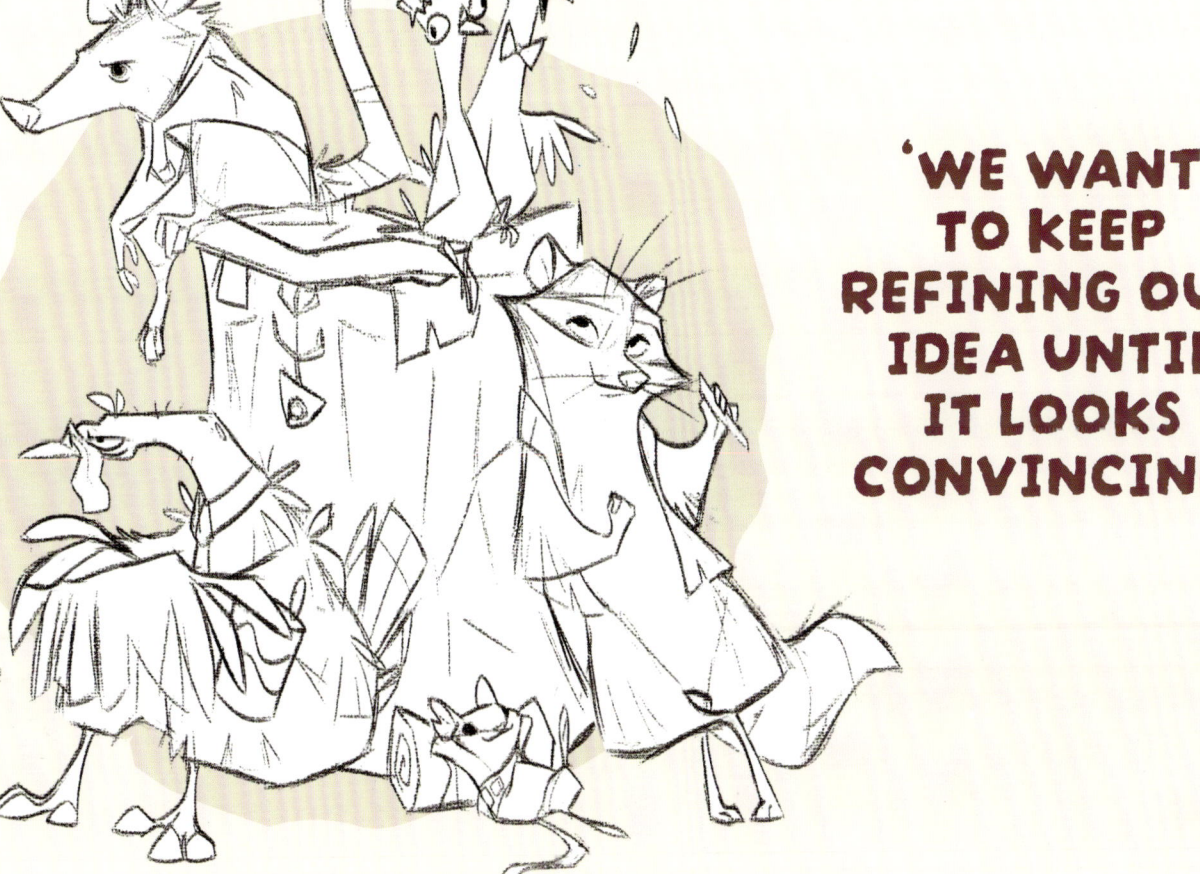

'WE WANT TO KEEP REFINING OUR IDEA UNTIL IT LOOKS CONVINCING'

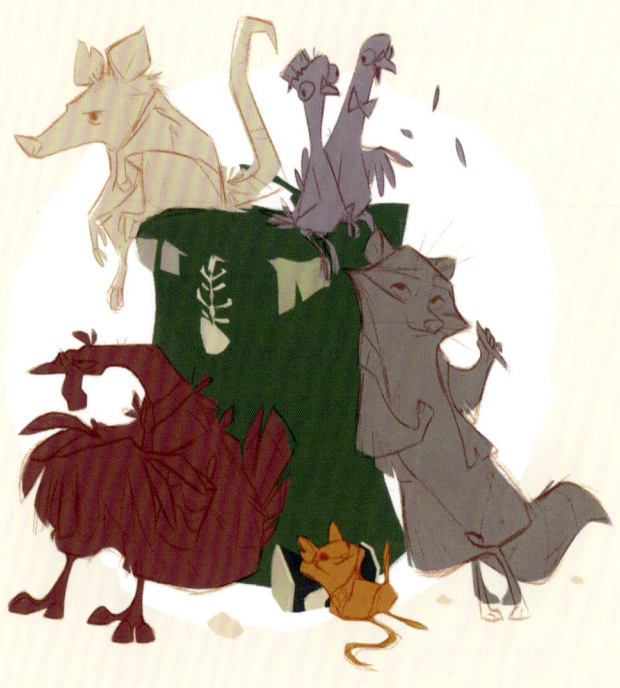

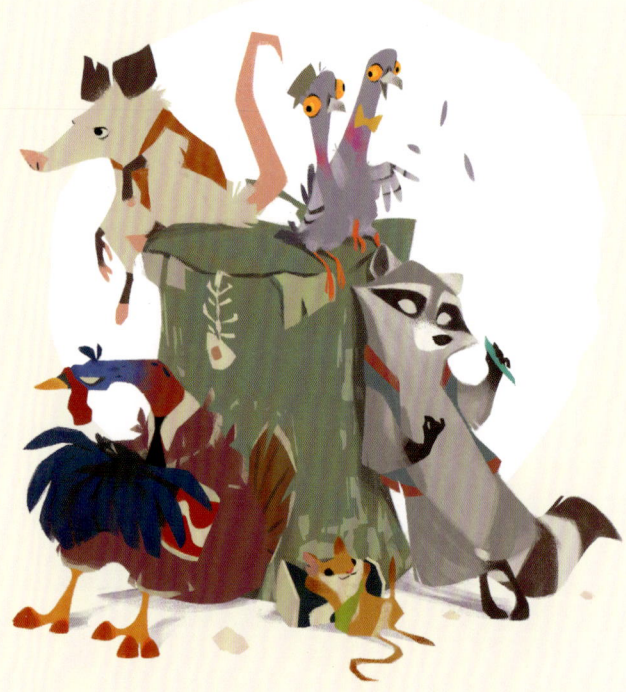

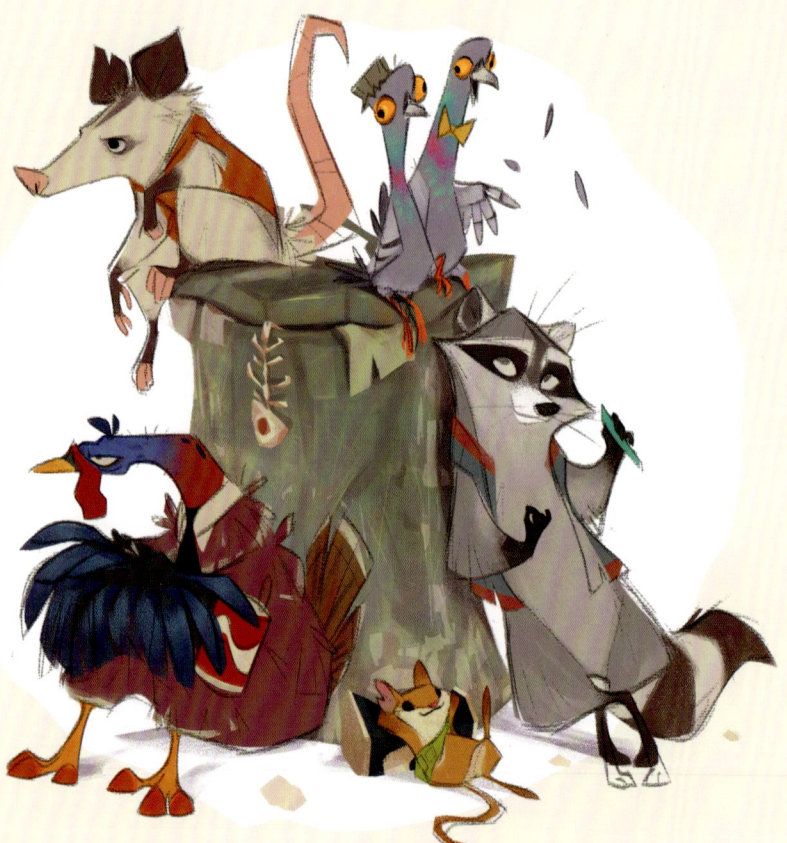

CREATING CONTRAST

Colour and contrast often go hand in hand. In this case, I use colour blocking to create contrast, separating the characters from the trash can. You can also use contrasting colours to create the same effect.

TEXTURE AND DEPTH

Adding texture is one of my favourite steps. The challenge for this image is communicating that these creatures dig through trash cans and dumpsters, without making them look gross. Texturing gives me the ability to add depth to the composition and to create the illusion of different materials and surfaces, such as wood, fabric, metal, or fur. Textures can help make a drawing look gritty or smooth, rough or soft. I personally love to texture human skin and rusty metals.

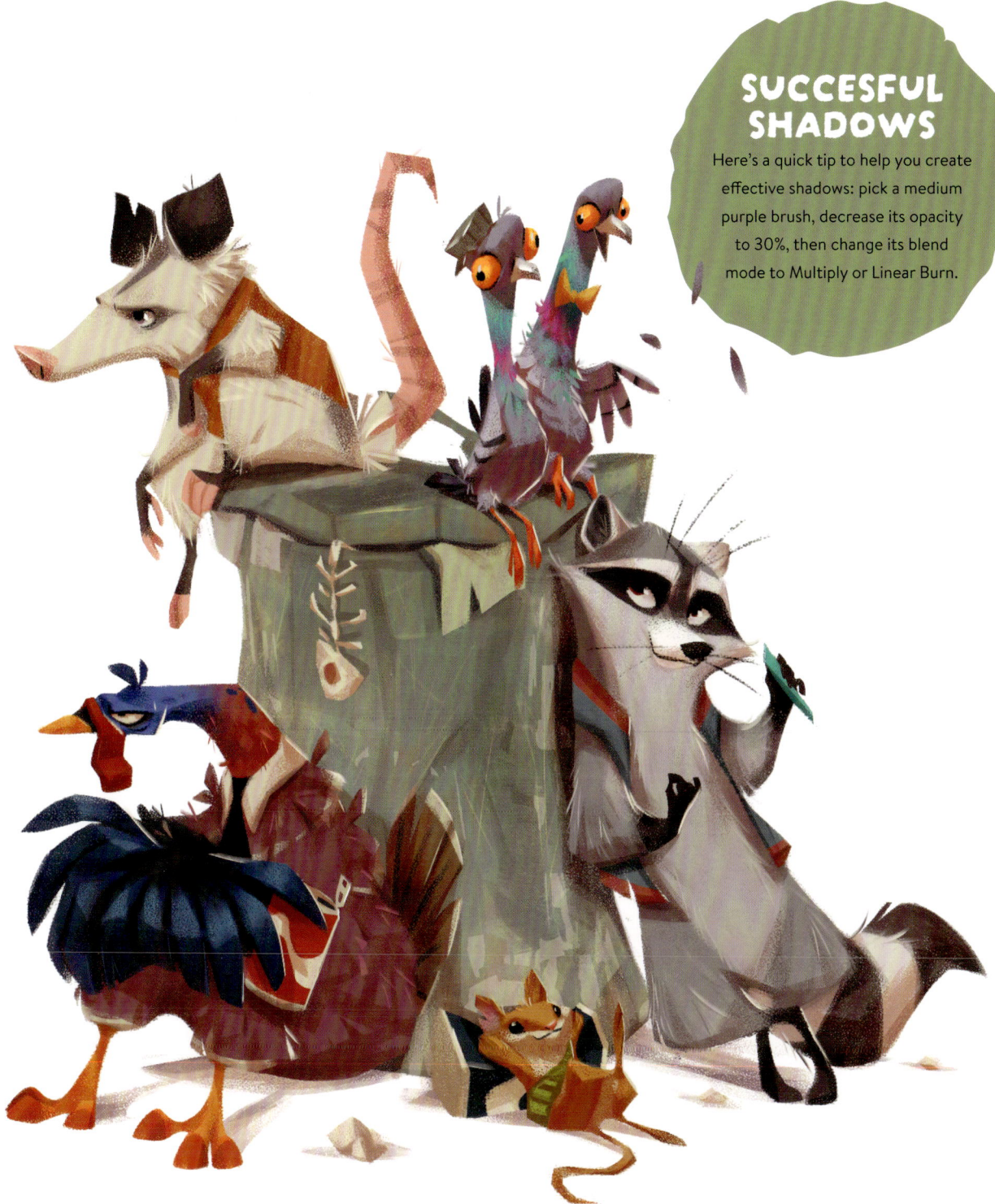

SUCCESFUL SHADOWS

Here's a quick tip to help you create effective shadows: pick a medium purple brush, decrease its opacity to 30%, then change its blend mode to Multiply or Linear Burn.

ADDING EMPHASIS

Our gang of animals have assembled – now it's time to make them feel alive. How? All you need to do is to think and act with emphasis! The colours, the textures, and the details can be adjusted in this final phase – even the lines from the sketch-refining step. Add shadows, thinking about what time and type of atmosphere you want the drawing to evoke. Remember, strong visual impact and good storytelling go hand in hand.

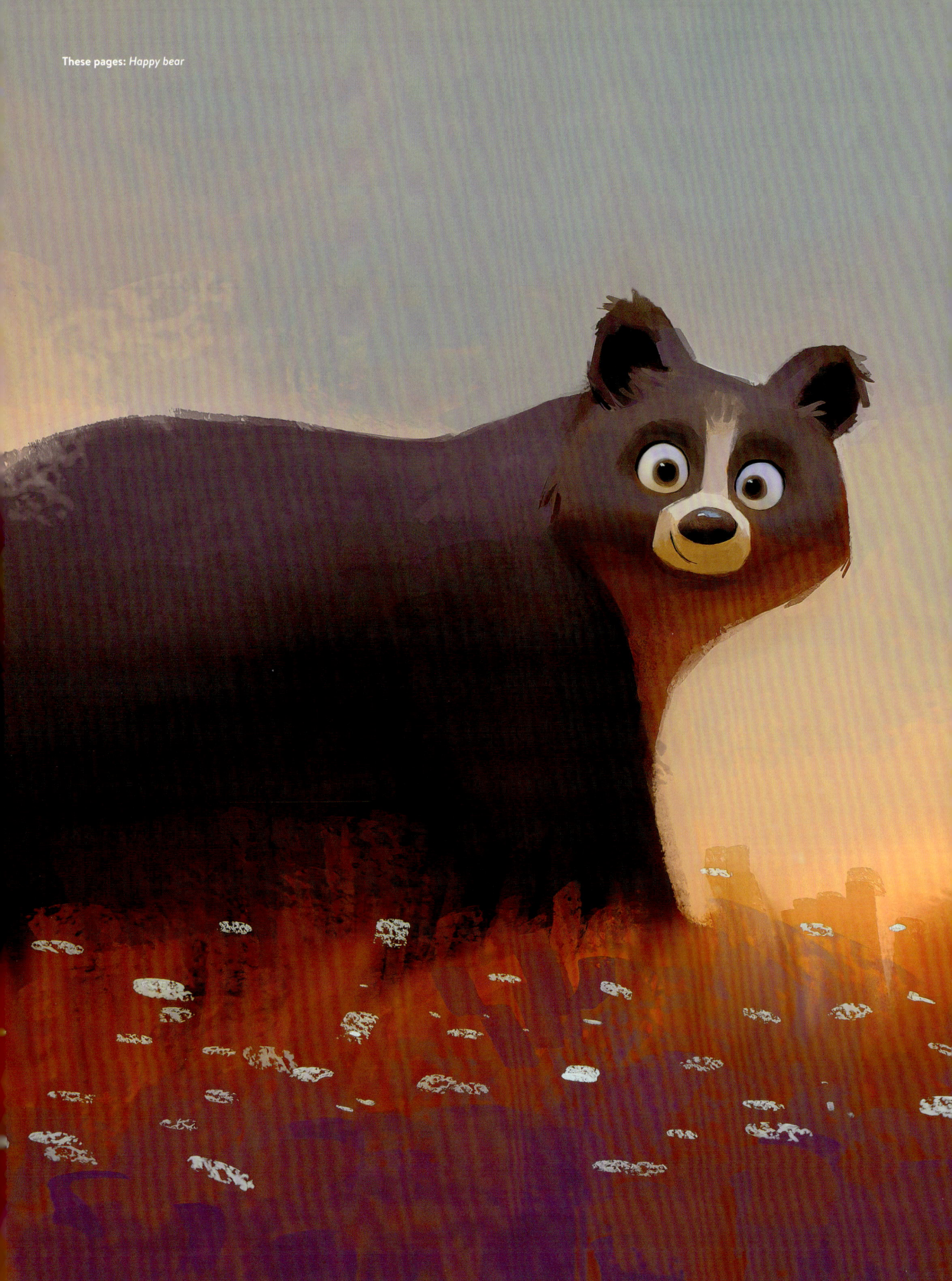

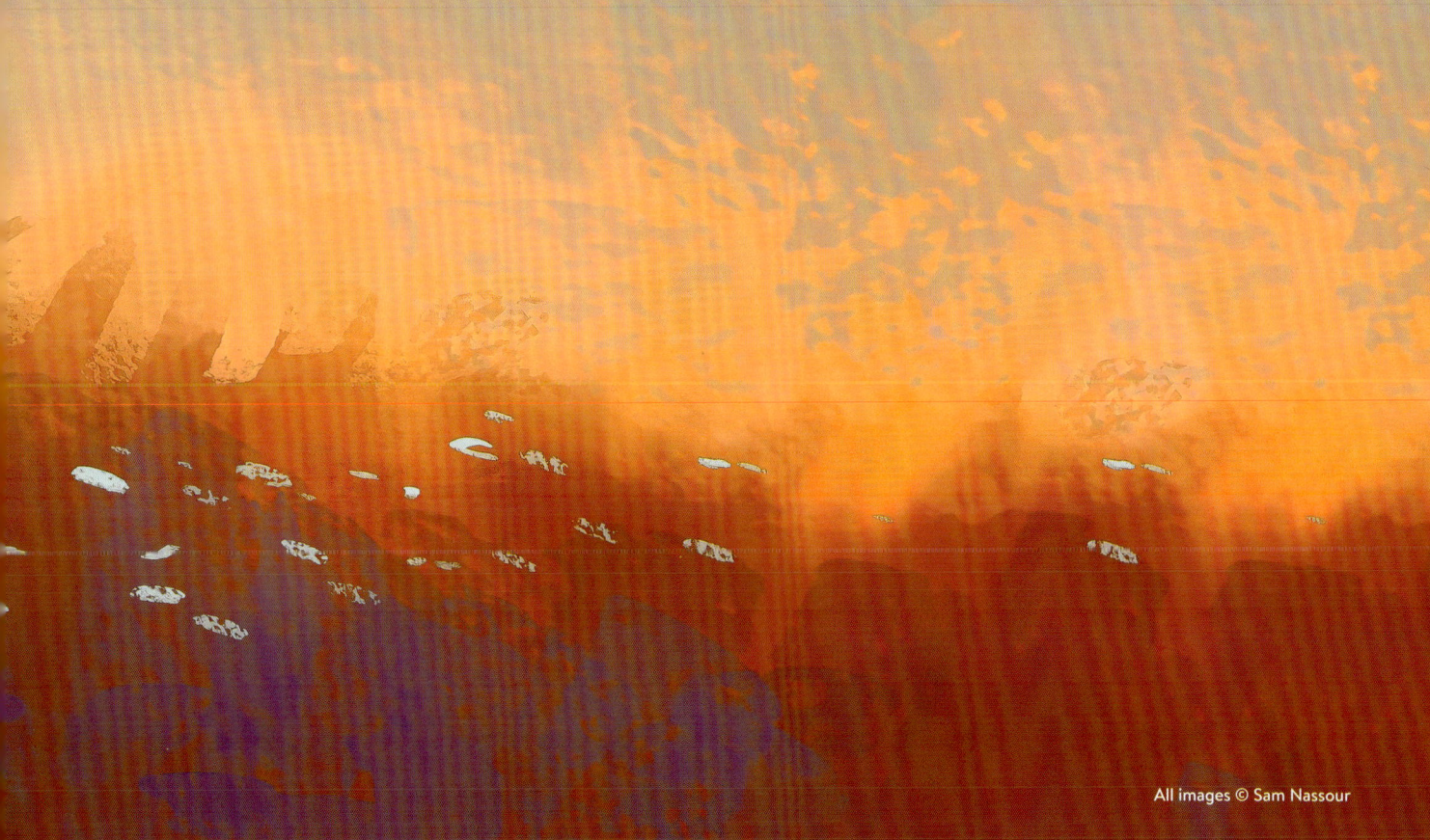

ARTIST CATCH-UP:
SAM NASSOUR

Sam Nassour is an art director and visual development artist who we last spoke to for
CDQ 11's cover feature. We caught up with Sam to see how his career has developed,
lessons he has learned, and the key ingredients behind his incredible character designs.

This page:

Green Dragon

Opposite page:

Beard Buddies

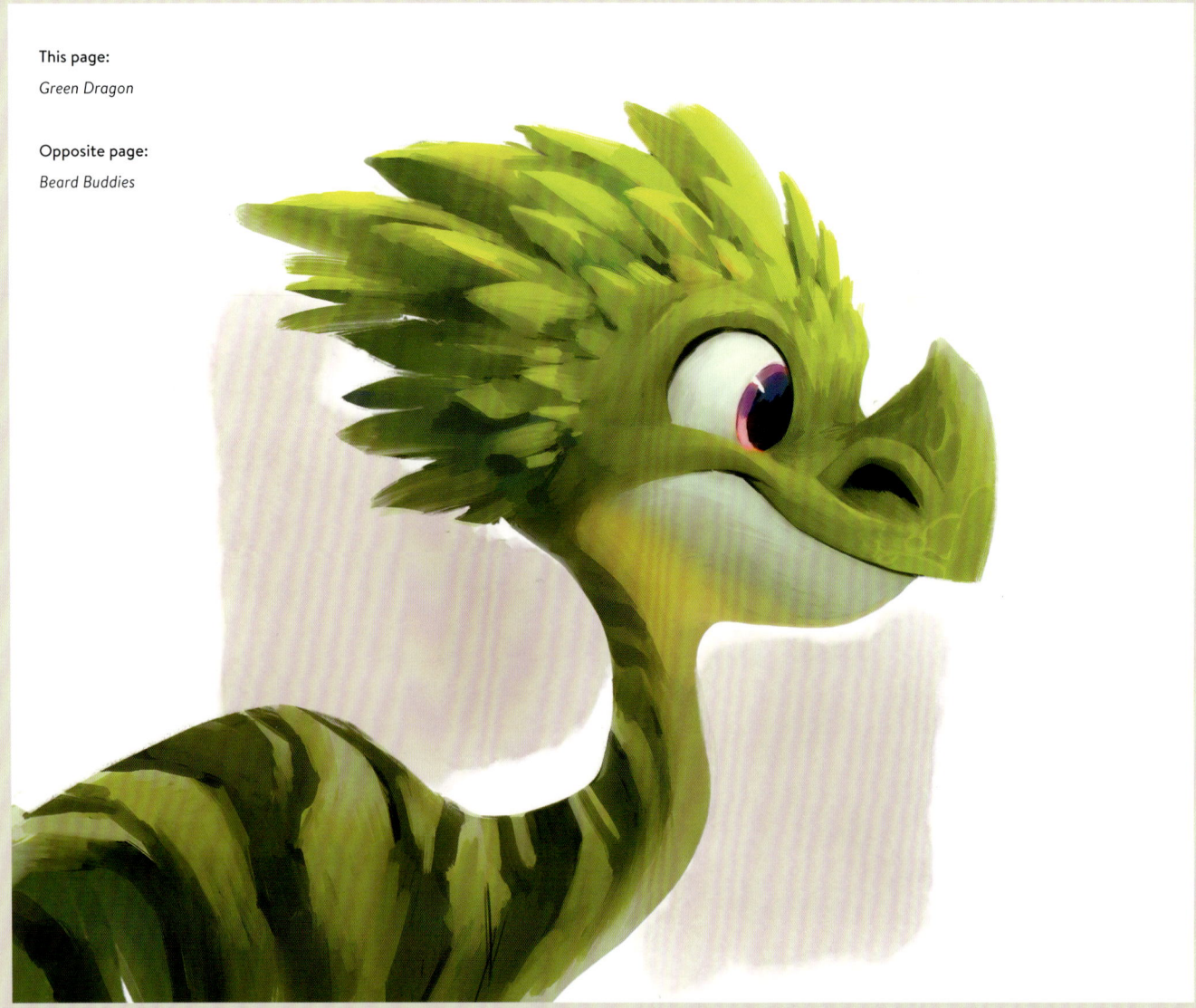

Hi Sam, welcome back to *CDQ*! Can you tell us a bit about what you've been up to lately?

Hello, it's great to be back in *CDQ* – I check out every issue and get a good dose of inspiration each time! I've been keeping busy working on a couple of animation projects and commercials. More recently I've been working on mobile games like Rovio's *Angry Birds Journey* and Metacore's *Merge Mansion*. It's been quite enjoyable to alternate between designing for animation and games. Interestingly, the thinking process for both is quite similar in terms of coming up with appealing-looking scenes and characters. I've also been teaching visual development and character design workshops at IDEA academy and CGMA, which has been quite fun, as well.

How did you get started as a professional artist?

I first started working in a graphic design agency while studying in college, which led me to learn how to use Photoshop professionally and how to think creatively. This was super helpful in the beginning of my career. I worked in multiple design boutiques and always kept sharpening my character-design skills. I just loved creating characters from an early age and wanted to focus more on animation and games that were based around characters and stories. I started building a portfolio and, after I felt I had enough good work to show, I started applying for studio jobs. I got hired to work at Cartoon Network studios in the UAE as an art director, which was my break into the animation industry. I gained lots of great experience working with fantastic directors and talented artists in the field.

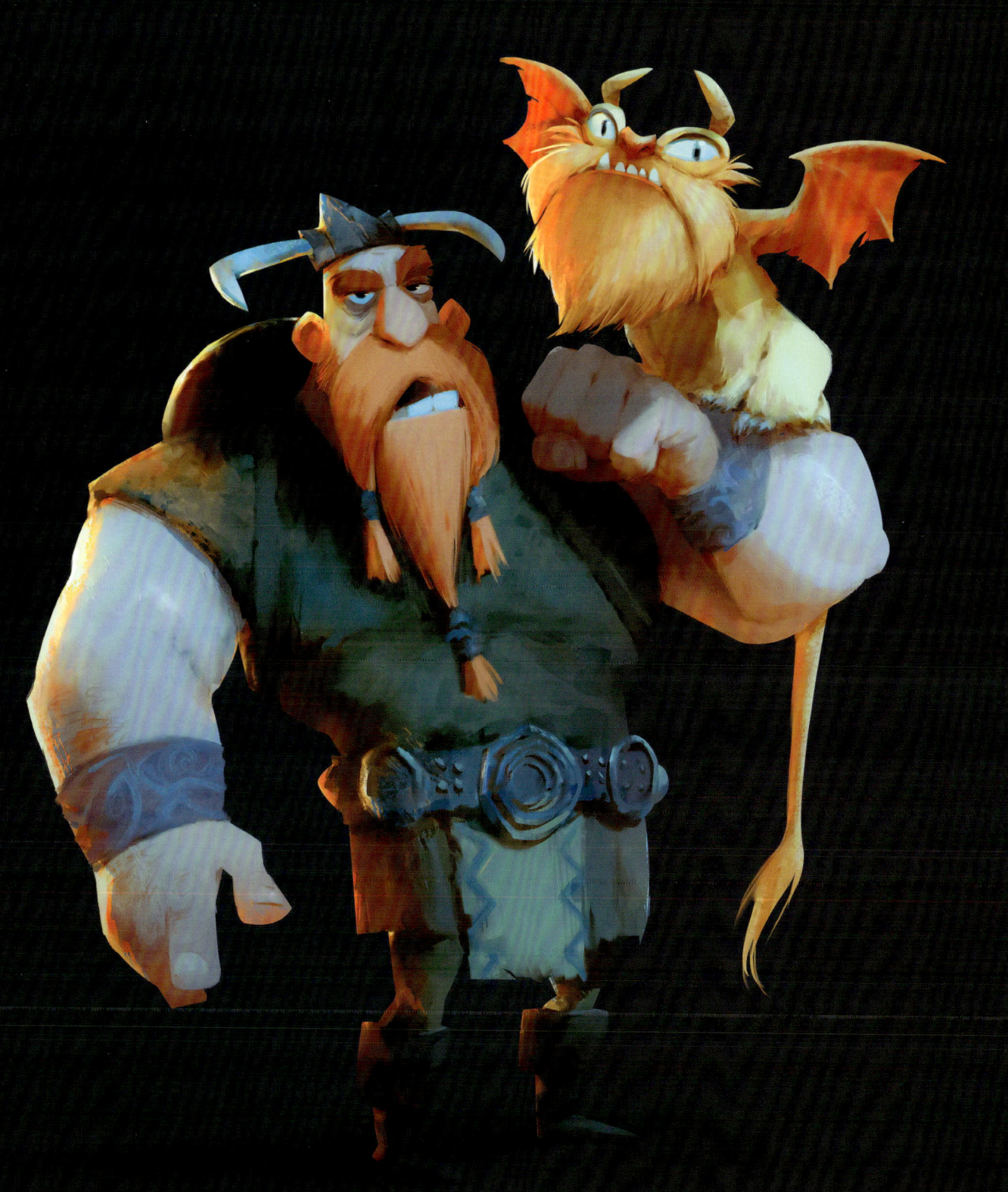

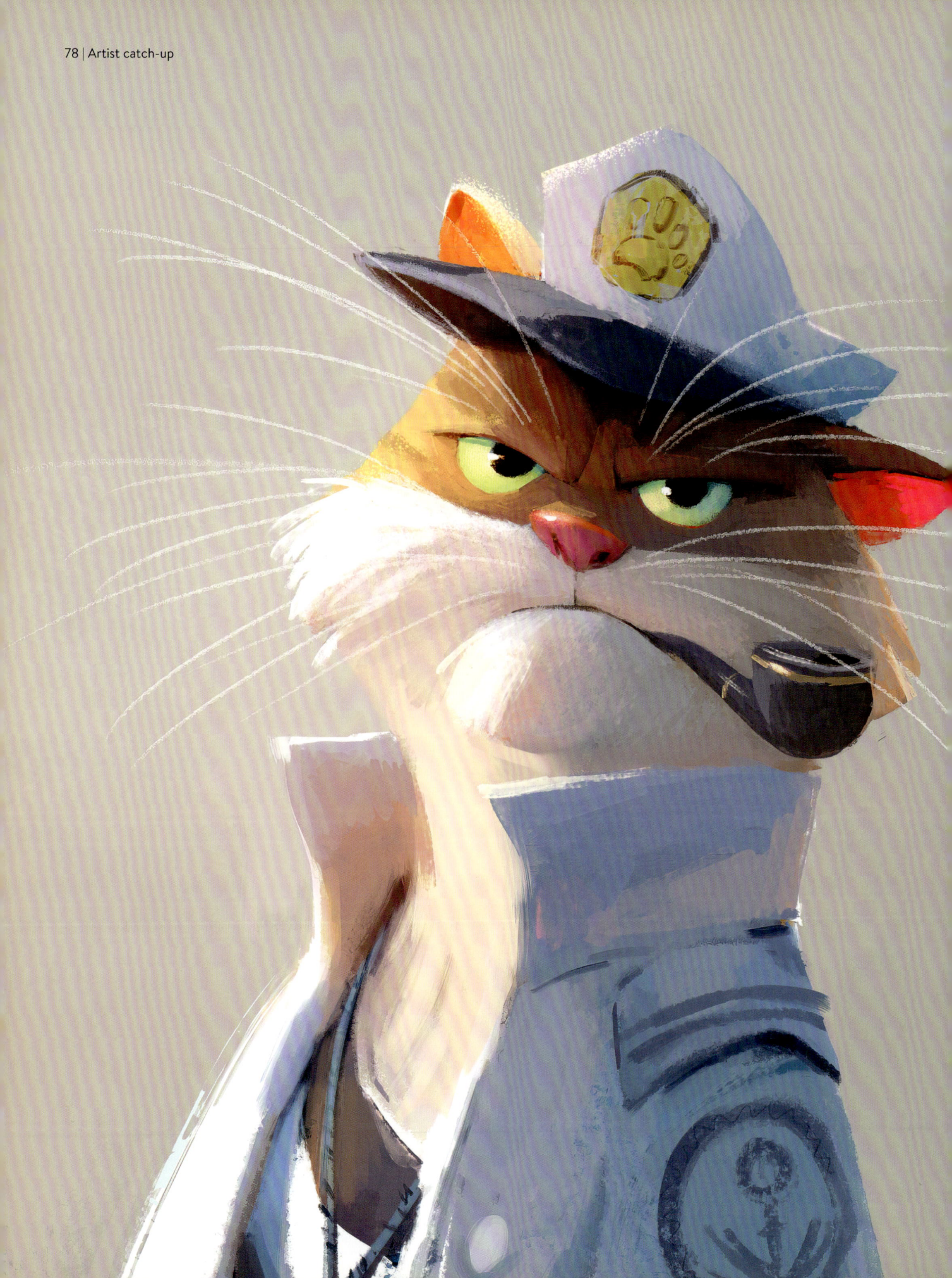

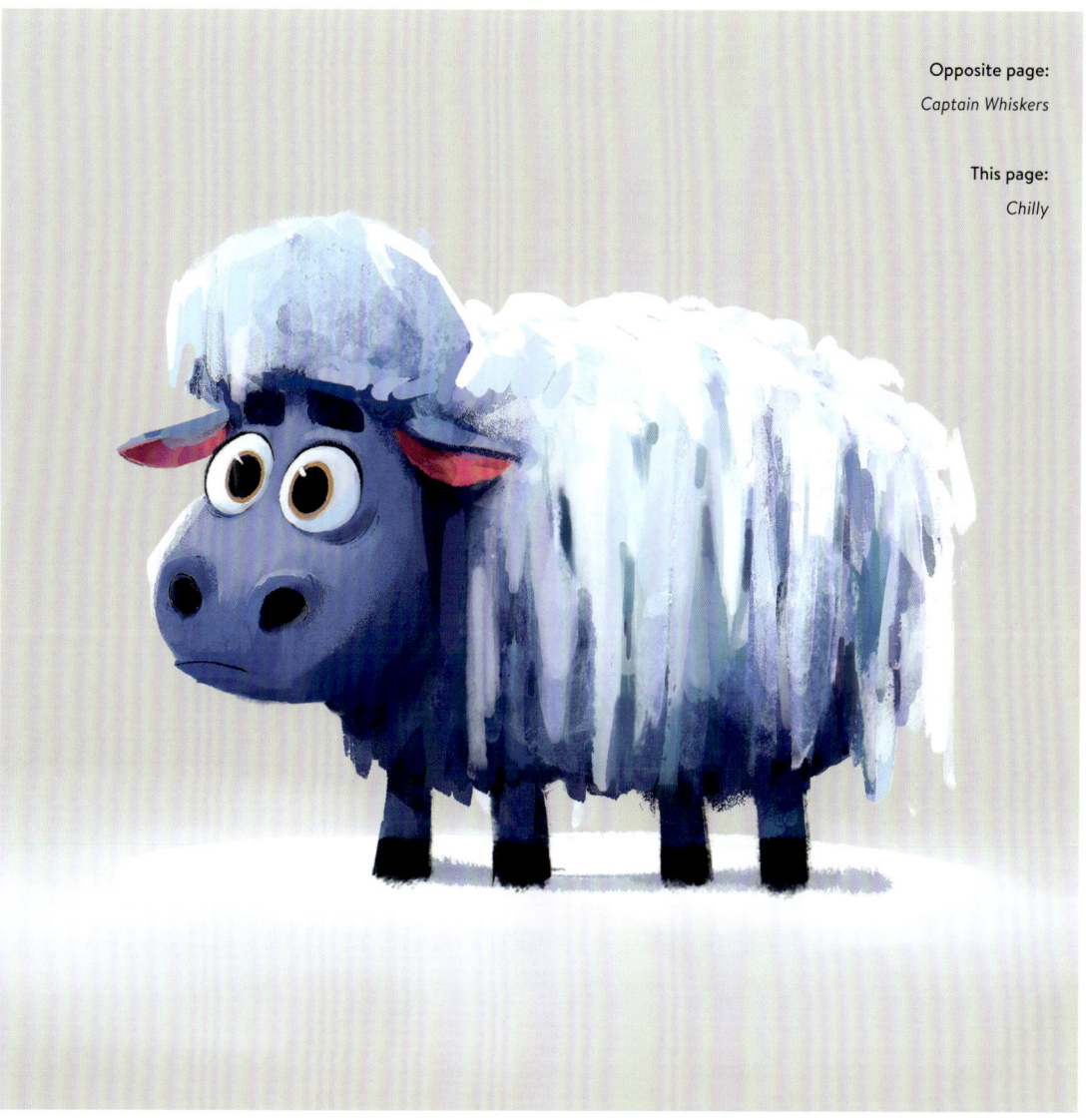

Opposite page:

Captain Whiskers

This page:

Chilly

Are there many differences in designing characters for animation and for games?

Great question! Whether it's animation or games, each project requires a certain level of research and exploration. In general, the animation pipeline – especially for feature films – requires a bit more work on character breakdowns, character model sheets, turnarounds, poses, facial expressions, and so on. Working on games, the process is a bit more focused on shape language, appeal, and the 'cool factor'. Of course, so many games have an interesting story and complex characters, but I feel there's usually deeper research that goes into the animation. However, the thinking process and design and rendering techniques are very similar across both mediums.

Are there big differences in how different studios operate?

Yes, there is always a different way of working depending on the project, the time available, and the art direction. Some studios are more flexible than others, in the sense that they give you the freedom to bring your own taste and style to the project, while other studios or projects have a stricter direction that the artists should follow. I've learned to adapt and work in both scenarios, although I prefer situations where I'm able to have my own voice and bring something of my style to the table.

This page:

Dino

Opposite page:

On the Fence

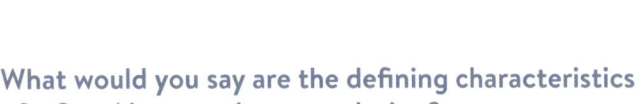

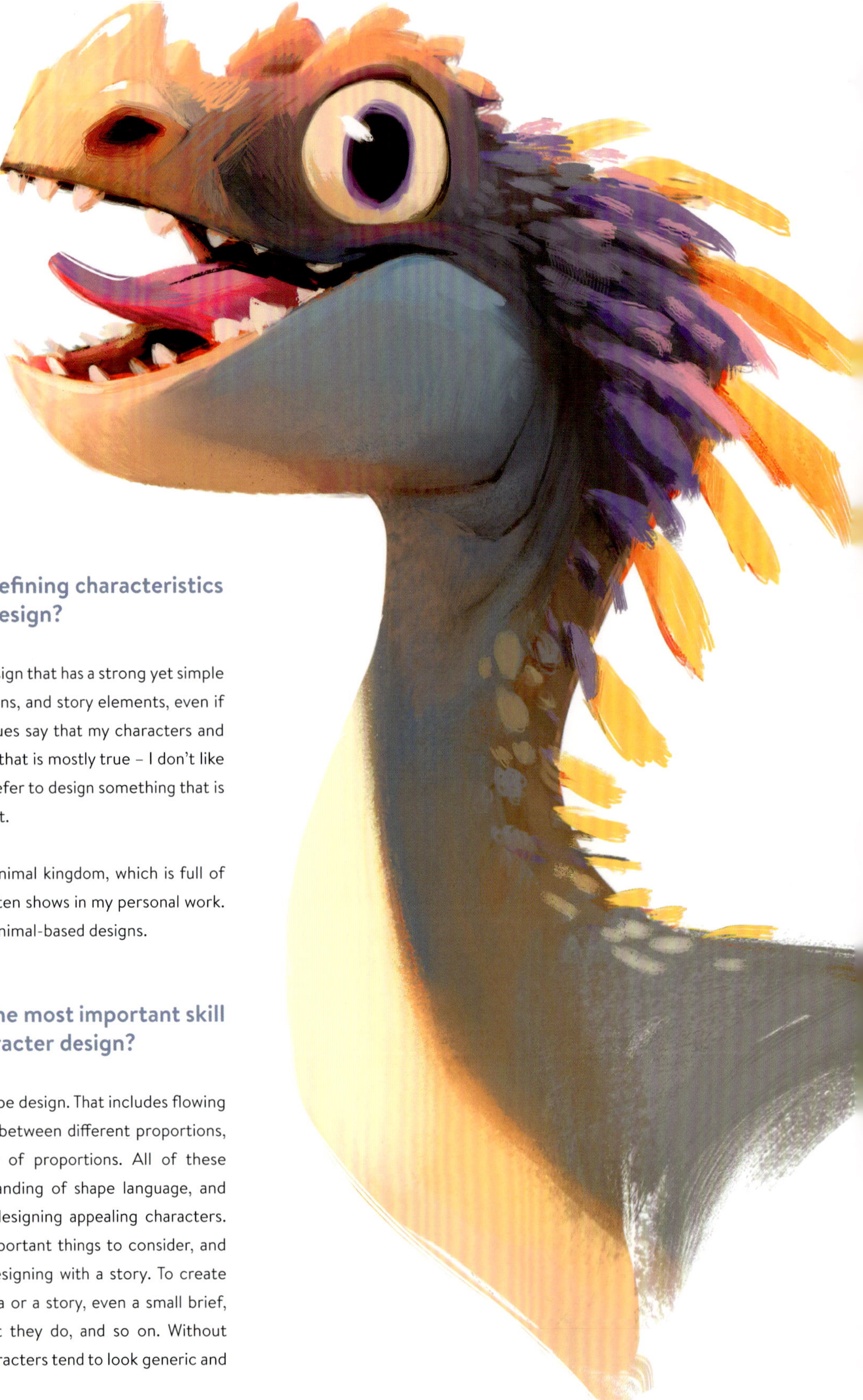

What would you say are the defining characteristics of a Sam Nassour character design?

I tend to enjoy creating any character design that has a strong yet simple shape language, good colour combinations, and story elements, even if they're minimal. My friends and colleagues say that my characters and art style look cute and appealing. I think that is mostly true – I don't like to create dark or violent characters. I prefer to design something that is quirky, fun, and has a positive energy to it.

I also love to get inspiration from the animal kingdom, which is full of amazing shapes and colours, and that often shows in my personal work. I love creating appealing creatures and animal-based designs.

What do you consider to be the most important skill to have when working in character design?

If I had to name one skill, it would be shape design. That includes flowing lines, interesting and appealing rhythm between different proportions, straights versus curves, and a variety of proportions. All of these factors are related to a good understanding of shape language, and I think they're a fundamental part of designing appealing characters. Of course, there are so many other important things to consider, and if I can name one more, it would be designing with a story. To create a believable character, you need an idea or a story, even a small brief, about the character's life, habits, what they do, and so on. Without a story (even if it's just in your mind) characters tend to look generic and not very relatable.

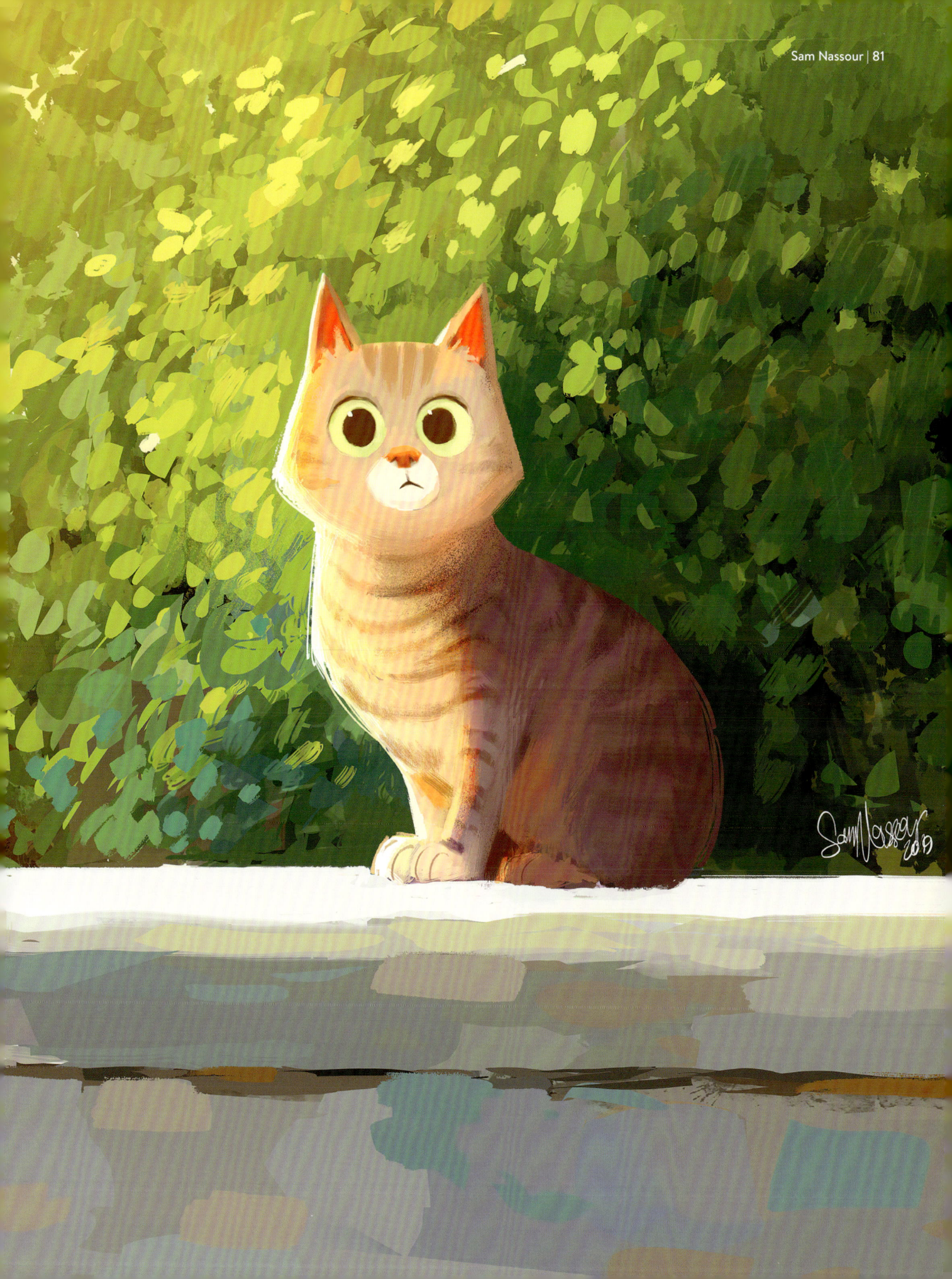

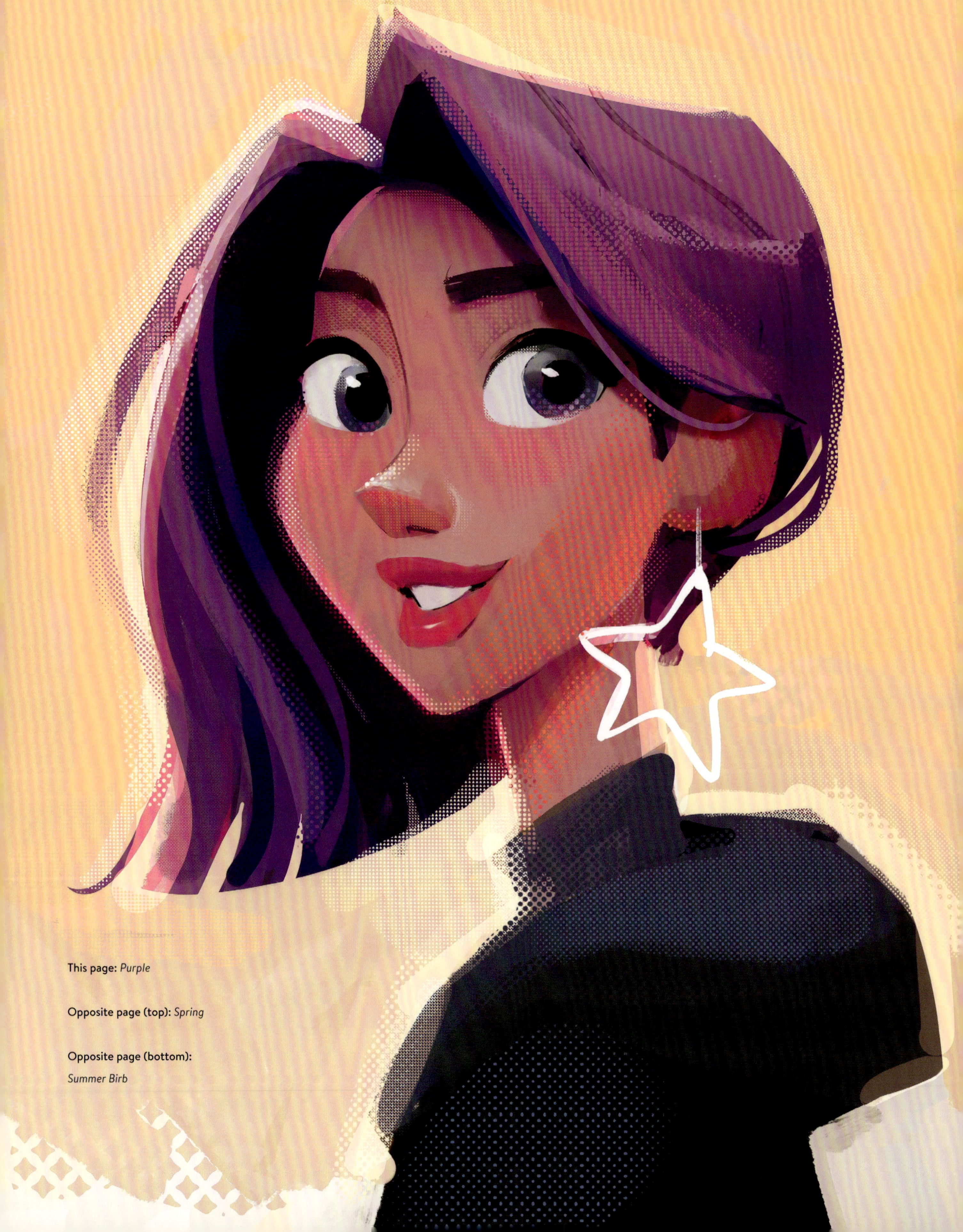

This page: *Purple*

Opposite page (top): *Spring*

Opposite page (bottom):
Summer Birb

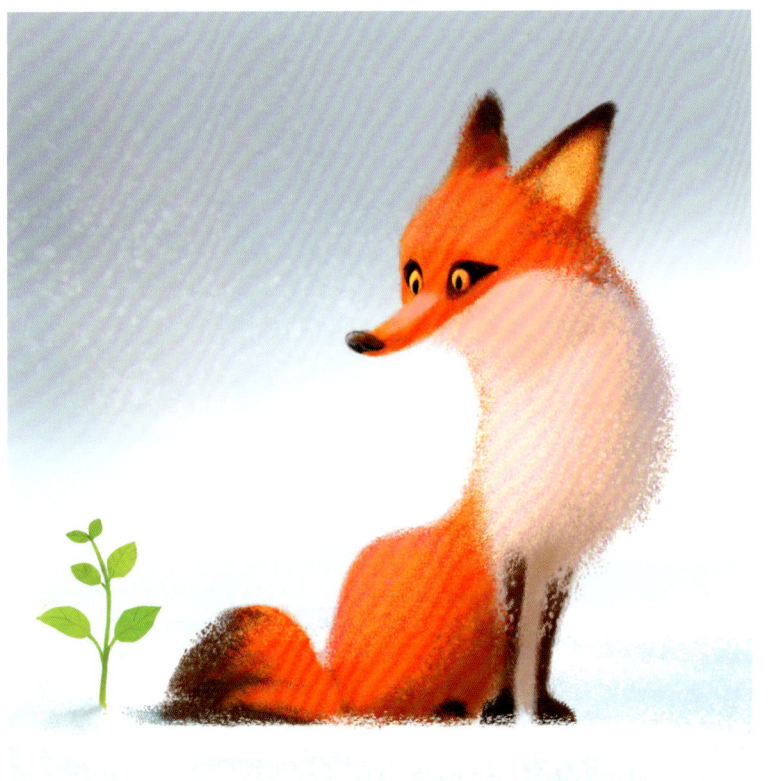

What are the big inspirations behind your art style?

Growing up, I think my biggest art inspirations were Franco-Belgian comics, like Uderzo's *Asterix and Obelix* and Hergé's *The Adventures of Tintin*. I loved the fun stories, the beautiful inks, and the art quality. I was also very inspired by some of my favourite classic Disney films, like *The Lion King*, *Hercules*, and *Atlantis*. Those stuck with me and really pushed me to try to practise drawing in a similar simplified way, pushing shapes and proportions, which is really fun for me. I also love taking and looking at photography of people, places, and wildlife. It's always inspiring to observe the world around me and study different lighting and time-of-day situations.

Do you have any advice for our readers who want to get into the industry or want to go further?

I think the main advice I can give is to never lose the inspiration and excitement in what you do. Find your true authentic voice and showcase it in your art – at least in your personal art you post online or share in your portfolio. Another important piece of advice I can give is to always aim for high quality in your art and, if you're just starting out, try to present yourself and your work as if you're already working in the field. Don't feel intimidated by artists who have more experience than you, but instead consider them your peers. I think this will push you forward faster.

Thanks for talking with us, Sam! Are there any upcoming projects we should look out for?

For a few months now I've been working on a new animated feature that hopefully will be announced next year. I also continue to work on creating characters and visuals for the mobile game *Merge Mansion* from Metacore Games. I'll be sure to post any updates on my Instagram!

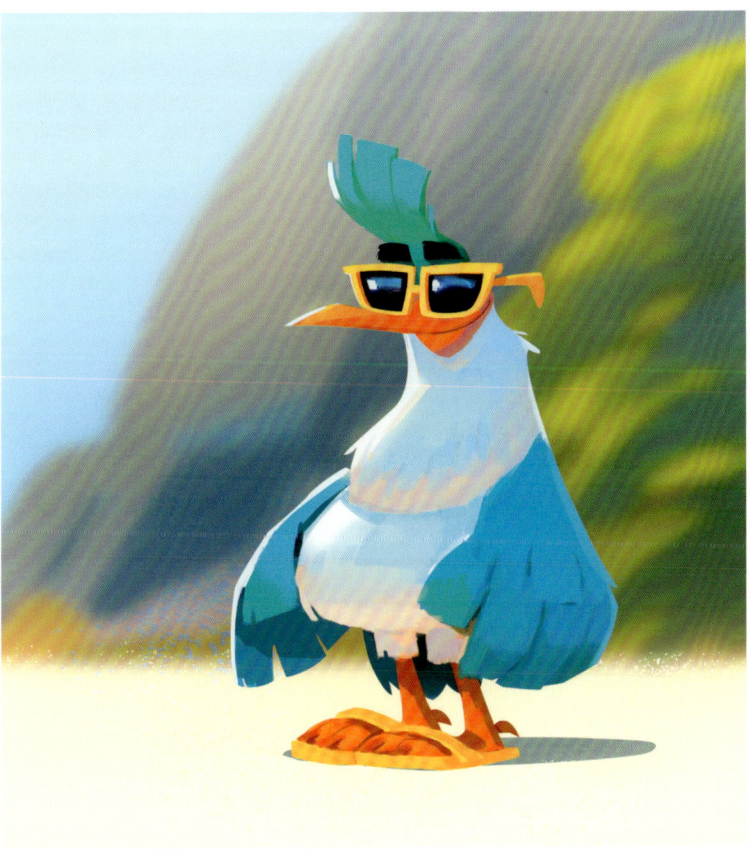

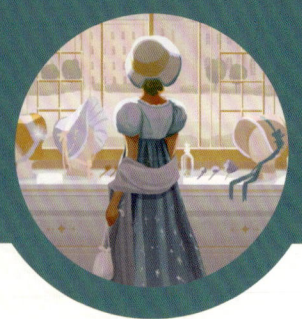

LETTING THE LIGHT IN
MAXINE VEE

Colour and light are two of the most important aspects of visual storytelling. Let me share with you some tips for quickly changing the mood of your painting by experimenting with Adjustment Layers. I will be using Photoshop, but other software will work just as well.

The painting I'll be working with is called *Starry Bonnet Shoppe* and is loosely inspired by a scene in the film *Emma* and other period dramas. I envisioned a store filled with bonnets in celestial designs and starry decor.

I will show you how I choose colour palettes and work through my process of finishing the painting. Then I will show you how to tweak the colour palette to create a soft and delicate pastel look that matches the decor and atmosphere. Whenever I adjust the colours of my painting, I like to imagine viewing the piece through a photographer's lens. I will change the raw image by using colour balance, selective colours, and gradient maps.

1. EXPLORING COLOUR PALETTES

To start, I test three different colour palettes using a Gradient Map. Using this tool is a quick way to explore a variety of different colour combinations. Since I want to match the colours of the regency period, I experiment with shades of pink and other light colours.

2. ROUGH AND READY

I decide to work with pinks and blues while adding a few gold accents to make certain sections of the image stand out. I try to keep this stage very rough – I'm trying to see how best I can create a contrast between the character and the surrounding objects and background.

3. DETAILS AND RENDERING

I start adding more details to the objects. Since I want to keep the focus on the character and the bonnets, I decide to desaturate the pinks to a more muted colour. This way, the image won't look too busy and it will place more emphasis on the darkest values of the painting.

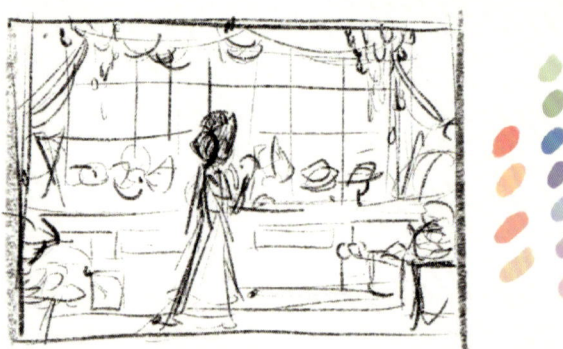

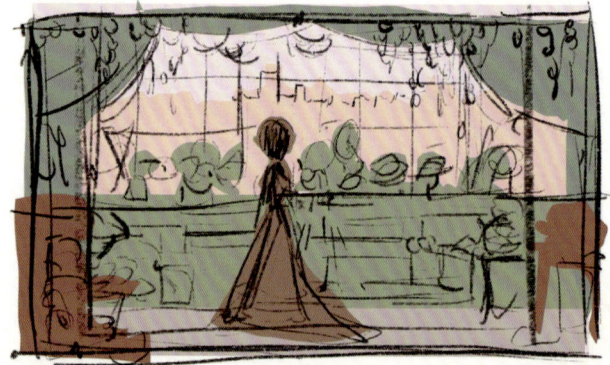

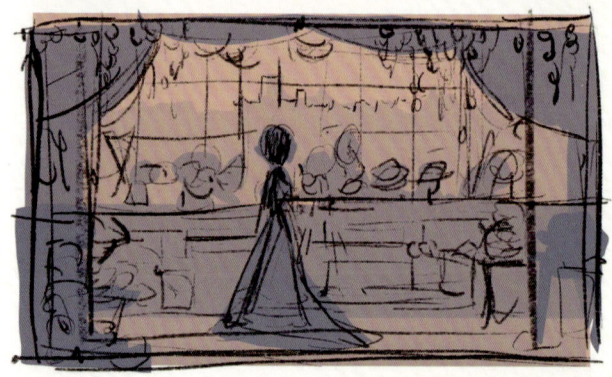

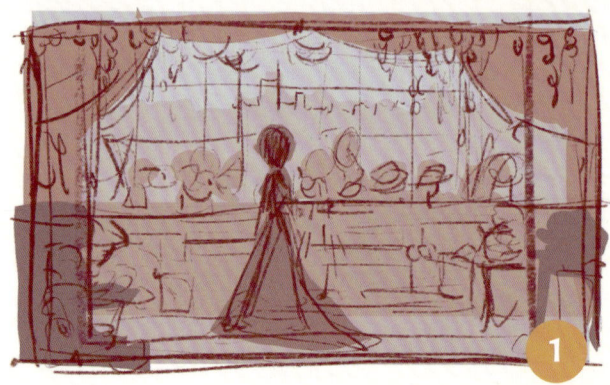

1

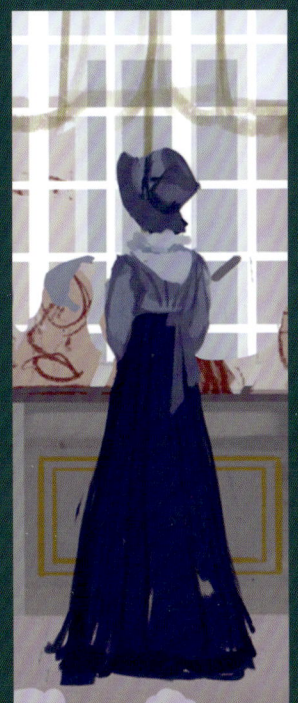

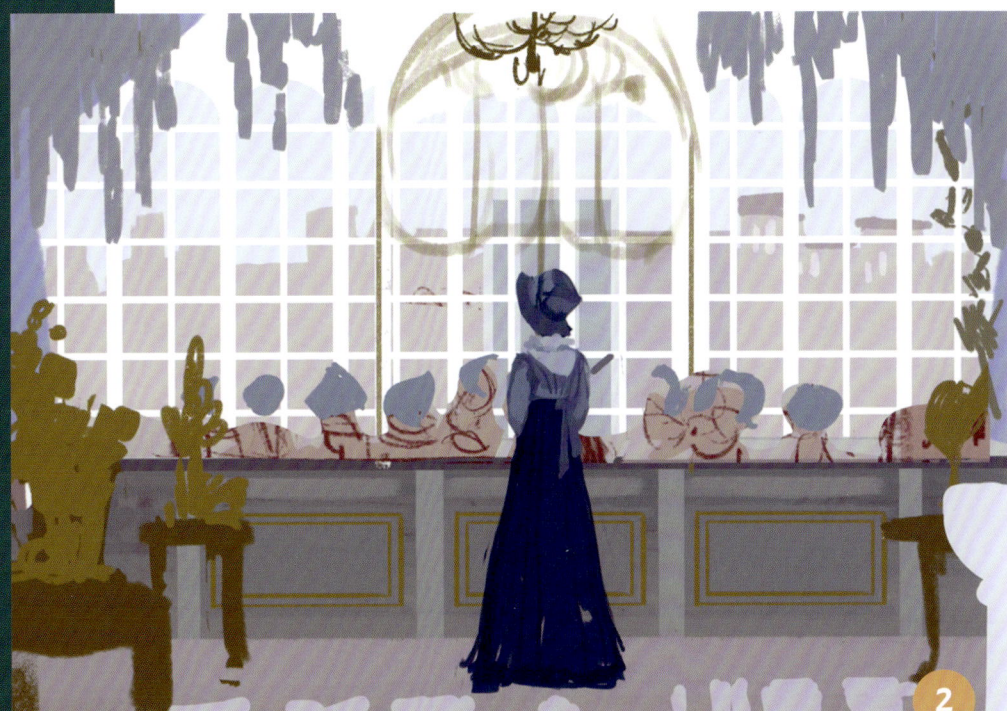

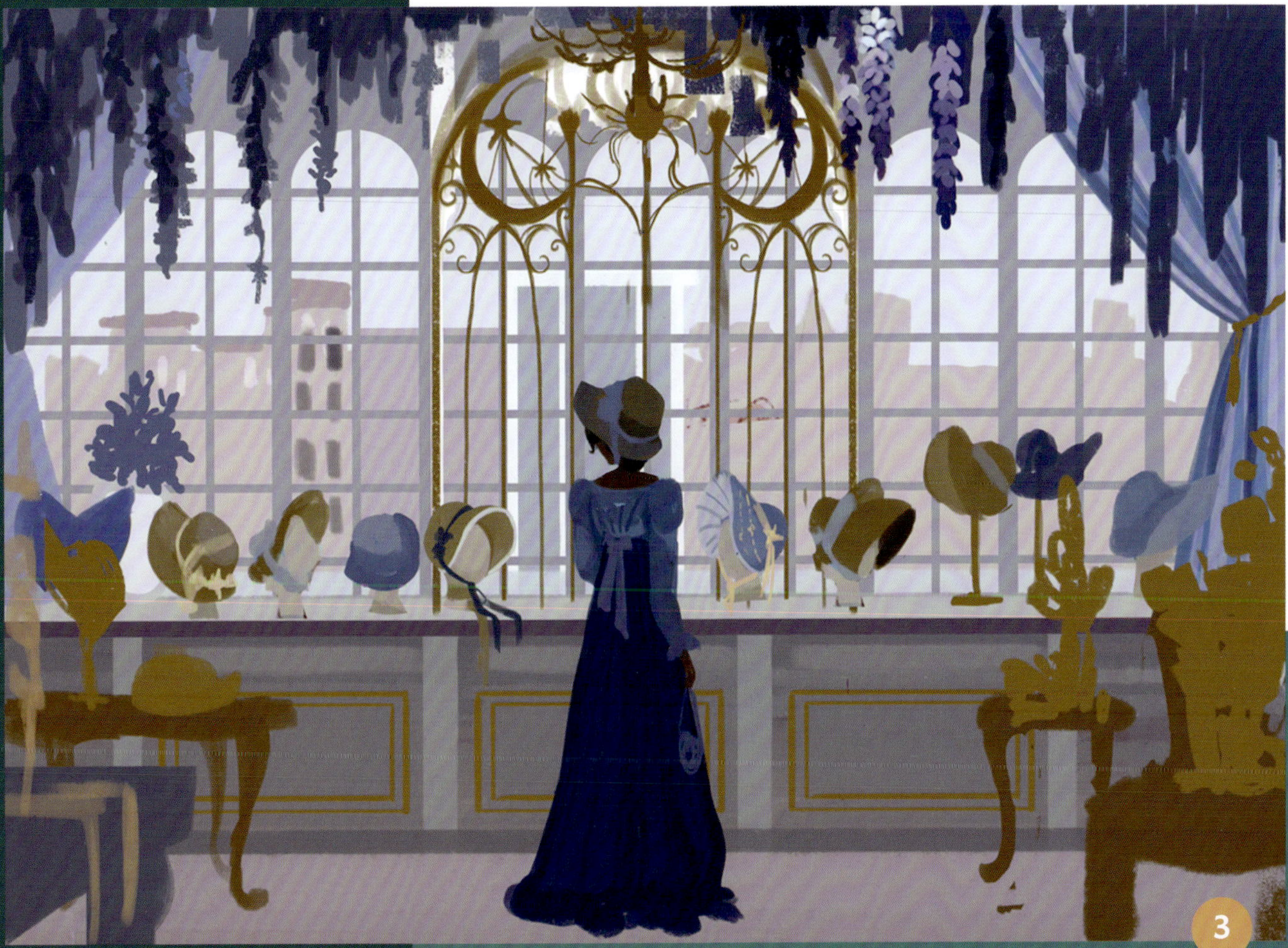

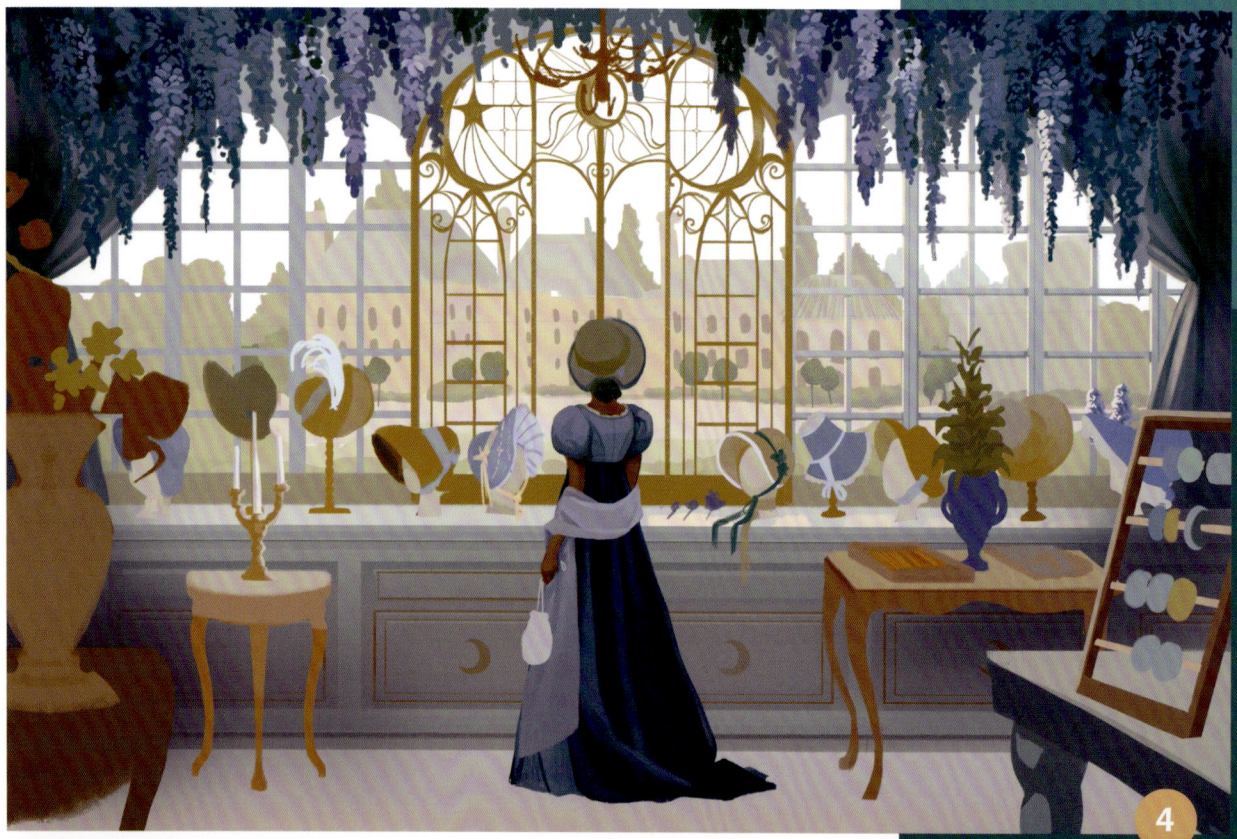

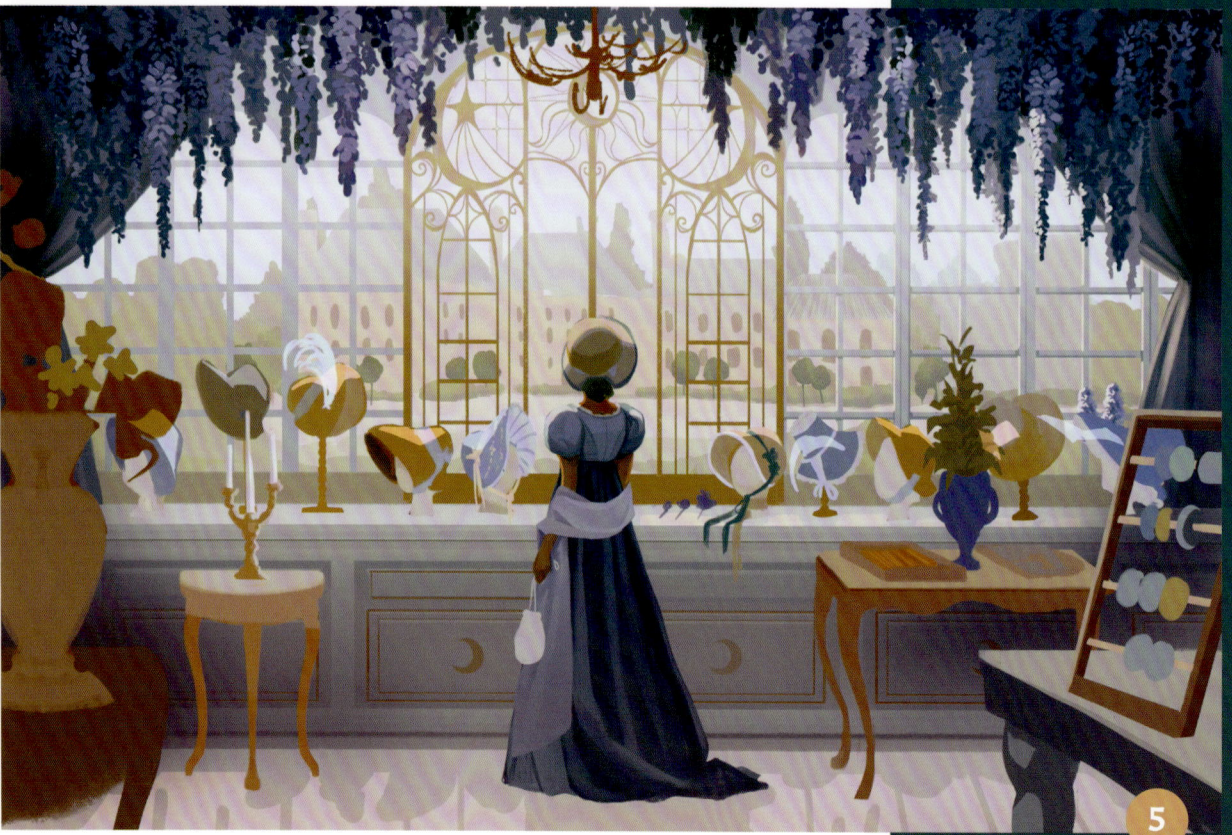

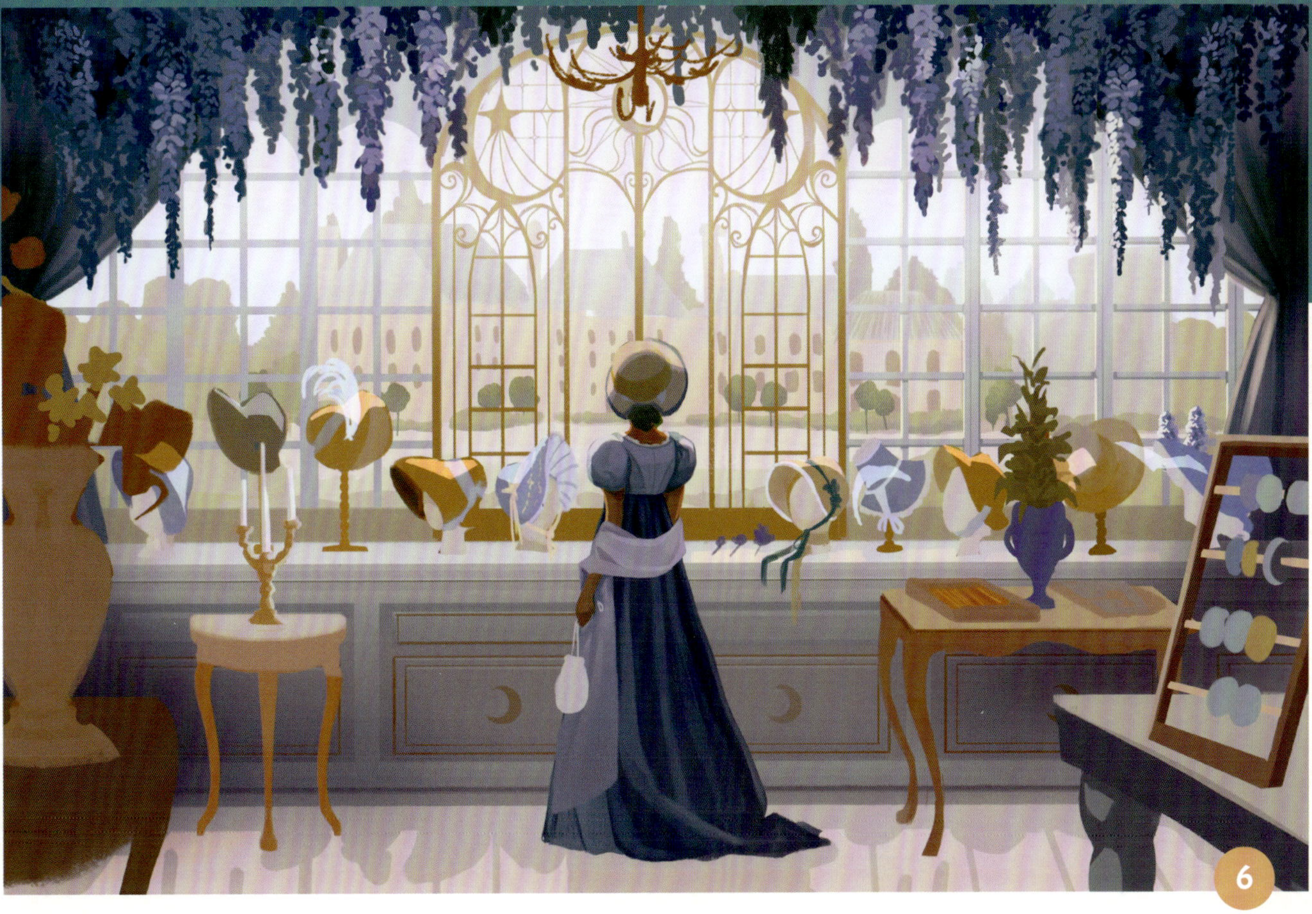

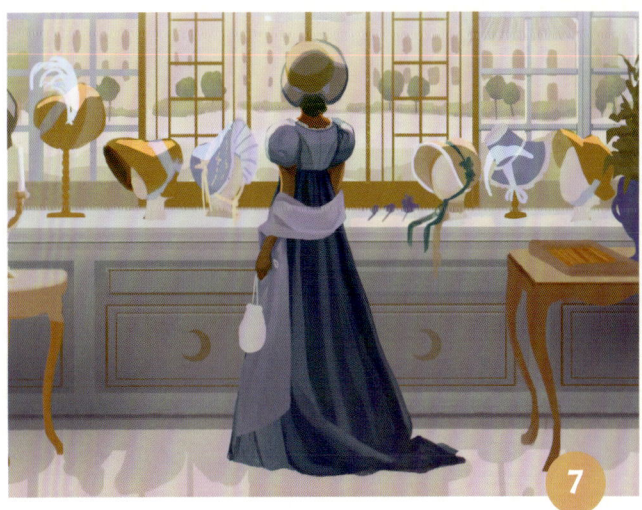

4. EVERYTHING'S GONE GREEN

I decide to completely change the background by adding more greenery and a warmer colour, creating a contrast against the blues. I also add more details to the flowers and more starry motifs into the window design and bonnets.

5. SOFTENING COLOURS

Now I'm happy with the painting, I can start to tweak the colours to create a softer, pastel look. I usually start painting by adding a Gradient Map using contrasting colours on top of my layers. I change the layer Blending Mode to Darker Colour and turn off the toggle for Reverse – this helps soften the highlights of the painting with the pink and blues from the Gradient Map.

6. REFINING THE SHADOWS

Using the Colour Balance tool, I adjust the colours of the shadows and highlights of the painting. For the shadows, I lean towards the reds to create warmer undertones. I also change the highlights to yellows to bring back some warmer lighting.

7. COMING INTO FOCUS

I create a Hue/Saturation Adjustment Layer and focus on the most prominent colours from the painting, in this case the blues and cyans. Since the cyans prominently appear at the centre of the painting, I bring up the brightness to increase the focus on the character.

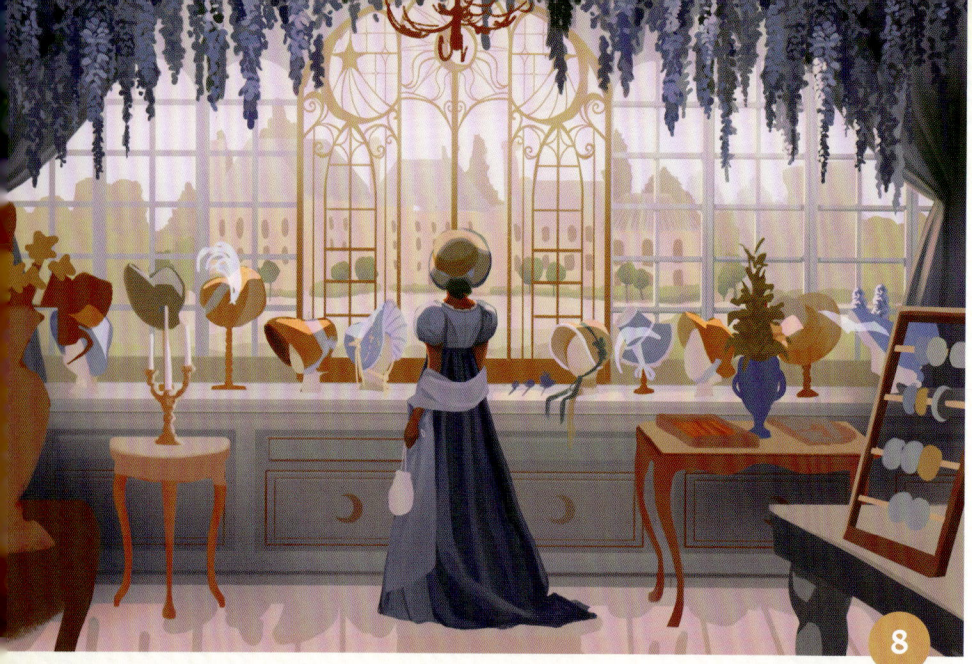

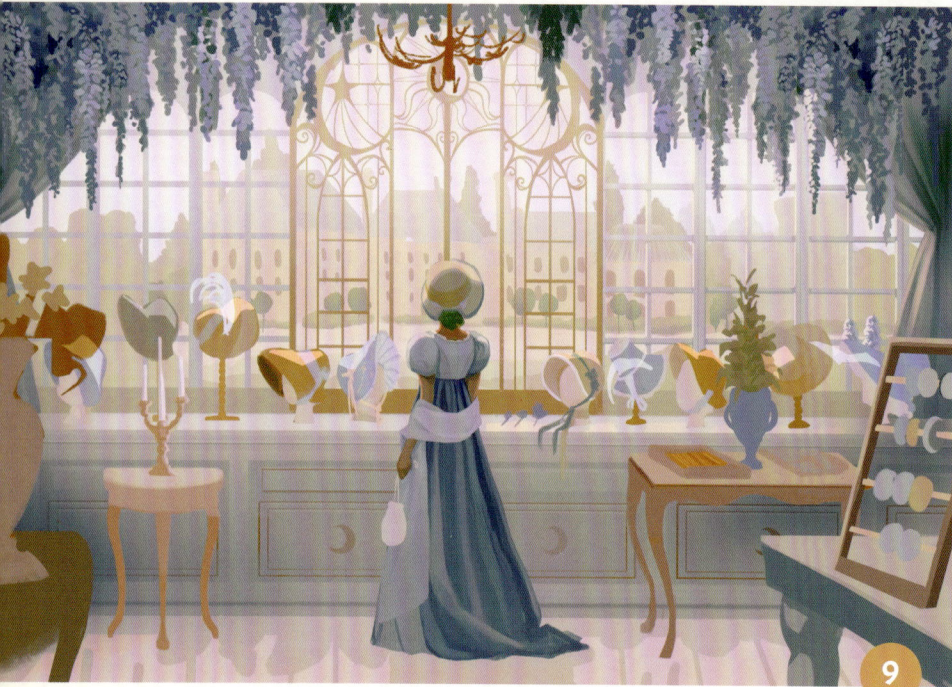

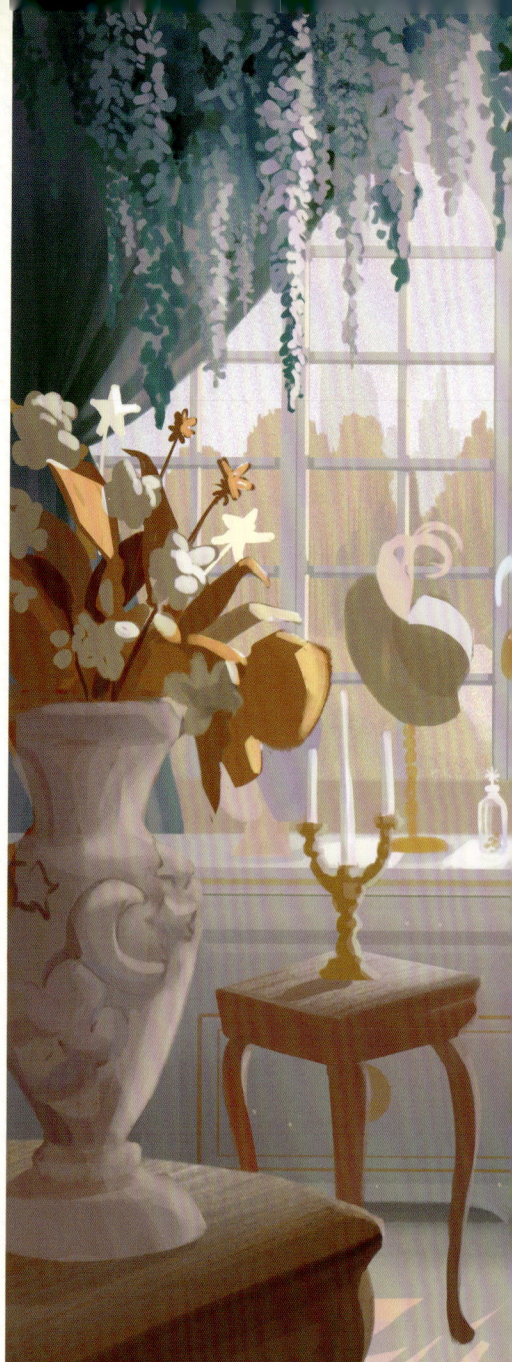

8. A WHITER SHADE OF PALE

Next, I experiment with the rest of the colours, moving the sliders and trying to find what looks best. The Selective Colour tool is one of my favourites in Photoshop because it can quickly transform your colours into different hues. I play around with the white selective sliders, nudging them towards pinks and yellows.

9. PICKING A PASTEL PALETTE

I add another Gradient Map during this stage, but set the layer Blending Mode to Divide. I use orange to contrast the pink and set the layer opacity to 25%. Not only will this brighten up the image, but it will create the soft pastel mood I'm looking for in this painting.

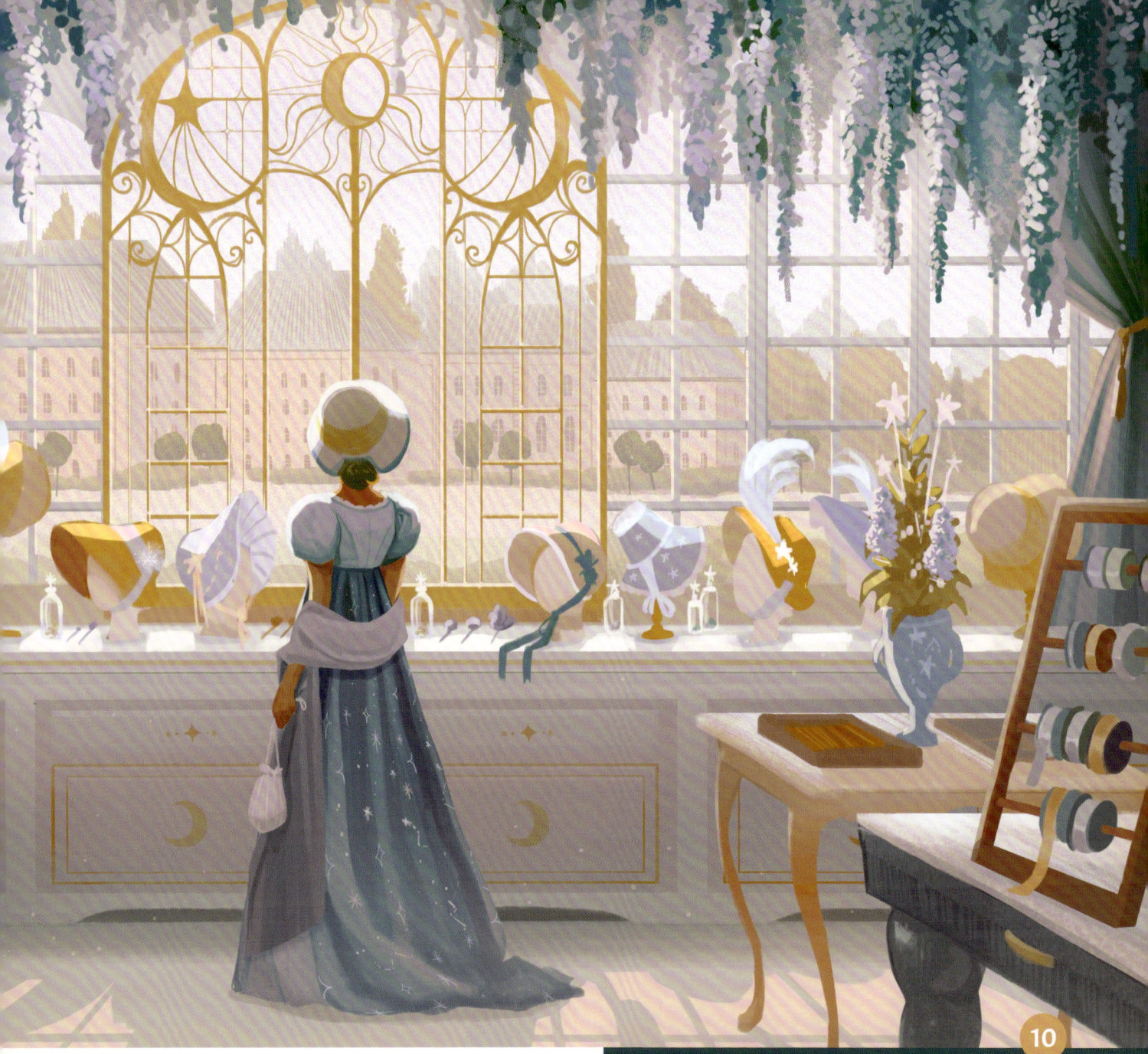

10. FINISHING TOUCHES

Once I'm happy with the image, I refine some of the details in the foreground and add more rim light to the edges of the objects to bring them out from the background. I also add highlights to the ribbons to indicate the silk texture and add a soft glow on top of the windows to create atmospheric lighting.

SIMPLIFY YOUR SHAPES

Most of the shapes and objects in the background are simplified. Notice how the trees and other organic shapes in the painting are created with large brushstrokes to indicate the form. Not all things need to be detailed – it's about finding where to add necessary embellishments to the painting that help enhance the focus on what you're showing to the viewer.

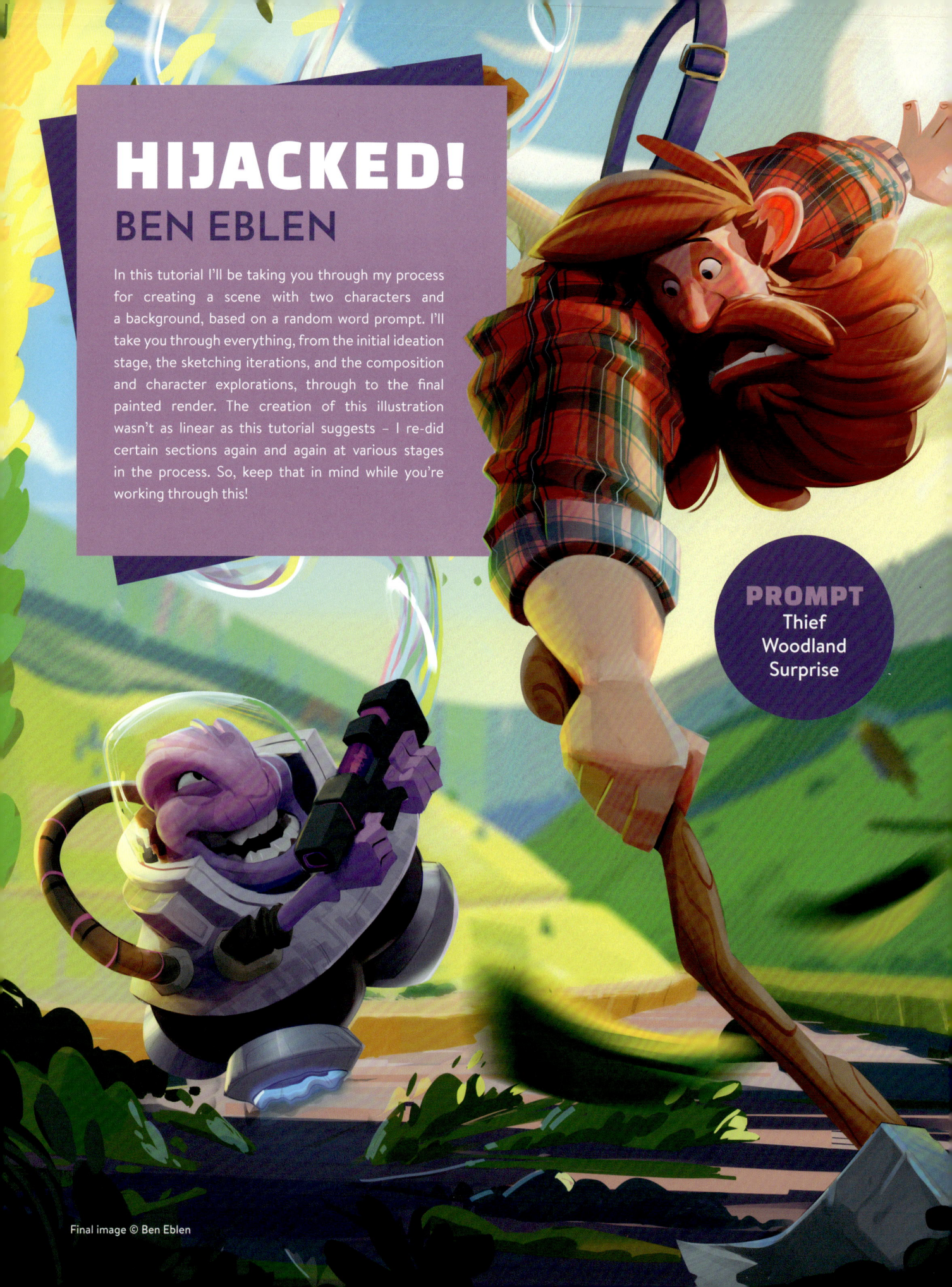

HIJACKED!

BEN EBLEN

In this tutorial I'll be taking you through my process for creating a scene with two characters and a background, based on a random word prompt. I'll take you through everything, from the initial ideation stage, the sketching iterations, and the composition and character explorations, through to the final painted render. The creation of this illustration wasn't as linear as this tutorial suggests – I re-did certain sections again and again at various stages in the process. So, keep that in mind while you're working through this!

PROMPT
Thief
Woodland
Surprise

Final image © Ben Eblen

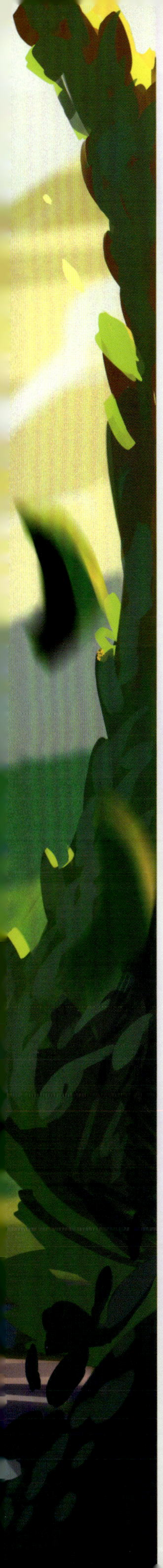

The big idea

First things first, I need to get some ideas down on the page. I start by writing down whatever comes to mind straight away, and I'll try to see if there's some less typical ways to explore the three prompt words. I end up landing on the idea of a lumberjack, who's surprised while out in the woods by an alien trying to abduct him! Now, this could easily become a little sinister, but I want to keep it light and fun. I make sure to keep this ideation stage as loose and non-committal as possible.

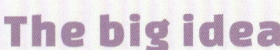

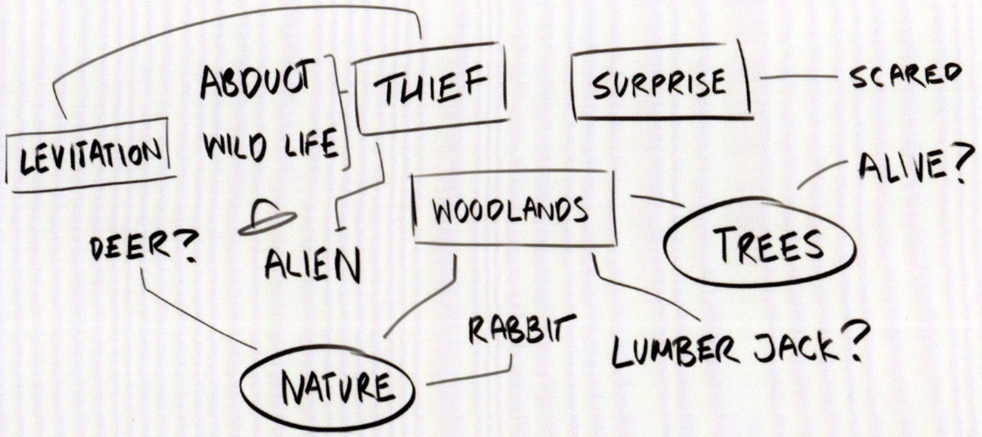

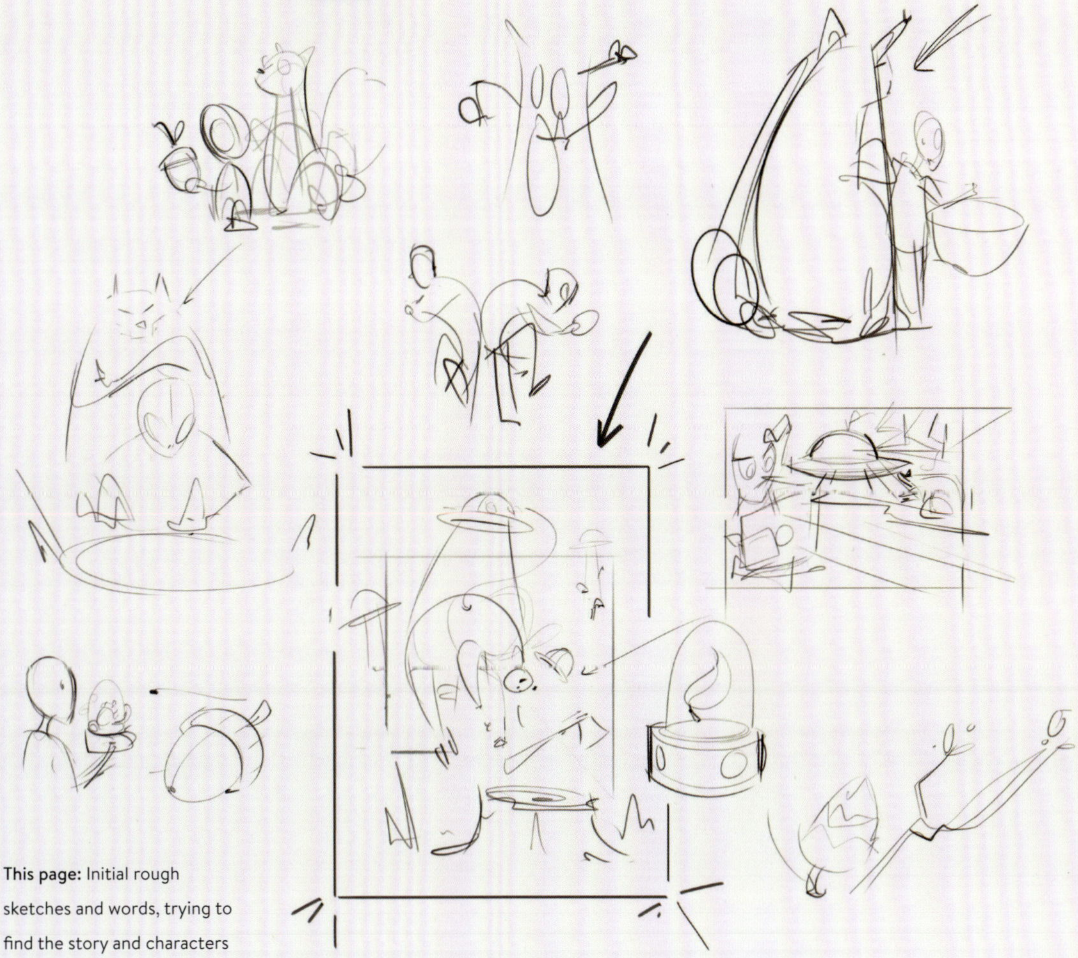

This page: Initial rough sketches and words, trying to find the story and characters

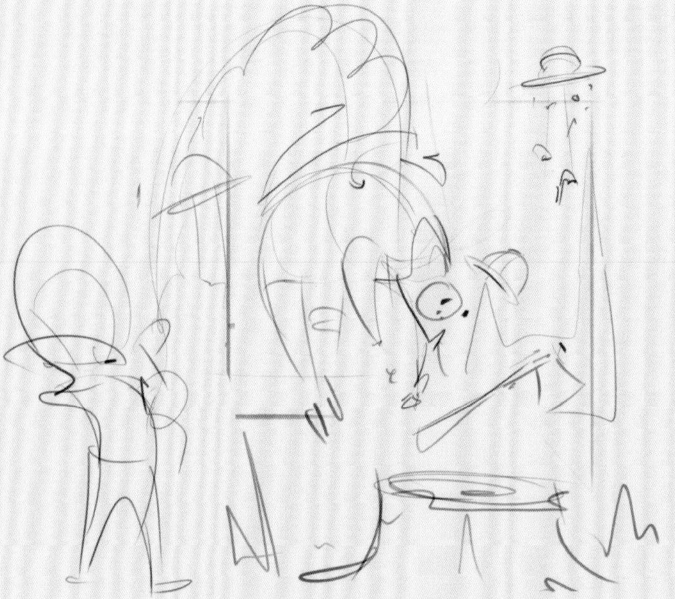

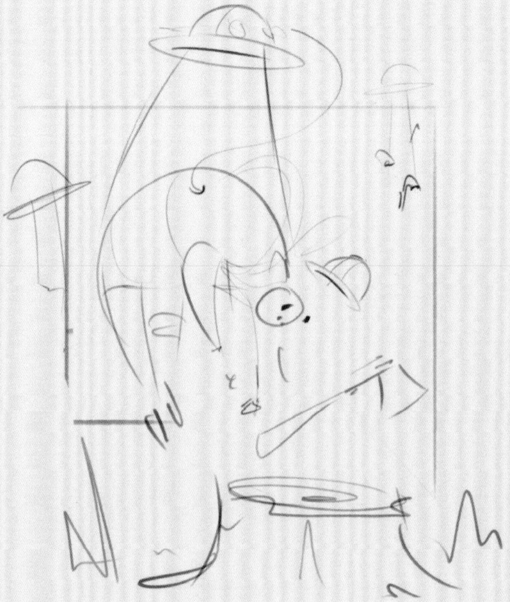

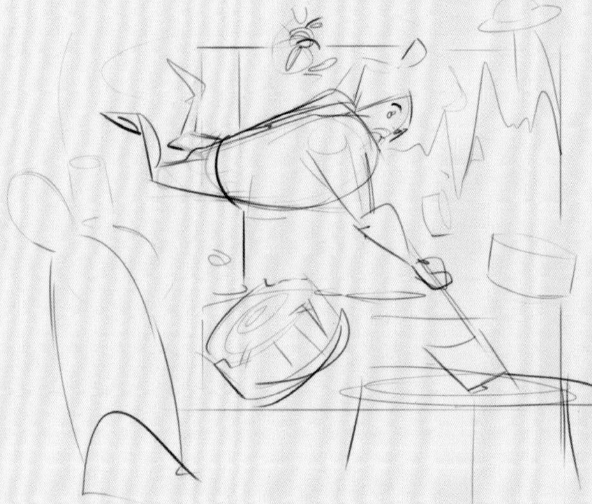

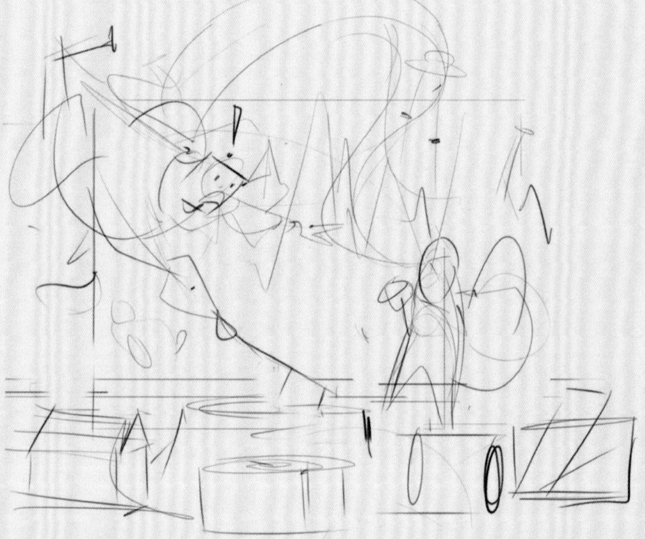

Refining
the scene

Next, I begin to refine this idea, playing around with different compositions, characters, and scenes. I'm still trying to keep it loose and sketchy, with only as much detail as I need to clearly convey the story I have in mind. Big simple shapes are the name of the game. If I start to get too into the details it makes it a lot harder for me to move things around and experiment freely.

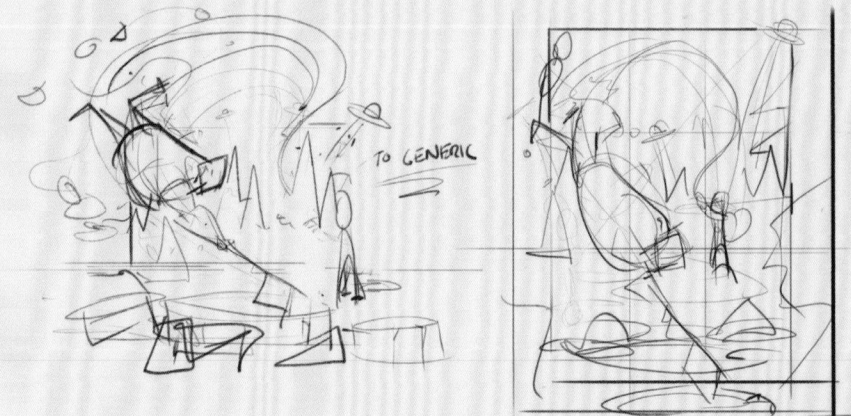

Meet the lumberjack

Before I go any further, I want to explore the characters a little bit more, so I have a better idea of who I'm putting in the scene and how they might interact with one another. I want the lumberjack to be quite robust and stocky, but also have a friendly, innocent feel to him. I play around with rounded shape language, rather than sharp or harsh shapes, to give him an approachable feel.

A close encounter

Time to take a look at the alien. I start off with a typical alien character design, but I want to experiment with the idea of anti-gravity. I'm thinking it could be cool to have the alien sitting within his spacecraft, giving him the agility and tools to overpower the much larger lumberjack. Again, I keep the shapes very simple and the ideas loose. This is all about experimentation – I'm exploring ideas, using references of different animals and existing alien designs to see what might fit the world I'm creating.

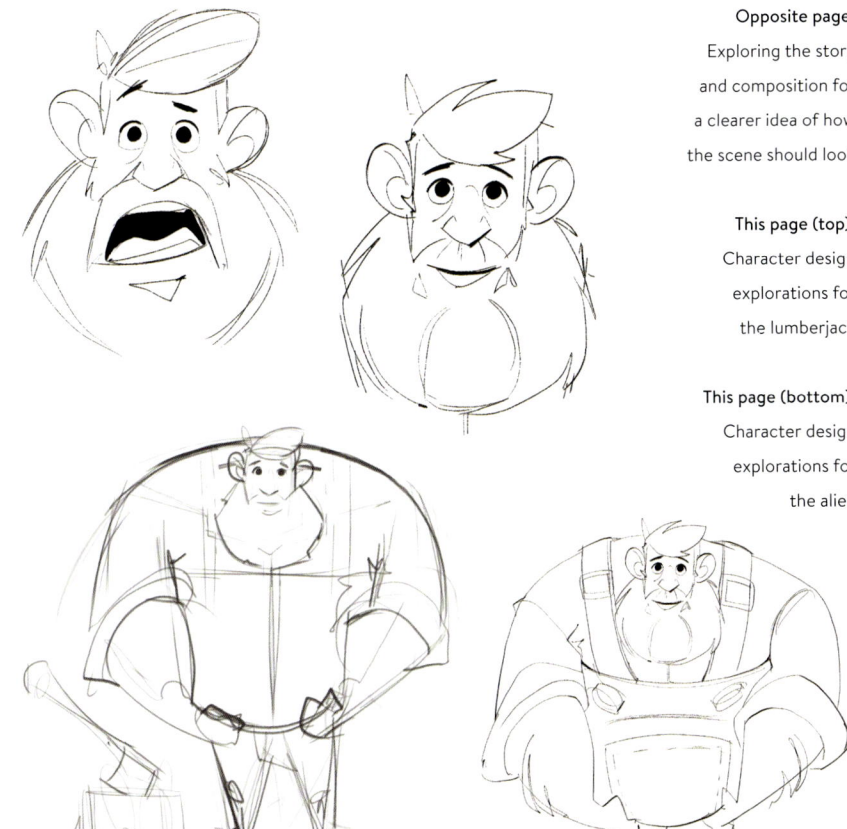

Opposite page:
Exploring the story and composition for a clearer idea of how the scene should look

This page (top):
Character design explorations for the lumberjack

This page (bottom):
Character design explorations for the alien

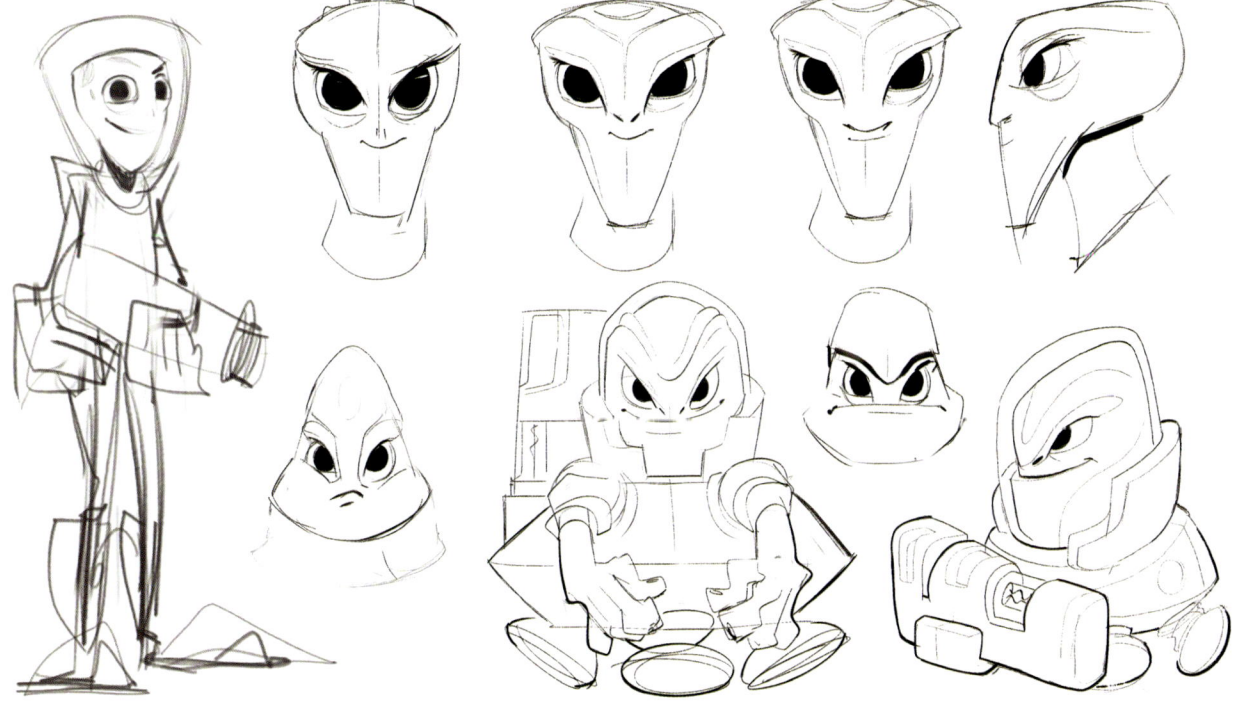

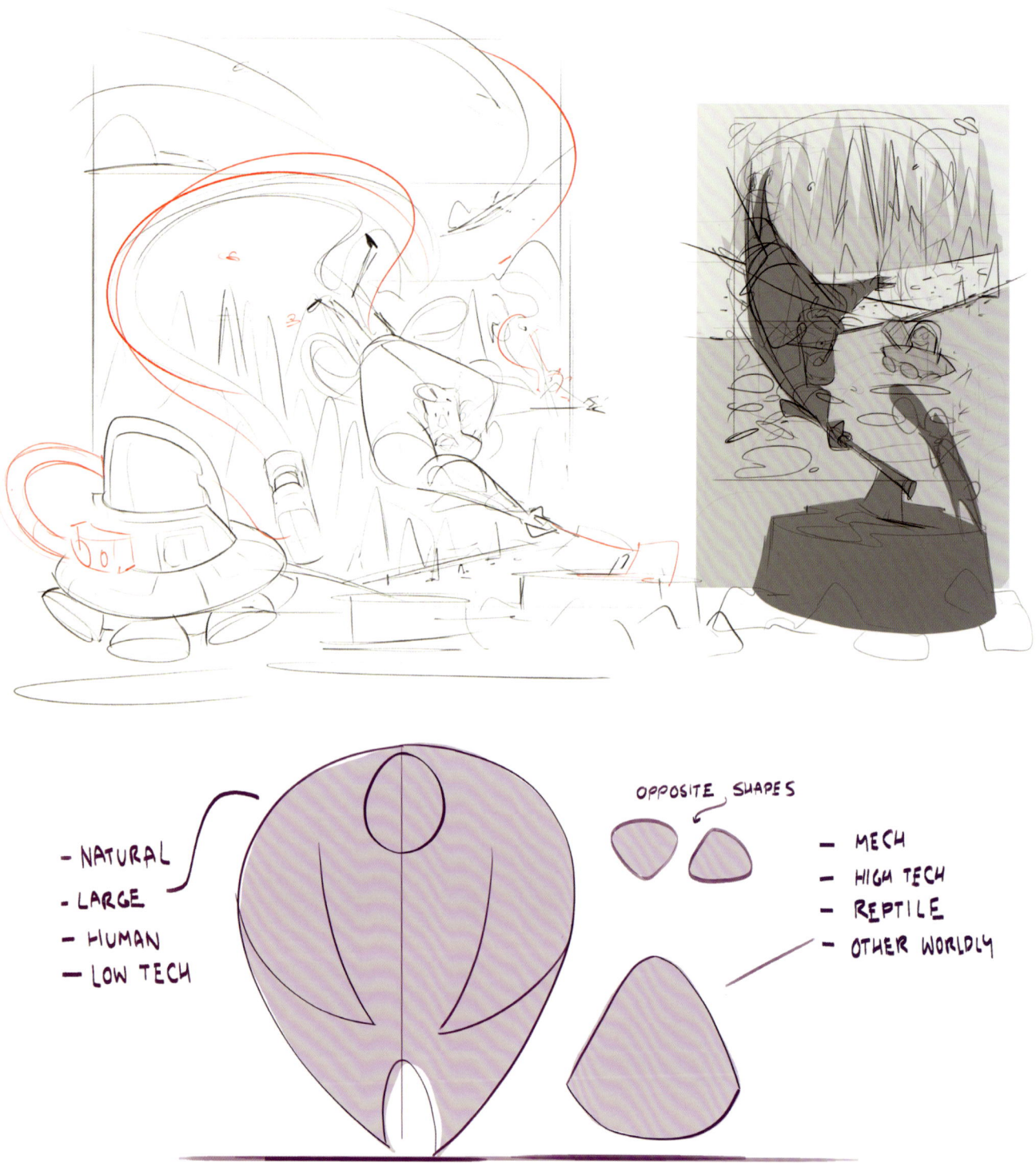

- NATURAL
- LARGE
- HUMAN
- LOW TECH

OPPOSITE SHAPES

- MECH
- HIGH TECH
- REPTILE
- OTHER WORLDLY

Character contrast and interactions

Now that I've started to flesh out the characters, I can see more clearly how they can contrast with one another. They have shape, size, and material contrast, while still sharing that 'rounded corner' vibe that appears fun. I play with how they interact with one another and make

notes of where things are working and where things aren't. Ultimately, I'm trying to figure out how to lead the eye of the viewer through the scene and clearly show what's going on in this unlikely interaction.

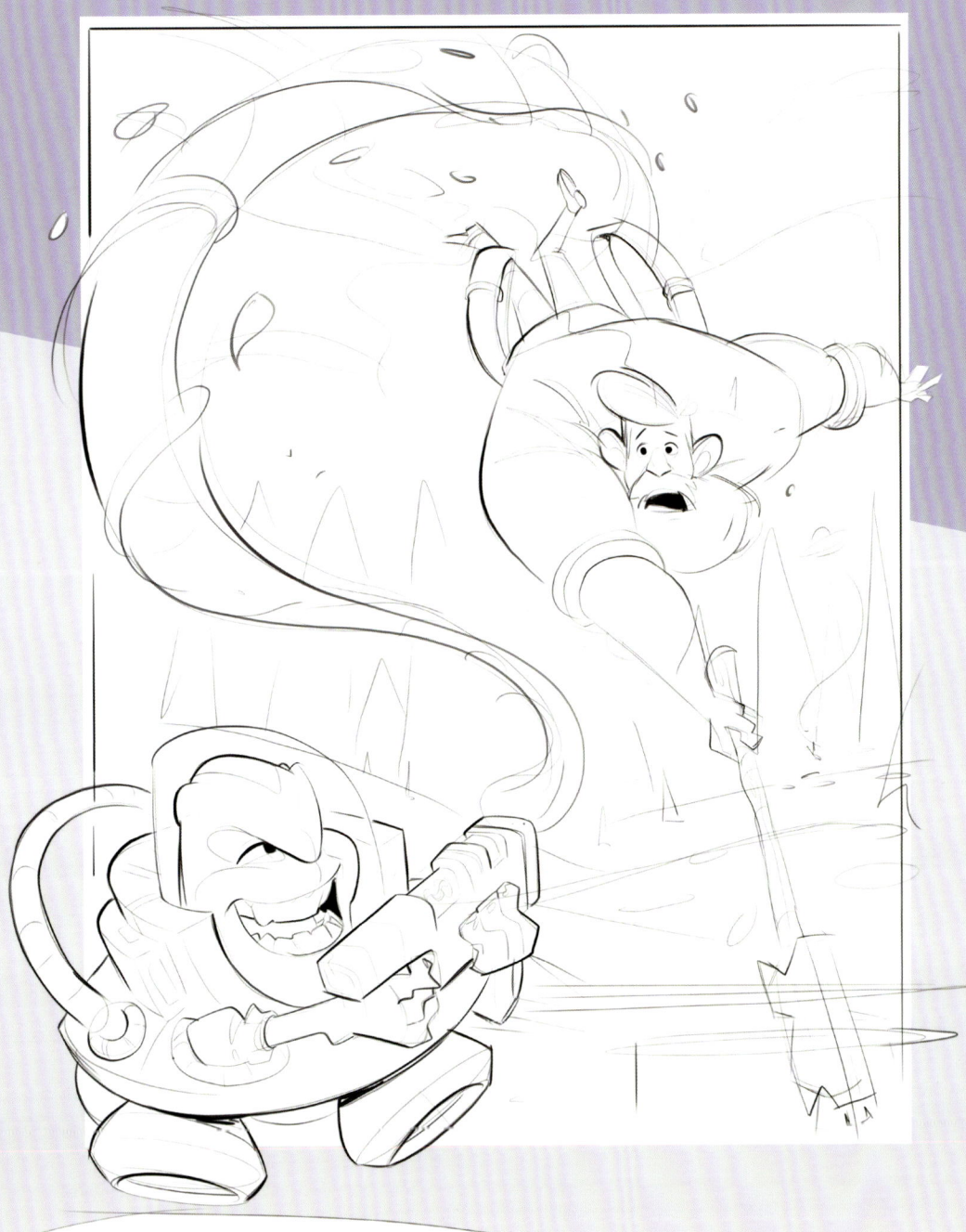

Cleaning up

Next, it's time to clean up the line work. This not only tidies up the drawing, it also helps clarify my thoughts and tie up any ambiguous shapes and ideas that may have appeared in the sketching phase. For instance, I clearly define the lumberjack's braces, which have been pulled off his shoulders, and the beam firing from the anti-gravity gun. The beam also works to lead the eye from one character to the other. I tidy up the line work just enough so that it acts as a guide when I start to add values and colours to the characters.

Setting the scene

For this project, I think of the environment as just as much of a character as the alien and lumberjack – after all, 'woodland' is a third of the brief. I want to focus on really setting the scene. After cleaning up the sketch, I begin to block in really simple shapes, in greyscale first, thinking about the idea of darker elements in the foreground and lighter elements in the background. I consider how these shapes can support – and even highlight – the action that's taking place. I then start to add some test colours to these shapes using the Colour layer mode on top of the black-and-white shapes to give me something to experiment with.

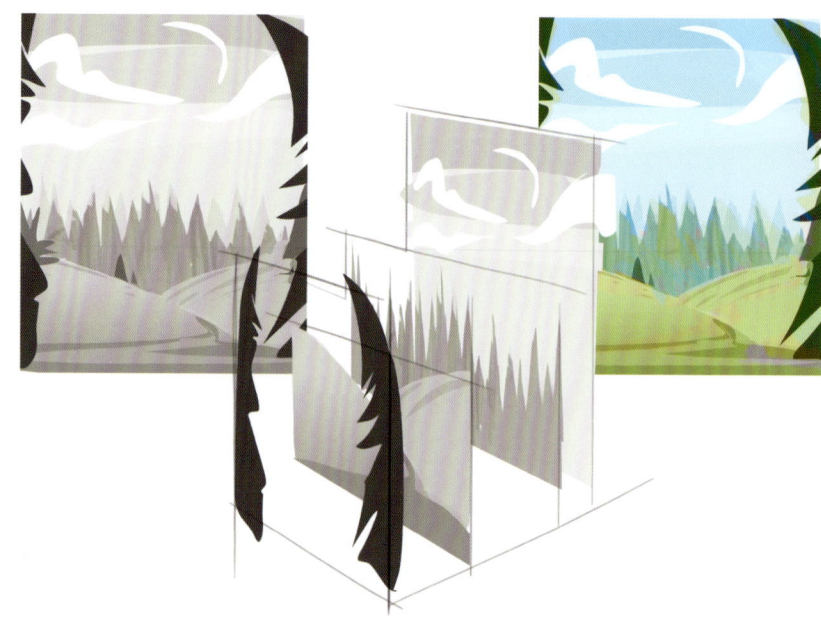

Low risk colour tests

Using the cleaner line work as a guide, and the coloured background test from the previous step, I start to experiment with different colour schemes by painting with a Normal layer mode underneath my line work. I add other layer modes like Colour, Overlay, and Multiply and play with the light source, shadows, and different times of day. I want to keep these tests small, loose, and experimental, with minimal detail. I'm thinking about how the lumberjack's red shirt will contrast nicely with the blue sky and how the cooler colours of the alien will contrast with the lumberjack as well.

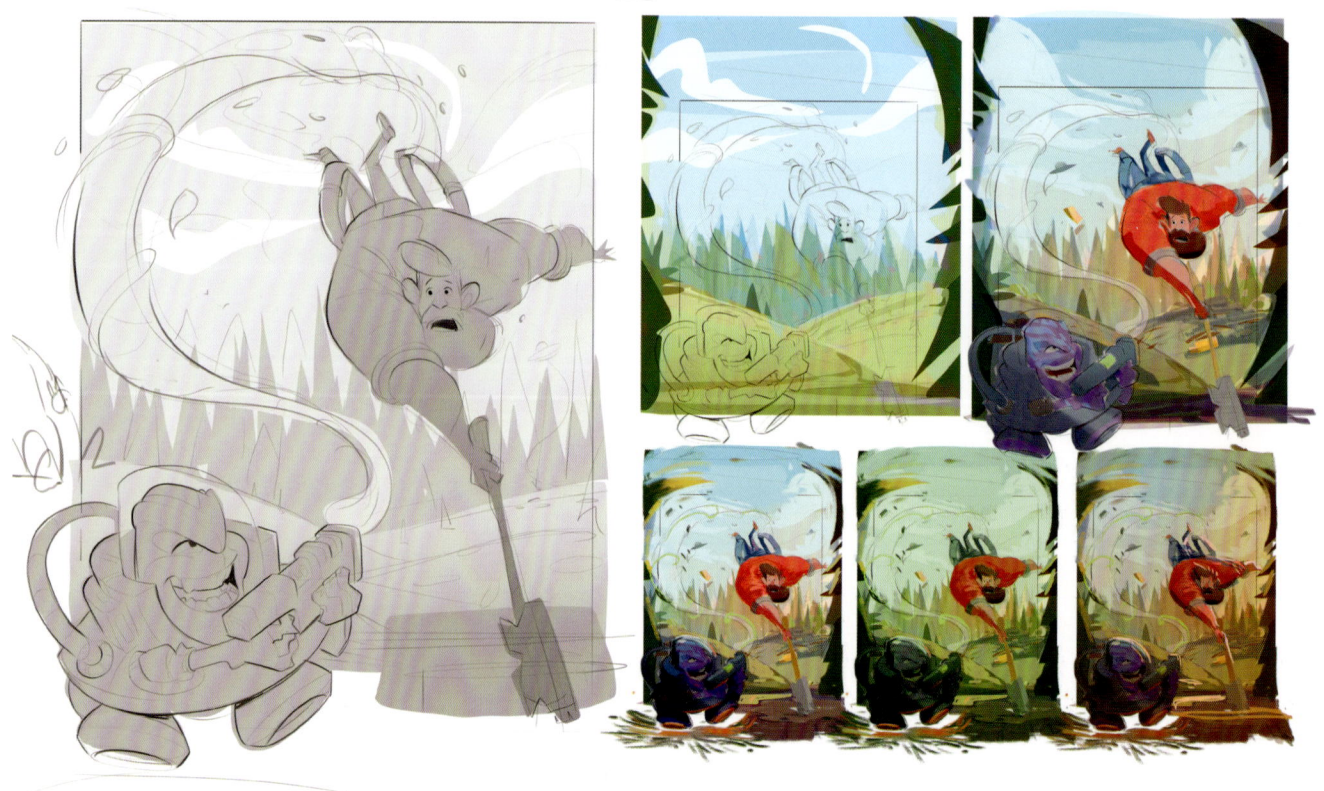

'Darker elements in the foreground and lighter elements in the background will help give a sense of depth'

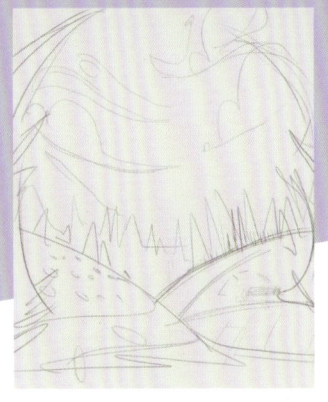 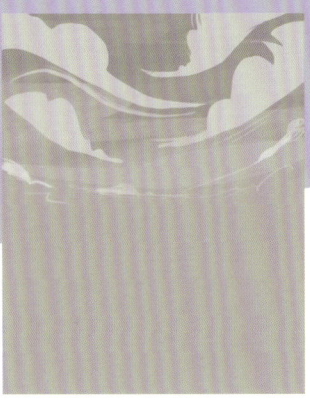 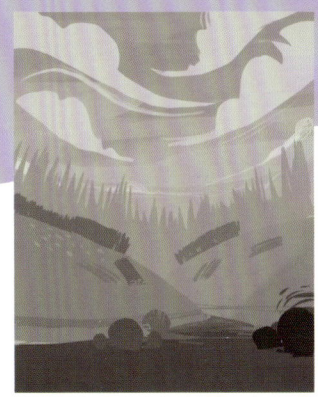 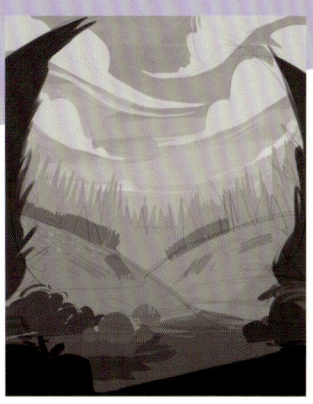

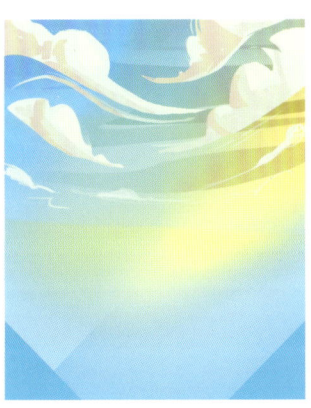 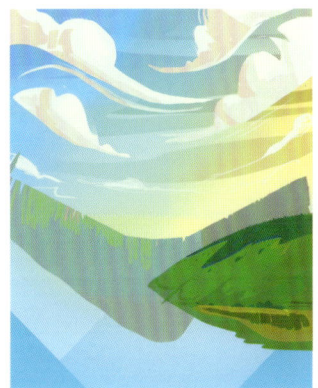 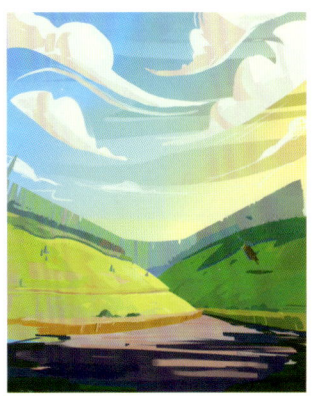 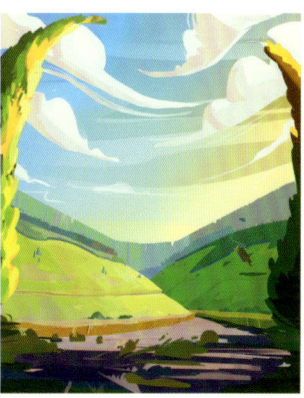

The background takes shape

Now things are cooking! We've got our characters, environment, and different colour schemes to reference, so it's time to clean up the background for the final piece. I use a cleaner sketch and do a black-and-white pass, using as simple shapes as possible to create depth in the scene. Again, using the idea of darker elements in the foreground and lighter elements in the background will help give a sense of depth. I use the Lasso tool and brushes with a hard edge to keep the shapes simple and clear. I refer to a lot of references of woodlands, pine forests, and hills.

Sun setting the mood

Why would an alien fleet fly down and abduct their subjects in the middle of the day? I think it would make more sense within the story for the scene to be set at the end of the working day. I try to think about the type of light source that will convey that 'dusk' feeling. A warmer sunlight source and cooler shadows are going to affect every element in the finished drawing. Understanding this up front gives us a lot of information to work with when rendering our characters, so we can ensure they feel like an integral part of the scene.

Opposite page (top): Background elements showing the depth that I'm thinking about

Opposite page (bottom): Colour thumbnails, experimenting with different character and environment colour schemes

This page (top): Black-and-white pass at the final background design

This page (bottom): Colour pass of the final background design, showing light direction and time of day

Chopping and changing

I ended up replacing the original lumberjack pose with a more dynamic stance that added a little bit more depth and contrast to the interaction between him and the alien. Having him pushed more into the foreground gives a greater sense of scale between the two. He's also now twisting in a more natural way to make eye contact with his abductor.

This page:

Steps showing the rendering process for the lumberjack

Opposite page:

The rendering process for the alien and his spaceship

Refining the design

I follow a similar rendering process for the lumberjack. I start with black and white to help show where the lights and shadows will be, then add Colour, Multiply, and Overlay layers to add to the base colours. I continue to refine the painting, often merging all the layers down into one layer and painting on top. You'll notice in the more finished rendering the lumberjack has different light sources hitting him – these light sources are coming from the environment, such as reflections from the green bushes and the blue sky.

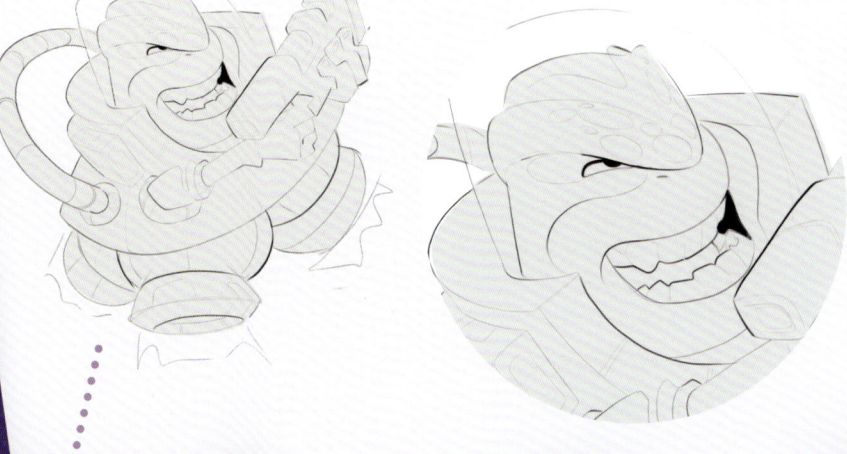

Softening the sinister alien

At this stage I noticed that the alien was looking too sinister and not playful enough, so I decided to make his eyes bigger and his smile a little bit cheekier. I made this change at quite a late stage and painted over the top of everything that I previously laid down – this is an easier way to make adjustments than going back through and resketching and painting the whole thing again.

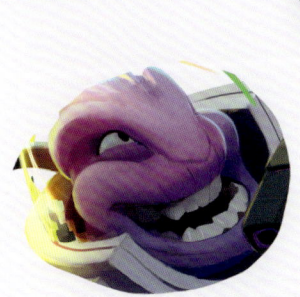

SUBTLE TEXTURE

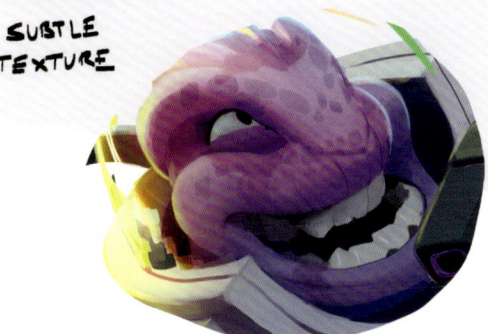

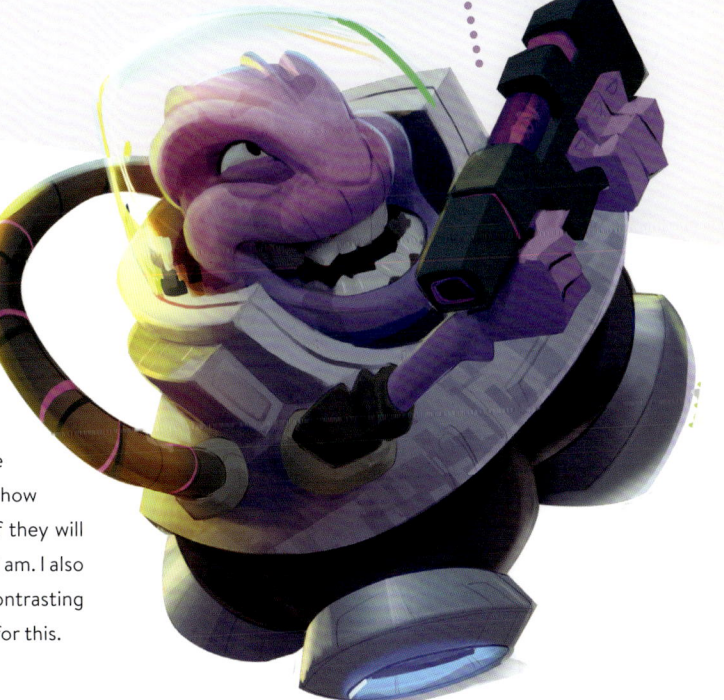

Alien alterations

I use the 'black-and-white-to-colour' rendering method for the alien, starting with an initial greyscale painting, keeping in mind the light source. I then add colour on top and continue tweaking the character as I go. Even during the rendering stage you will notice how much the alien's face changes. I'm not afraid to make adjustments if they will improve the overall character, no matter how far through the process I am. I also want to add a little more personality and texture to his face, further contrasting him from his abductee – Multiply and Overlay layer modes are great for this.

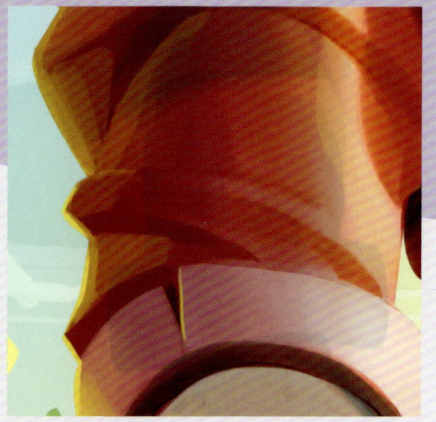
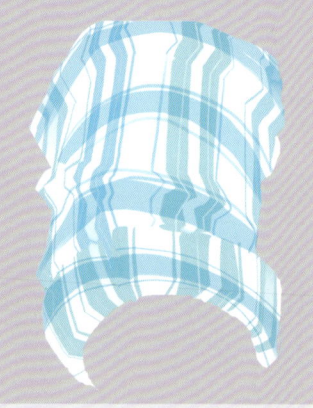
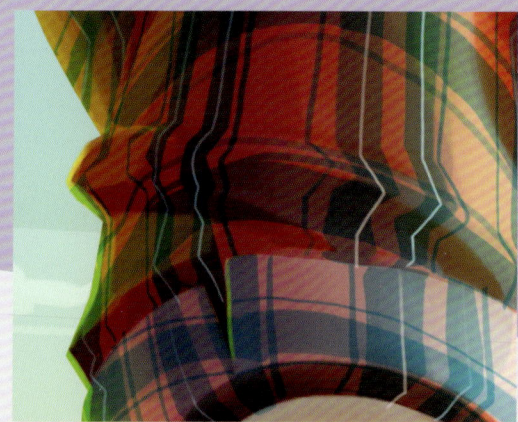

All clad in plaid

What's a lumberjack without a little plaid? Just like with the alien's face texture, I follow the same process here, using Multiply, Overlay, and Screen Layer modes over the top of the base-rendered red shirt to make this plaid pattern. Like with most things, I don't have an exact mental image of what the pattern is meant to look like, so I grab a bunch of different references of plaid patterns and attempt to replicate them with a slightly chunkier look to fit the overall shape language. I also make sure the pattern wraps over the contours of the shirt.

Attention to detail

Next, I focus on the little details that will complete the image; things like the subsurface scattering on his ear where the light is passing through the skin, the reflections on the alien's helmet of the surrounding environment, and the translucency of the anti-gravity vortex. These are small tweaks, but they work together to bring the piece to a new level, helping to sell the idea that these two characters are actually living in the scene.

I'm a lumberjack and I'm bokeh

Finally, I like to add special effects to help sell the character and scene just that little bit more. I use the Lens Blur filter on the background elements to help give the illusion of depth of field, as if this image has been taken by a camera. I use the Liquify tool to create some wobbles on the thrusters of the alien's rockets. These elements are the cherry on top that help further bring the scene to life. Remember, these are completely optional and no amount of filters or special effects will help fix an unclear character design or story moment.

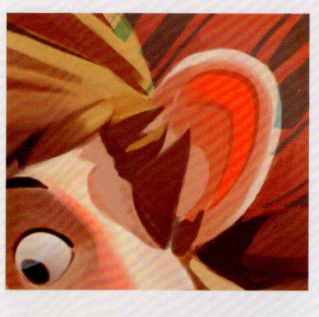
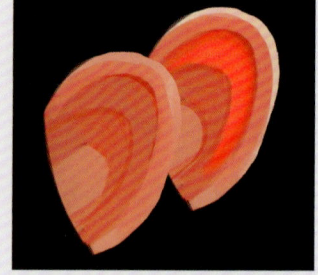
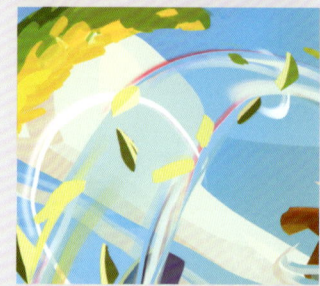
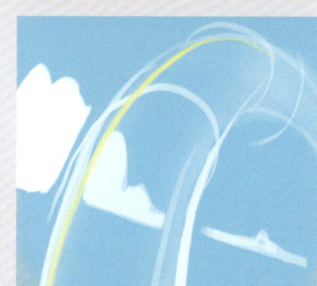
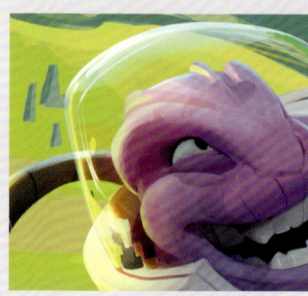
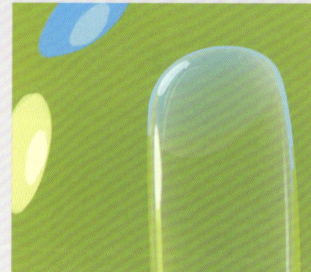

This page (top): Adding texture to the plaid clothing using layer modes

This page (bottom): Examples of details that I paint in after most of the ground work is complete

Opposite page: The final illustration

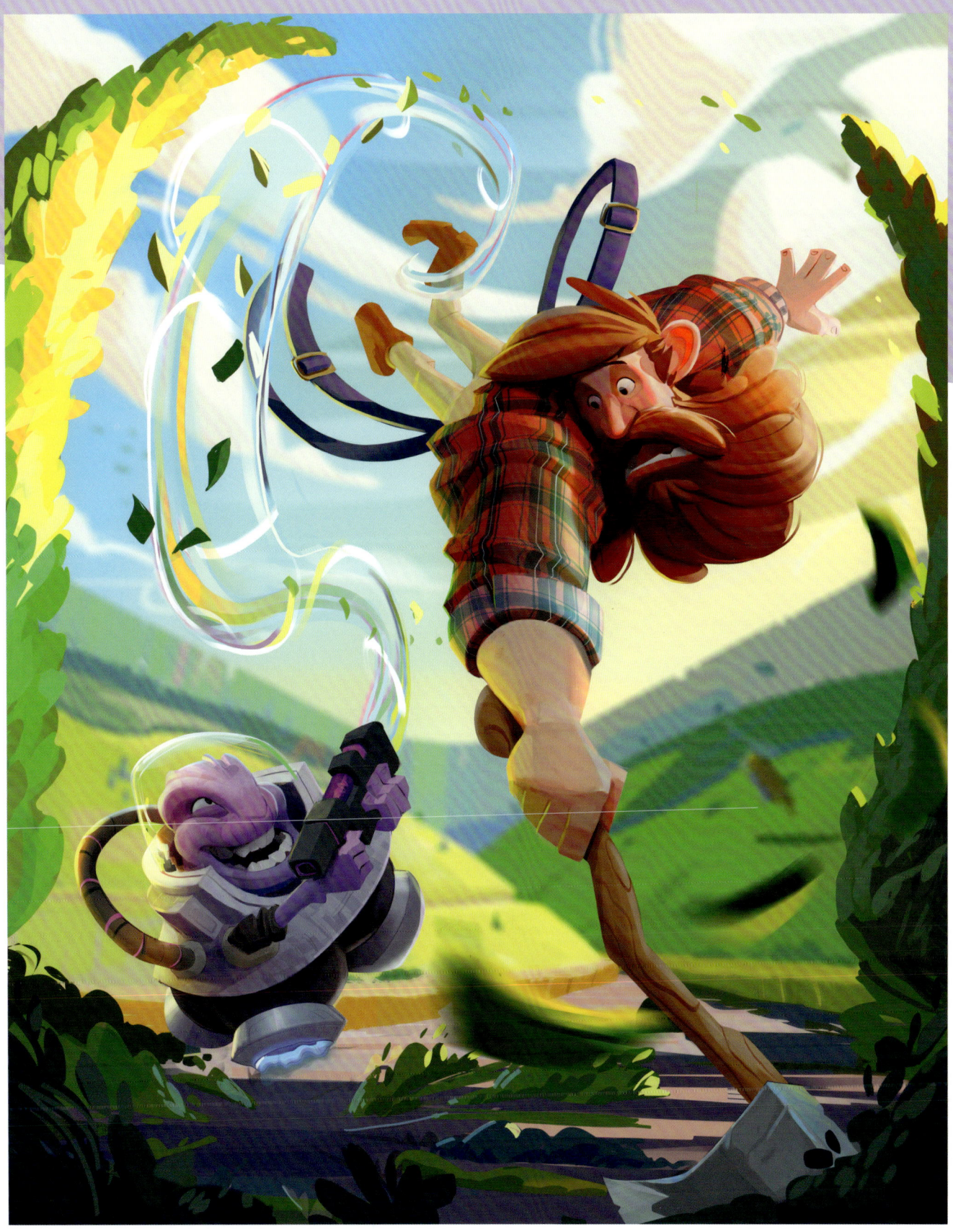

CONTRIBUTORS

BEN EBLEN
Illustrator, character designer, and content creator
beneblen.com

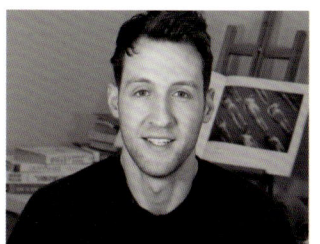

Ben is an Australian illustrator, developer, podcast host, chaser of 'aha!' moments, and loves sharing his process and findings online.

ALEX JENSEN
Character designer
alexjensenart.com

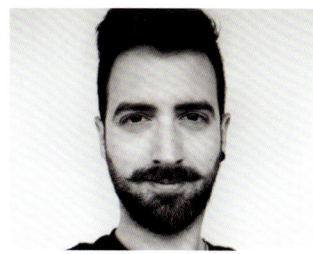

Alex Jensen is a character designer from Spain who has worked in the animation and game industry for the past seven years.

RAAHAT KADUJI
Freelance illustrator
raahatkaduji.com

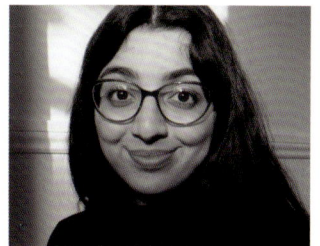

Raahat is an illustrator and children's author from the UK. Her work is inspired by nature, wildlife, and the English countryside where she lives.

SAM NASSOUR
Visual development artist and art director
samnassour.com

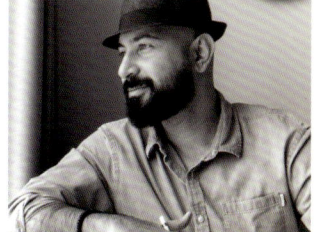

Sam Nassour works in the animation and games industries, with a focus on character design and keyframe painting.

SARA PAZ
Freelance illustrator and character designer
sarapazdesign.wordpress.com

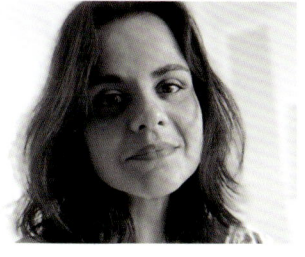

Sara was born in Lisbon, Portugal, and graduated from IADE in 2002. She has worked in publishing, but has been freelancing since 2010.

ABRAHAM REYES
Character designer and visual development artist
abrahamreyes.com

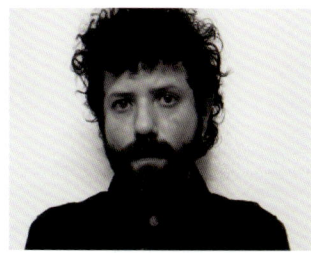

Abraham lives in the SF Bay Area with his cat, Pumpkin. He's worked for clients such as Pixar, Sony Pictures Animation, and Nickelodeon.

SAULO NATE
Art director and 2D artist
saulont.com

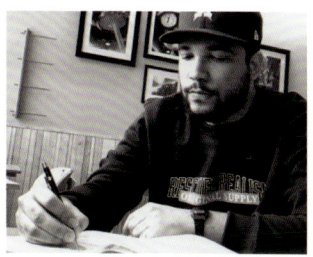

Saulo was born and raised in Brazil, but is currently based in the US. He loves wildlife and character design, and can't survive without a hot coffee.

RACHELLE JOY SLINGERLAND
Visual development artist and freelance illustrator
instagram.com/rachellejoys

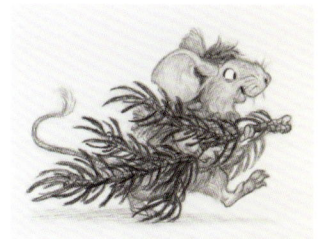

Rachelle works as a freelance vis dev artist, with a focus on character design. She draws every day in her studio in Rotterdam.

MILA USECHE
Artist and director
milauseche.art

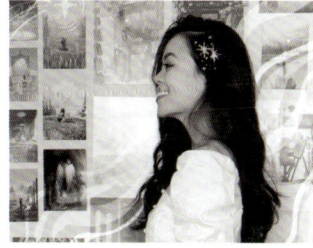

Mila is originally from Colombia, but is currently based in Berlin. She's a director, character designer, illustrator, and lover of cute things.

MAXINE VEE
Illustrator and independent artist
maxinevee.com

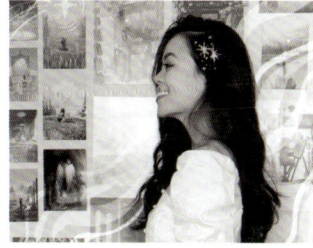

Maxine is an illustrator based in the Greater Toronto Area. She loves creating whimsical illustrations, quiet moments, and magical scenes.

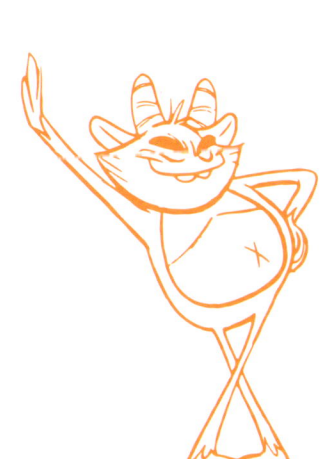

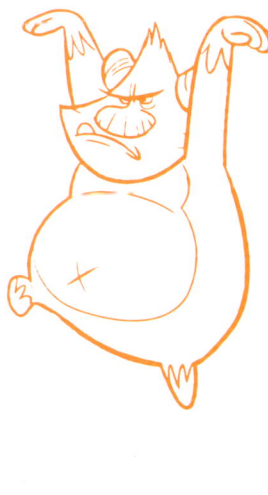

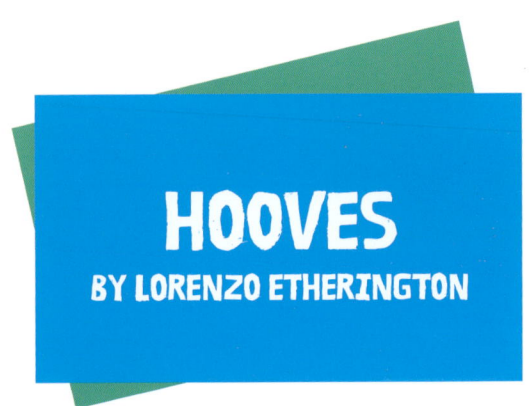

HOOVES
BY LORENZO ETHERINGTON

THE MORE YOU MAKE STUDIES FROM *REAL LIFE...*

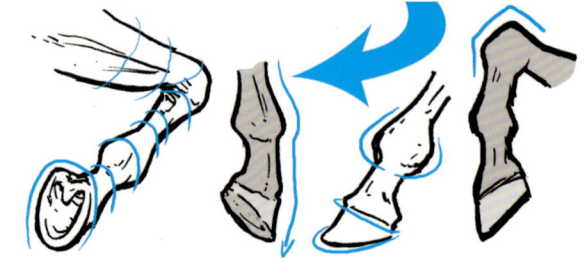

ALTHOUGH WE'RE PRIMARILY FOCUSED ON *HOOVES* ALONE IN THIS TUTORIAL, IT'S WORTH THINKING ABOUT THE *BASIC STRUCTURE* OF THE *LOWER LEG* AS WELL.

...THE MORE YOU CAN *EXAGGERATE* AND *STYLISE.*

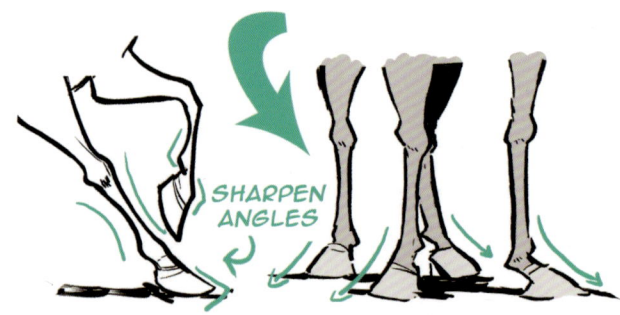

SHARPEN ANGLES

THE LOWER LEG CAN BE SIMPLIFIED INTO TWO MAIN *BONE* AND *TENDON* LINES. THE SPACE BETWEEN THESE CREATES A *CHANNEL.*

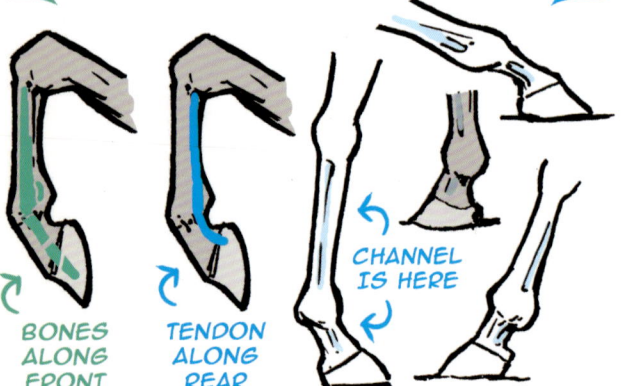

BONES ALONG FRONT

TENDON ALONG REAR

CHANNEL IS HERE

CLOVEN HOOVES HAVE A *DIFFERENT STRUCTURE,* THOUGH THEIR OVERALL FORM IS SIMILAR...

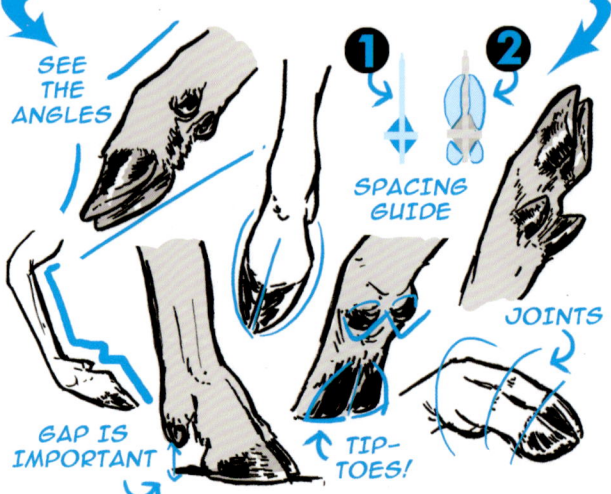

SEE THE ANGLES

1 **2**

SPACING GUIDE

GAP IS IMPORTANT

TIP-TOES!

JOINTS